OPEC and the World Oil Market:
The Genesis of the 1986 Price Crisis

OPEC and the World Oil Market: The Genesis of the 1986 Price Crisis

Papers by Contributors to the
Oxford Energy Seminar

EDITED BY
ROBERT MABRO

Published by the Oxford University Press
for the Oxford Institute for Energy Studies
1986

Oxford University Press, Walton Street, Oxford OX2 6DP
Oxford New York Toronto
Delhi Bombay Calcutta Madras Karachi
Petaling Jaya Singapore Hong Kong Tokyo
Nairobi Dar es Salaam Cape Town
Melbourne Auckland
and associated companies in
Beirut Berlin Ibadan Nicosia

Oxford is a trade mark of Oxford University Press

British Library Cataloguing in Publication Data
OPEC and the world oil market: the genesis of the 1986 price crisis.
1. Organization of the Petroleum Exporting
Countries
I. Mabro, Robert   II. Oxford Institute
for Energy Studies
338.2'3   HD9560.1.066
ISBN 0-19-730003-0

Typeset by Joshua Associates Limited, Oxford
Printed in Great Britain by
Billing and Sons Ltd., Worcester

CONTRIBUTORS

Nordine Aït-Laoussine	President, Nalcosa, Geneva
Ali Attiga	Secretary General, OAPEC
Mario Ramón Beteta	Director General, Petróleos Mexicanos
Fadhil Al Chalabi	Deputy Secretary General, OPEC
Jack Crutchfield	Vice President, Esso Middle East
Vicomte Etienne Davignon	Formerly EEC Commissioner for Industry and Energy
Edward R. Fried	Senior Fellow, Brookings Institution
Ali Jaidah	Formerly Secretary General, OPEC, and Managing Director, Qatar General Petroleum Corporation
Arve Johnsen	President, Statoil
Robert Mabro	Director, Oxford Institute for Energy Studies
Alirio A. Parra	Director, Petróleos de Venezuela SA
Francisco R. Parra	Formerly Secretary General, OPEC

Franco Reviglio

Chairman, ENI

Ian Seymour

Editor, *Middle East Economic Survey*

Ibrahim Shihata

Formerly Director General, OPEC Fund for Economic Development

E. Allan Wendt

Assistant Secretary, US Department of State

Sheikh Ahmed Zaki Yamani

Minister of Oil and Petroleum Resources, Saudi Arabia

The *Oxford Energy Seminar* is an international conference designed for government officials, industrialists, managers and other professionals engaged in the field of energy. The Seminar is sponsored by St Catherine's College and co-sponsored by OPEC and OAPEC. It was established in 1979 and its sessions are held annually at St Catherine's over a two-week period in September.

The Seminar, which is fully residential, has educational objectives. Its aims are to enhance the professional qualifications of participants; to improve the understanding of factors and forces which influence the operations of energy markets and the behaviour of policy-makers and economic agents; and to provide a privileged opportunity for contacts and debate between participants from petroleum exporting and importing countries.

A most distinctive feature of the Seminar is the balance of speakers and participants between nationals of petroleum exporting and importing countries and between representatives of government and industry. Each annual session of the Seminar involves fifty to sixty participants and approximately forty speakers. The organization is delegated by the co-sponsors to a Board of Management consisting of the Secretary General of OPEC, the Secretary General of OAPEC, Mr Wilfrid Knapp and Mr Robert Mabro.

The *Oxford Institute for Energy Studies* was established in 1982 to pursue through research and advanced study of problems of international energy the same objectives as the Seminar. The Institute is an association of members, including Oxford University and three of its constituent colleges, OAPEC, the EEC, the UK Department of Energy and other national or regional institutions from Sweden, Norway, France, Japan, Mexico and the Arab world.

The Institute is committed to the idea of co-operation between scholars representing different sides of the international energy debate. This international character is reflected in the composition of both the membership and the research staff of the Institute. The Institute is also committed to achieving high academic standards in the study of real-life problems in the energy world. The aim is to combine excellence in research and relevance to important policy issues.

The Institute has a board of governors representing all members. Dr Ali Attiga is the Chairman, Sir Rex Richards the Vice-Chairman and Robert Mabro the Managing Director.

ACKNOWLEDGEMENTS

Many of the papers in this collection have been presented at various sessions of the Oxford Energy Seminar. In the interest of rapid dissemination, the Seminar has long-standing arrangements with *Middle East Economic Survey*, *OPEC Review* and *Petroleum Intelligence Weekly* for immediate publication of a few contributions without prejudice to the rights of the Seminar for eventual publication of these papers in book form. I wish to thank the Editors of these journals for their valuable co-operation. My paper (Chapter 2) was published in 1975 in *Millennium*. Dr Fadhil Al Chalabi has revised, and considerably enlarged, for the purpose of this book, one of his earlier contributions to the Seminar (Chapter 17). I also wish to thank David Guthrie for sub-editing the papers and following its progress through all the production stages, and Gordon Davies for designing the jacket.

Robert Mabro

CONTENTS

Introduction   1
Robert Mabro

Part I: The Uneasy Relationship between OPEC and the Market

1 Can OPEC Hold the Line?   13
Robert Mabro

2 OPEC after the Oil Revolution.   23
Robert Mabro

3 The Marker and the Market, the Heavy and
the Light.   35
Robert Mabro

4 The Nature of the Energy Problem.   45
Robert Mabro

5 OPEC's Future Pricing Role may be at Stake.   57
Robert Mabro

6 Statement of Saudi Policy (1982).   67
Sheikh Ahmed Zaki Yamani

7 The Changing Nature of the Oil Market and
OPEC Policies.   75
Robert Mabro

8 Oil Prices in 1983: a Critical Year.   91
Research Group on Petroleum Exporters' Policies

9 OPEC in a Longer-Term Perspective.   111
Alirio A. Parra

10 Oil Market Stability: Time for Action?   121
Ali Jaidah

11 The Role of OPEC in Market Stabilization.   131
    Fadhil Al Chalabi

Part II: The Oil Consumers' Views: Security and Free Trade

12 Market Stability and Market Security.   141
    Edward R. Fried

13 Energy Trade: Problems and Prospects.   151
    E. Allan Wendt

Part III: Prelude to the 1986 Oil Price Crisis

14 Debate at the Oxford Energy Seminar,
    13 September 1985.   165
    Final Panel Speakers

Part IV: Stabilization and Long-Term Strategies

15 The Economic Development of the Oil-Exporting
    Countries.   197
    Ali Attiga

16 The Need for an OPEC Central Trading Agency.   207
    Robert Mabro

17 Options for OPEC Long-Term Pricing Strategies.   215
    Fadhil Al Chalabi

TABLES

1.1 Oil Production of OPEC Countries, 1973–4,
and Percentage Changes.   17
1.2 Hypothetical Distribution of Output for the
OPEC Countries.   20

8.1 Energy and Oil Intensities. Percentage Change.
1981 over 1978.   96
8.2 Components of the Reduction in OPEC
Crude Oil Production. 1979–82.   100
8.3 Forecasts of 1983 Oil Demand.   102

17.1 Forecasts of Non-Communist World Demand for
Energy, Oil and OPEC Oil for the Year 1990.   240
17.2 Adjusted OPEC Prices. 1974–84.   266

FIGURES

17.1 Nominal and Adjusted Prices of Arabian Light.
1974–84.   228
17.2 OPEC Oil Reserves/Production Ratio. 1970–84.   234

ABBREVIATIONS

AFRA	Average Freight Rate Assessment
AGIP	Azienda Generale Italiana Petroli
API	American Petroleum Institute
bcm	billion cubic metres
b/d	barrels per day
BNOC	British National Oil Corporation
boe	barrels of oil equivalent
BP	British Petroleum
CIA	Central Intelligence Agency (USA)
CIEC	Conference for International Economic Co-operation
c.i.f.	Cost, insurance and freight
CPE	Centrally planned economy
EEC	European Economic Community
ENI	Ente Nazionale Idrocarburi (Italy)
f.o.b.	Free on board
GATT	General Agreement on Tariffs and Trade
GDP	Gross domestic product
GNP	Gross national product
GSP	Government Selling Price
IEA	International Energy Agency (OECD)
kWh	kilowatt hours
mb/d	million barrels per day
mboe/d	million barrels of oil equivalent per day
mBtu	million British thermal units
n.a.	not available
NGLs	Natural gas liquids
NYMEX	New York Mercantile Exchange
OAPEC	Organization of Arab Petroleum Exporting Countries
OECD	Organisation for Economic Co-operation and Development
OPEC	Organization of the Petroleum Exporting Countries
PSBR	Public Sector Borrowing Requirement (UK)
SBM	Single buoy mooring
SPR	Strategic Petroleum Reserve (USA)
UAE	United Arab Emirates
WAES	Workshop on Alternative Energy Strategies
WTI	West Texas Intermediate

INTRODUCTION

Robert Mabro

Like all international organizations, be it the United Nations or the EEC, OPEC is continually facing some crisis. And like all other organizations it enjoys on occasions successes and achievements. Crises are as much a feature of OPEC's history as successes, and the latter cannot be properly understood without a study of the problems and tensions that the organization encounters or generates as it endeavours to fulfil its objectives.

The analysis of crises is as important for an assessment of OPEC's role in the world petroleum market as that of its achievements. Recent events, in 1985 and 1986, have plainly shown that the behaviour of economic agents – oil companies, traders, consumers, producers – remains deeply influenced by news and perceptions of OPEC, whether the organization is in crisis or in command, whether it is believed to be losing its sense of direction or regaining the initiative. A proper understanding of the nature of OPEC, the interests and objectives of its members, the dynamics of their relationships, the problems faced by the organization and its behaviour during crises, the policies and strategies it seeks or fails to implement, is as important today as it was in 1973 and 1979 when OPEC appeared to lead the rise in oil prices.

This book is about the crises that have faced OPEC regularly since 1974 and which culminated in the big crisis of 1985–6 and about the policies and strategies that can solve the difficulties. It purports to contribute to a better appraisal of the issues raised by these crises and the remedial policies. Their correct assessment has always been difficult to attain, partly because of economic and political prejudices, partly because simple half-truths appeal to the busy decision-makers and become embedded in the conventional wisdom, and partly because of incomplete information. Yet such an improved understanding would be of great value not only for academic endeavours in the field of petroleum economics but for all those concerned in different operational or policy-making capacities with the oil market and the oil industry. It would be of great value for all those involved within OPEC with the affairs and objectives of the organization, simply because improved knowledge about problems and tensions and thorough analysis of policy options improves their capability of managing crises.

There are two main phases in the history of OPEC. We shall not be concerned with the first phase, between 1960 and the early 1970s when OPEC's objective was to protect the economic interests of its members through bargaining with the major oil companies. This phase has little direct relevance to the issues of today. The second phase, which provides the time framework for the contents of this book, begins in the early 1970s when OPEC initiated fundamental changes in the structure of the oil market and when its main task became the administration of oil prices in international trade with the aim of increasing the income and wealth of its members.

The task, despite the successes of 1973 and the apparent achievements of 1979–80, was never an easy one. The administration of oil prices requires very strong intervention in the market against the opposing tendencies of powerful economic forces. OPEC seeks to set prices at a certain level and these forces are continually pulling these prices towards other levels, sometimes higher as in 1979, but often lower as in 1974–5, 1977–8 and throughout 1981–6.

When we mention in this Introduction, and generally in this book, OPEC's problems we are indeed referring to the diffi-culties of price management, to the perpetual tension between an institutional intervention in the market and the opposite tendencies of that market. When we mention the term 'crisis' we refer to situations when these difficulties became acute, either because the forces opposing OPEC's price administra-tion acquired additional momentum or because the difficulties themselves caused tensions between OPEC members, disagreement on policies or threatening breaches of discipline. In that sense the problems have always been there, even at times of much heralded successes, and the crises, fairly benign at first (1974–5 and 1977–8), have recurred with increasing gravity in 1982, 1984 and 1985–6.

The papers presented in Part I of this book are closely related to each other by common themes. They all address, in one way or another, the question of OPEC's behaviour in a slack oil market, a market in which the demand for OPEC oil falls below the aggregate volume that members are technically able and economically willing to produce. All these papers were written at the time of the events they analyse. Put together they constitute a retrospective which reveals, among other things, the perennial characteristics of the problems facing OPEC and of the organization's behaviour. It is instructive, for example, to read in Chapter 1, written in 1975, that OPEC's 'lack of concern about distribution [of revenues between members] can be detrimental in the new situation of falling demand',[1] that 'OPEC members, including the market leader Saudi Arabia, value for both economic and political reasons the survival and the cohesion of the group. Their ability to compromise and reach agreement should not be underestimated.'[2] The significance of the distributional issue was not fully appreciated by OPEC until 1982 when more serious difficulties than those encountered in 1975 led to the first attempt at allocating output under a quota system. And had oil experts remembered in 1986 the points made as early as 1975 about OPEC's 'ability to compromise' they would have been less surprised by the outcome of the Geneva meeting of July/August 1986 when the compromise was proposed by the most unlikely member, revolutionary Iran.

Chapter 2, also written in 1975, proposes a practical solution to the oil price differential problem which was ignored by OPEC and rejected by the oil companies at the time. In a system of administered prices, rigidly determined differentials cause distortions and lead to shifts in the distribution of exports among member countries because of rapid changes in the relative demand for different varieties of crude. The problem of price differentials getting continually out of line and causing tensions between member countries in periods of slack market conditions has plagued OPEC for most of the period 1974–85.

---

[1] See below p. 15   [2] See below p. 19

A simple, though not absolutely perfect solution, is for OPEC to administer the reference price and determine differentials *ex post* on the basis of actual product prices and tanker freight rates. Buyers will settle the price differential one or two months in arrears after they have been calculated on the basis of uniform and previously agreed formulae. The presumption is that they will be indifferent as regards the purchase of this or that crude variety since relative prices (but not the reference or base level, say the price of the marker crude) would closely relate to market realizations. Such an idea has become much more acceptable today than at the time of its first formulation, partly because of experience with analogous schemes (e.g. for Alaskan oil and for some non-oil commodities), and partly because the recent netback deals in oil (1985–6) have familiarized both OPEC and the industry with the idea of relating prices to realizations. If OPEC were to return to a policy of administered prices, and I believe it will, it would be well advised to consider this or similar schemes for the solution of the problem of price differentials.

A central aspect of the OPEC story relates to the role, the objectives and the policies of Saudi Arabia. Most, if not all the papers in Part I refer to this aspect. The importance of the Saudi role was naturally perceived from the beginning and was already analysed in 1975 (Chapter 2). The dictum 'One could almost say without too much exaggeration that OPEC *is* Saudi Arabia', was coined then.[3] More interestingly this early study identified the situation in which Saudi Arabia was to find itself ten years later in 1985 and the possible response. 'The only course of action open to Saudi Arabia if it wishes to regain control over the volume of its exports is to vary the marker price. But this is tantamount to dissolving OPEC.'[4] The paper also pointed out that although Saudi Arabia did not seem unduly disturbed in 1975 by the sharp movements in the volume of its oil exports 'in a few years' time, as absorptive capacity and commitments to aid and external investment rise, the Saudis may begin to place greater value on the stability of revenues'.[5] In 1985, Saudi Arabia abandoned the marker price

---

[3] See below p. 30
[4] See below p. 30   [5] See below p. 31

in response to a very sharp drop in the volume of its oil exports 'partly due to the actions of other producers and partly to the movements of aggregate demand for OPEC oil which it tends to shoulder to a much larger extent than other producers'.[6]

Saudi Arabia's policies are the main subject of Chapter 3 which analyses in some depth the 1978 decision to apply a 65/35 ratio of light and heavy crudes to oil exports. The policy was introduced for two main reasons: first to help Nigeria which was then badly hit by the emergence of North Sea production, and secondly to regulate the depletion of light crudes which are scarcer relative to heavy oil reserves. The application as a depletion device of a ratio rather than a ceiling on the production of light crudes was a clever device to avoid an international outcry against restrictive policies. The significance of this episode in the history of OPEC is in revealing that sophisticated policies can be usefully adopted in certain circumstances either by individual members or by the organization as a whole. There may be a lesson in this episode for those who, both within and outside OPEC, are always inclined to reject outright new ideas about policies when they are more subtle or more complex than conventional schemes.

The Saudi 'export ratio' policy, however interesting, was not of fundamental significance in later developments. The crucial issues relate to the events of 1979–81 and to the crises of 1982–3 and 1985–6. Saudi Arabia's policies in 1979–81 were motivated in a first phase by a desire to moderate price increases fuelled by buyers deeply concerned by the effects of actual supply disruptions and deeply affected by fears of a continuing supply shortfall. In 1979 there was a market imbalance, not because consumption requirements were higher than available supplies, but because companies and governments of the consuming countries were scrambling for additional oil as a result of: (a) 'structural changes ... which led to the withdrawal of the majors from the third-party market ...', and (b) 'uncertainty about future developments in Iran which induce a very significant inventory build-up'.[7] However the attempts at moderating prices made persistently by Saudi Arabia in 1979–80 were not successful. When the supply/demand balance was

---

[6] See below p. 30   [7] See below p. 53

tight there was no other leader than the market. All that happened was that Saudi Arabia's prices, instead of providing a target as a ceiling to other oil prices, lagged persistently behind them.

In a second phase (late 1980 and 1981), when demand began to decline and the market balance to slacken, Saudi Arabia placed a high priority on the need to restore order to the distorted oil price structure which emerged after the momentous events of the preceding year. The oil price explosion of 1979 not only pushed prices up to high levels but, in a literal sense, 'exploded' the price structure. Every country could sell its own crudes to the maximum of its productive capacity at virtually any price it dared to ask and no producer had to worry about the need to maintain its price in an 'equilibrium' relationship with the prices of competing crudes. When desired demand is higher than available supplies, there is no competition between producers or between different crude varieties. It is the buyers who compete and this is what an 'explosion' is all about.

Distortions of the oil price structure, inevitable during the boom, do not matter so long as the market remains tight. The difficulties arise when the recession sets in and when OPEC enters the slack period with a price structure inherited from the boom. This happened in 1974–5 (as noted in Chapters 1 and 2) and in 1980–81, that is after each of the two oil price revolutions. In both instances the distortions caused problems, more serious of course on the second occasion than on the first. As indicated above Saudi Arabia was determined in 1980–81 to restore order to the structure of relative prices. It was undoubtedly aware that OPEC would be unable to manage the slack market without a unified price policy, and that a very high price level would aggravate, through adverse effects on demand and non-OPEC supplies, the adverse market conditions affecting OPEC.

However, Saudi Arabia met strong political resistance from virtually all OPEC members when it attempted to obtain an agreement on an orderly price structure. OPEC countries were victims of mistaken beliefs about the nature of their oil power. They failed to see 'that their power does not reside in their ability to raise prices . . . independently of each other when the

market is tight, but in the ability to hold a unified price structure when the market is slack . . .'. This 'mistaken belief. . . .
has turned every Government Selling Price (GSP) into a political symbol.'[8] The delay in the resolution of this conflict for a
while maintained Saudi prices below the levels applied by
other OPEC members. Naturally companies lifted large
quantities of this relatively cheap and abundantly available oil
and added them to their stocks. They guessed correctly that the
agreement on the price structure that OPEC was likely to reach
later would probably involve some matching compromises on
the part of all concerned and, more specifically, that Saudi
Arabia would raise its own price by a few dollars in exchange
for a similar reduction of all other prices. In such circumstances
private commercial entities had an interest in buying quantities
in excess of their immediate requirements in anticipation of an
inventory profit.

This is precisely what happened in the end but considerable
harm was done. A huge inventory overhang cast its shadow
over an increasingly weak market until late in 1985.

In this context, it is important to stress that Saudi Arabia's
moderation does not reflect a systematic preference for very low
prices. Several papers in this collection are very revealing on
this issue which is widely misconstrued by oil experts. The
conventional wisdom today involves a totally misleading
picture of Saudi Arabia's motivations and objectives, and I can
only suggest that the two statements made by Sheikh Yamani
at the Oxford Energy Seminar in 1982 and 1985 (Chapters 6
and 14) be read without preconceptions and with great attention to the actual wording of the texts. He thus said in 1982 'I
think that it would be extremely harmful to reduce the price of
oil in money terms as was envisaged by the major consumers
when they started their campaign against OPEC earlier this
year to force us to reduce the price of oil.'[9] His preference was
for a freezing of the money price for a while leaving the necessary adjustments to the real price to the inevitable reflationary
process.

More important is his statement to the Seminar on 13
September 1985 which marked the historic turning-point for

---

[8] See below p. 49   [9] See below p. 72

Saudi and OPEC oil policy. This statement, which was wrongly interpreted as reflecting an interest on the part of Saudi Arabia in bringing about a price collapse and maintaining the oil price at a very low level for a long period, in fact reads very differently. The message, which is also the key to a correct assessment of Saudi Arabia's position was simply that 'Saudi Arabia is no longer willing or able to take that heavy burden and duty, and therefore it cannot be taken for granted.'[10] The burden was placed by 'the non-OPEC producers relying on OPEC to protect the price of oil' and by 'most of the OPEC member countries [which] depend on Saudi Arabia to . . . protect the price of oil.'[11]

Sheikh Yamani then defined the terms of two alternatives. The first, which he judged as immediately inevitable but which he clearly disliked, was described as follows: 'Either it is left for everybody to produce as much as he can, and sell at any price dictated by the market and we will see real *chaos*, we will see a sharp drop in the price of oil – maybe to within the range of $15 per barrel, maybe less . . .' (our italics).[12] It is well known that Saudi Arabia never relishes the prospect of chaos. He said indeed 'I am worried, and I think that the situation should worry everybody'.[13]

The second alternative, which he could not see materializing without the shock of a threat to the oil price, but which expresses his real objective is 'some sort of co-ordination between the non-OPEC producers and the OPEC producers, and also among the member countries within OPEC.'[14]

Saudi Arabia's oil policies, about which so much has been already said, are largely reactive. This is suggested by the quote stating that Saudi Arabia 'cannot be taken for granted'. The crisis of 1985–6, which this book aims to place in correct perspective, is the culmination of developments starting at the time of the 1979 boom. The initial causes of the current crisis and the real factors that brought it about in the end through their own gathering momentum are economic forces unleashed both by high oil prices and by consuming countries' fears of excessive dependence on OPEC oil supplies in an

[10] See below p. 166
[11] See below p. 166
[13] See below p. 168
[12] See below p. 166
[14] See below p. 167

uncertain world. Saudi Arabia's actions in 1985 were a late response to a situation which had already become intolerable to all OPEC members who try to mitigate it by placing additional burdens on Saudi Arabia. It is fair to say, if the matters are assessed in the correct time framework and in proper perspective, that Saudi Arabia was reacting to a crisis that was already there rather than causing it. To take an analogy from history: battles are lost when the last bastion falls, but the fall of the last bastion is never interpreted by military historians as the cause of the defeat since it is the surrender of all the previous posts which isolated the last one and destroyed its ability to resist.

To assess the role of the economic forces which brought about the 1986 price collapse and the flaws in OPEC's policies which aggravated the problems, the reader is referred to almost all chapters of Part I and to Part III of this book. Of particular significance is the paper by the Research Group on Petroleum Exporters' Policies written in late 1982 and reproduced here because its message remains topical despite the drastic change in circumstances.

To examine and analyse crises is a sterile exercise unless the issues of policy and strategy are addressed. In the same vein, we should add that the examination of the past has more than intrinsic value if it can help us with current problems and with the issues of the future. All the papers in this book discuss policies. Common themes seem to persist throughout the ten years during which these papers were written. The central idea is that price administration is the only policy consistent with OPEC's objectives in a slack market. A production policy based on quotas (not necessarily fixed) is a necessary adjunct, but it is a second line of defence and it cannot, on its own, stabilize the market. The aim of the production programme is to ensure that the allocation of output shares, and hence of revenues, is tolerable and that it will not become so distorted by shifts of buyers' preferences for this or that source of supply to the point that price discipline becomes intolerable. The ability to hold the oil price along a preferred path when the market is slack is the real test of OPEC's power. This is emphasized in one paper which goes as far as saying that the true manifestation of OPEC's power was in the time of crises and not in 1973 and

1979 when OPEC gained the recognition but when the tightness of the market was the real cause of the price increases.

It remains true, however, that OPEC price policies lacked sophistication. It proved simpler, largely for political reasons, to hold prices at the levels reached during the boom rather than to bring them back on a path determined by a long-term strategy. If the current crisis is resolved, OPEC will need to address again this issue which has been 'temporarily' shelved since the beginning of the decade. For that reason Al Chalabi's paper in Part IV is both important and topical. It examines the complex aspects of the issue and suggests lines of thought for further debate and consideration.

OPEC is not the only important agent in world oil. On policy matters non-OPEC exporters and the industrial consuming countries have a major role to play. In several papers OPEC's views on the desired co-operation with non-OPEC producers and the consuming countries are forcefully expressed. The reader will also find in Parts II and III thoughtful expressions of the positions of responses of these other parties to the debate. The papers by Fried and Wendt, and the interventions of Davignon, Beteta, Johnsen, Reviglio and Crutchfield in the 1985 Oxford Energy Seminar (Part III of this book) are important documents in this respect.

The purpose of this Introduction was to present some of the themes developed in the various contributions of this book. It is not a summary and much is left for the reader to discover for her or himself. The other aim is to give an idea of the coherence of the book's structure which is both chronological and thematic. It may not be necessary to add more.

PART I

THE UNEASY RELATIONSHIP BETWEEN OPEC AND
THE MARKET

1 CAN OPEC HOLD THE LINE? (1975)*

Robert Mabro

Introduction

The view that a reduction of world demand for oil will force lower prices and lead to the disintegration of OPEC is frequently expressed in the USA and elsewhere. These propositions are not meaningful predictions because they are open-ended. They beg many questions. When? How? What is the size of the expected fall in price? What would be the relevance of price reductions to the solution of international monetary and economic problems if these reductions were immediate but small? Or, if they were significant but occurring after an interval of several years? Nobody cares to be explicit. Yet, these views are becoming influential in some political and academic circles and may play an important role in the formulation of policy.

The purpose of this paper is to examine the validity of these propositions within a specific time period, say, the next five years. It involves a short discussion of the nature and policy instruments of OPEC, an analysis of the distribution of oil production capacity within OPEC, a study of the *present* effects of slack demand on oil supplies and prices, and an evaluation of OPEC's problems and OPEC's likely responses and strategies.

The Nature of OPEC

OPEC is often referred to as a cartel. This is at best an approximation which pre-empts qualified thinking about the nature of this organization. It is fair to say that neither OPEC as a group

* Lecture delivered at the oil seminar of Professor Edith Penrose, School of Oriental and African Studies, London, 13 February 1975. Published in *Middle East Economic Survey*, Supplement to Vol. XVIII, No. 19, 28 February 1975.

nor its individual members have acted in the monopolistic fashion that consists of 'selling less than would be in one's economic interest at the going price in order to raise the price'. The production cut-backs of October 1973 were imposed by Arab oil producers for a specific political purpose; and the subsequent price rises were largely the consequence of the cut-backs rather than their objective.

The term 'cartel' may suggest to the uninformed that output controls in the form of pro-rationing or an agreed cut-back by a significant producer are the instruments applied by OPEC. Our audience here is informed and knows that OPEC has on occasions discussed production programmes but never implemented such measures. Its preferred instruments are taxes and/or prices.

Two simple economic interpretations, not mutually exclusive, account for OPEC's behaviour. The first is that OPEC tries to do what a primary producer faced with a less than perfectly elastic demand curve for its products would always be recommended to do: impose an export tax. That recommendation is legitimate and relates to a respectable concept in economics – the optimum tariff argument. There are practical difficulties in determining the correct rate of taxation and problems of trading off short-term objectives and long-term economic interests, but no other objections to the argument. The right of a country, especially a developing country, to give precedence to its economic welfare over the welfare of other countries is seldom questioned. The second interpretation recognizes a special characteristic of mineral resources, namely the interdependence of production and future availabilities. A case for fiscal measures or a production plan arises, whether monopoly power exists or not, when present prices diverge from expected future prices properly discounted. The oil price rises of 1973 may have been partly motivated by such considerations and thus may be construed as an attempt by oil-producing countries to react to long-term interests endangered by non-economic rates of production.

These interpretations may not catch the popular imagination with the same impact as the word 'cartel'. But they do not carry the same emotional connotations and they are closer to the truth.

The Policy Instruments of OPEC

Fiscal and price measures, the preferred instruments of OPEC, have certain advantages over pro-rationing and output restrictions. They are more acceptable to the rest of the world. Other things being equal, consumers generally prefer the freedom of buying any desired quantity at given prices to restrictions on the quantities offered. Markets tend to function in an orderly fashion in the first case; speculation and a scramble for available supplies will tend to characterize the second instance. There are certain advantages to producers too. Taxes and prices are easier to agree upon and administer than production programmes. Finally, in markets operated by intermediaries, output controls have unpredictable distributional effects which can infinitely complicate the relationship between producers and market intermediaries, namely the oil companies.

In an imperfect world, policy instruments relate imperfectly to objectives. Difficulties arise even if the instrument used is theoretically the best of several available alternatives. The difficulties are of two sorts: (a) the definition of objectives; and (b) the choice of the correct parameters (say the price or the tax rate) to maximize these objectives. They are further compounded when the decisions have to suit a group of governments. Up to the present, OPEC seems to have set itself a simple objective: to increase (rather than to maximize) members' revenues when circumstances are favourable and to check a fall in revenue per barrel when circumstances are adverse. OPEC has not been explicitly concerned with the distribution of gains among members. Price or tax increases have generally resulted in higher revenues for all members though some often gain significantly more than others. The wisdom is to accept that significant gains, unequally distributed, are better than no gains. And OPEC was wise to build its cohesion in the pursuit of feasible objectives, as another course might have entailed paralysis. We shall see, however, that the lack of concern about distribution can be detrimental in the new situation of falling demand. There is a case for policies more sophisticated than those pursued to date.

The use of fiscal or price measures, instead of pro-rationing, means that OPEC has no *direct* control over the distribution of supplies between producers or the distribution of gains resulting from a price or tax increase. This distribution reflects buyers' responses to the prices set by OPEC. Buyers' responses, of course, are subject to a variety of economic, technological, contractual and other constraints. OPEC can indirectly influence the distribution by varying the price structure for crudes of different types and origins.

The distribution of supplies between producers – or, if one prefers, their market shares – would tend to remain stable if buyers were faced by uniform prices from all sources. The relevant price in this context is the cost to the buyer, not the f.o.b. price. The fiscal and pricing systems of OPEC are imperfect and do not lead to such an equalization of buyers' prices for three main reasons. First, in many producing countries the same physical crude is sold at two different prices – one price for company oil, one price for government oil. In such a situation, companies tend to lift relatively more from countries where they hold concessions than from countries engaging in direct sales. Secondly, OPEC tax formulae do not equalize the tax-paid cost of any given crude if costs of production differ. This has a distributional effect in favour of countries with lower costs of extraction. Thirdly, the major complication arises from differences in the quality and transport costs of different types of crude. Price or tax differentials are imposed to allow for relative advantages. But the value of these advantages varies with market conditions (i.e. with changes in the spot freight rate and in the relative demand for crudes of different gravity and different sulphur content) while price differentials tend to remain sticky or to adjust imperfectly after long lags. The formulae that express these price differentials do not involve the correct economic variables (e.g. AFRA, which is an average freight rate, is used instead of the spot, or marginal, rate) and hence adjust imperfectly. Some governments are reluctant to adjust the differentials – which are *meant* to be variable – because prices have become sacrosanct. In most cases, smooth and rapid responses are impossible because of the very nature of administered prices. Thus, differentials can easily get out of line and they do. These distortions may have a significant influence on the distribution of market shares.

OPEC can afford to ignore such a phenomenon during a boom. Dangerous situations may arise when demand is slack.

The Recent Fall in Oil Demand and its Effects

The slack in oil demand of late 1974 has been accompanied by interesting shifts in the distribution of supplies. Taking September 1983 as a base and comparing average production levels of July–December 1974 and December 1974 with the base, average OPEC output in July–December 1974 was some 10 per cent lower than in September 1973. But this global reduction was far from being equally distributed among producers. The data are presented in Table 1.1. Two features stand out: first, production increased slightly in the two largest producing countries – Saudi Arabia and Iran; and secondly, two countries alone seem to have taken the brunt of the fall in demand: Kuwait and Libya. Output in July–December 1974 compared with September 1973 was 37 per cent down in Kuwait and 47 per cent down in Libya. In fact 74 per cent of the total fall in demand was absorbed by these two countries (2.39 million barrels out of 3.23 million).

Table 1.1: Oil Production of OPEC Countries, 1973–4, and Percentage Changes. Million Barrels per Day.

Country	Sep 1973	Average Jul–Dec 1974	% Change Over Sep 1973	Dec 1974	% Change Over Sep 1973
Saudi Arabia	8.57	8.63	+0.7	8.05	−6.1
Iran	5.83	5.90	+1.2	5.94	+0.6
Kuwait	3.53	2.21	−37.4	2.32	−34.3
Iraq	2.11	1.94	−8.0	2.18	+3.3
Abu Dhabi	1.40	1.36	−2.8	1.21	−13.6
Qatar	0.60	0.52	−13.3	0.52	−13.3
Libya	2.29	1.22	−46.7	1.00	−56.3
Algeria	1.10	0.97	−11.8	0.90	−18.2
Venezuela	3.39	2.82	−16.8	2.70	−20.3
Nigeria	2.14	2.24	+4.7	2.10	−1.8
Indonesia	1.42	1.34	−5.6	1.10	−22.5
Total	32.38	29.15	−9.97	28.02	−13.46

A closer look at the production trends over July–December 1974, extended to January 1975, reveals other interesting features. Libyan output declined steadily month after month during this period. Abu Dhabi followed the same trend with a 25 per cent reduction between the peak in July 1974 and December 1974 output, sharply aggravated in January 1975 by a further dramatic drop in output (37 per cent in one month). In Kuwait, on the contrary, there is no trend but a once-for-all fall between June and July 1974. Output behaviour in Kuwait is attributable to a producer's decision. It seems that in Libya and Abu Dhabi the market or other agents played the major role.

The economic explanation is simple. Product differentiation provides the clue. Both Libyan and Abu Dhabi crude command quality and transport differentials. In 1974 these differentials, fixed in relation to conditions or expectations pertaining to special circumstances, became increasingly out of line. There was a collapse in spot freight rates, a change in demand for light and heavy products, increasing excess capacity in desulphurization plants, and a relaxation of sulphur regulations in certain countries. The freight and quality advantages of Libyan crude eroded faster than its supply price. This is probably true of Abu Dhabi too. Algeria and Nigeria were less affected because they tend to sell to captive markets – France and the USA respectively.

Taking $10.46 as the price for the marker crude (December 1974/January 1975) we may roughly compute that Libyan 40 °API crude with a sulphur content of 0.45 per cent would appear attractive at around $11.54, assuming a Worldscale freight rate of 40. It was offered at $16.00 in January 1974, $13.48 in July, $12.50 in October and $11.86 in January 1975. Despite these adjustments, Libyan crude has probably always been overpriced. A similar argument could be made for Abu Dhabi.

Are market forces solely responsible for these shifts in market shares? *The Economist* suggested that other factors may be at work.[1] A deliberate attempt to break the 'cartel' by exerting pressure on producers one by one? I know not. If such a plot

[1] 8 February 1975, p. 69.

existed it would be logical to pick on Abu Dhabi. Abu Dhabi has considerable productive capacity. A sudden drop in liftings would be aimed, in the first instance, at undermining the base price in the Gulf. If Abu Dhabi succumbed and lowered its price by more than was warranted by differential adjustment, liftings would be resumed and rapidly increased to very high levels. Demand would be sucked off from other major sources in the Gulf, thus further undermining the price structure.

Plot or no plot, it is essential for OPEC to avoid distortions in the price structure which could undermine, because of undesirable distributional effects, the cohesion of the group.

Strength and Weaknesses

The natural strength of OPEC arises from the distribution of oil production capacity among members. Countries with large populations and considerable development needs tend to have either small oil reserves (Algeria, Nigeria, Indonesia) or large reserves but small installed capacity (Iraq). The only large producer with considerable expenditure needs is Iran. But Iran is unlikely to engage in competitive undercutting in order to increase its share of the market. If historical precedents have any meaning, one could recall that Iran avoided such a course of action in the late 1960s when it was much poorer and in greater need of money than at present. Countries with large oil reserves or fairly large installed capacity such as Saudi Arabia, Kuwait or Abu Dhabi are cushioned in a falling market by financial reserves.

It is important to recall that OPEC members, including the market leader Saudi Arabia, value for both economic and political reasons the survival and the cohesion of the group. Their ability to compromise and reach agreement should not be underestimated. It is founded on the belief that all members – including the largest producers – would be worse off without OPEC. This belief is both rational and deeply felt. It should also be recalled that OPEC was created in a time of crisis and that crises are more likely to cement the unity of the group than to weaken it. The real danger – exemplified by the drift of the price structure in 1974 – is carelessness after a major success.

OPEC can withstand a further fall in world demand for its

oil. No change in the nature of its policy is required. But the price/tax instruments must be made more sophisticated, with flexible and responsive differentials. An adjustment of price differentials need not result in a lower average price of crude, nor in a lower posting for the marker crude.

Let us assume very pessimistically that some time during the next five years demand for OPEC oil falls to as low a level as 22 mb/d. OPEC could still hold on a simple pro-rationing programme that would allow small producing countries such as Algeria, Indonesia and Nigeria to maintain their present levels of production. Table 1.2 shows a possible distribution.

Table 1.2: Hypothetical Distribution of Output for the OPEC Countries. Million Barrels per Day.

Country	Output
Saudi Arabia	5.0
Iran	5.0
Kuwait	1.5
Abu Dhabi	1.0
Iraq	2.0
Qatar	0.5
Venezuela	2.5
Algeria	1.0

This ought not to be difficult to achieve. In any case few observers believe that demand will fall that low during the next five years. Substitution will only be felt in the 1980s and conservation is making slow progress. The level of economic activity in the industrialized world is already low and this is reflected in the present levels of demand for oil. Conditions may worsen still. The more severe and the longer the depression, the greater the chances of a generalized boom of exceptional magnitude. To hold tight during the impending depression would enable OPEC to take advantage of a likely recovery, forecast for the later years of this decade.

There is no reason why OPEC should collapse in the next five years. But members ought to watch and anticipate the market and adapt their pricing policies or contingency pro-rationing plans to expected conditions. Policy responses to depressed demand are within OPEC's capabilities. It would be absurd if OPEC allowed its cohesion to be undermined.

Different problems arise in the long term. But there is a period of grace because investment in alternative sources of energy has a long lead time and because consumers have great difficulties in formulating viable energy policies. Here again OPEC has an opportunity to take advantage of this period of grace to define its long-term objectives and policies. To miss this opportunity and waste time may be of grave consequence for the future.

2   OPEC AFTER THE OIL REVOLUTION (1975)*

Robert Mabro

The oil revolution is now two years old. The price increases, the temporary production cut-back of October 1973 and the seemingly permanent changes in the system of price determination from bilateral negotiations to direct administration by OPEC constitute a set of events which had, and may continue to have, far-reaching implications for the world economy and international relations. Much has already been written about the consequences of the oil revolution for international finance, trade and payments and about its adverse effects on economic growth in both advanced and developing countries. By comparison, much less has been said about the implications of the oil revolution for OPEC. In fact, the nature of the organization, its mode of operation and the behaviour of the petroleum market in which OPEC is a major agent are not always clearly understood.

Though two years is in some respects a short period, it may be appropriate to pause and ask how OPEC is faring after the oil revolution. Oil price increases have significantly transformed demand conditions in the world petroleum market. OPEC now faces an unfamiliar situation – decline or stagnation instead of steady growth in the volume of its exports. A depressed market tends to create strains and hence may represent a possible threat to the solidarity of the members. What are these strains and how serious is this threat? OPEC successes in late 1973, however impressive and significant, were achieved with simple means in very favourable circumstances. To preserve these successes in a strained market may call for new responses and more sophisticated policies. What is the nature of these policies and what are the difficulties involved in

* First published in *Millennium: Journal of International Studies*, London School of Economics, Vol. 4, No. 3, Winter 1975–76.

designing and implementing them? The purpose of this article is to provide some answers to these questions. The hope is to throw some light on the nature of OPEC and contribute to a balanced appraisal of its role.

The main characteristic of the world petroleum market before October 1973 was a steady and rapid growth of demand for OPEC oil. Growth and expectations of further expansion strained the price system agreed upon in Tripoli and Tehran in late 1970 and early 1971. Most oil-exporting countries within OPEC – with the notable exception of Saudi Arabia – were then operating either close to capacity or close to a ceiling determined by long-term conservation objectives. There was no reserve capacity outside OPEC. Oil production in the USA, both the top world producer and the country with the largest incremental demand, was on the decline. No relief could be expected from the North Sea before the late 1970s. Saudi Arabia was expected to supply on its own a very substantial proportion of world incremental demand for oil. In such a situation prices are bound to rise.

The mechanism is simple. Pressures on productive capacity in various countries signal the emergence of excess demand for specific varieties of crude oil. Excess demand leads to rises in the price of petroleum in arm's length transactions which in turn signal to oil-producing countries the opportunity for an upward revision of administered prices. The existence of excess capacity in one country – in this instance, Saudi Arabia – does not imply that countervailing pressures will be brought to bear to prevent price increases. On the contrary, the immediate presumption is that the country that enjoys a virtual monopoly over incremental supplies in this peculiar market structure would itself act as a price leader and set the mining tax at the level that maximizes long-term revenues. The optimum price for such a monopolist may be lower than the price that maximizes the income of small producers. The former has large petroleum reserves and must protect the long-term security of its market from the threat of substitutes; the latter have small mineral endowments and will gladly take the highest price oil can immediately fetch. The distinction between price leader (Saudi Arabia) and militants (producers with small reserves) is crucial to the understanding of OPEC.

The leader can afford to be quiet because he has real power and is ultimately the price maker; the militants are vocal but ultimately can be forced into the position of price takers. The moderating influence of the monopolist over the militants is often misconstrued as a vested interest in price inertia. This is not true. Saudi Arabia wanted a price increase in October 1973 and was instrumental in bringing about the concealed increases arising from participation agreements in 1974. Allowing for necessary compromises made for the sake of solidarity within OPEC, it is fair to say that the price of oil is as high as Saudi Arabia is prepared to allow.

In late 1973, OPEC acted from an economic standpoint in a perfectly predictable way. The combination of excess demand in markets served by small producers and of a monopoly in the incremental market provides a sufficient economic explanation of price increases. Political factors influenced the timing of the price hike and perhaps the size of the increase. They may explain the manner in which OPEC broke off bilateral negotiations with companies and took over as the sole price administrator. They are not, in my view, the cause of price increases.

Despite changes in the form of OPEC actions (the change from bargaining with companies to bargaining between members on the appropriate level of prices) and the enhanced significance of these actions, the events of 1973 did not transform the economic nature of the organization. OPEC used to be likened to a trade union and after October 1973 was labelled a cartel. This change in characterization is extremely misleading. The important point is that, both before and after October 1973, OPEC has been solely concerned with prices (or more precisely with unit revenues of oil exports). OPEC has, as yet, never behaved as an ordinary cartel. It administers prices rather than output. There is no control on aggregate supplies, nor is there any agreement between members on production shares. Price administration itself is limited to a single type of crude oil – Saudi Arabian Light, 34 °API – known as the marker crude. Attempts to administer the whole price structure for quality (gravity and sulphur contents) and location differentials have never been successful. The beauty and, in a sense, the main strength of the so-called oil producers' cartel lies in the extreme simplicity of its function and mode of operation: the periodic determination of a single oil price.

One may think at first sight that output controls and price administration are equivalent in their effects. This would only be true if the shape and position of the demand curve were known and if demand shifts over time could be correctly anticipated; but the real world is characterized by uncertainty and imperfect information. Further, administrative controls lack the flexibility necessary for prompt adjustment in the face of changes in demand. In practice, the use of a price instrument allows offtake to fluctuate; the use of quantity controls would lead to price variations.

The economic model of the market for OPEC oil exports may be characterized as follows. Buyers face a perfectly elastic supply curve at the administered price and shifts in demand are translated into fluctuations in the quantity purchased. One often reads – not only in the Press but, alas, in academic articles – that OPEC or Saudi Arabia maintains the price by restricting output. But in fact output is determined by demand given a fixed price. The difference between the two propositions is important. Had OPEC controlled output instead of fixing prices the very marked monthly variations in demand that have characterized the world petroleum market since mid-1974 would have led to very unstable prices. All things considered, the simple mechanism adopted by OPEC turns out to be preferable, from the consumers' point of view, to the alternative method of output control. Certainty about price levels over definite periods of time (the period between the two significant OPEC meetings) and freedom to match offtake to shifts in demand at the ruling price are the valuable features of the system.

Recourse to the price instrument has also been to OPEC's advantage. It is easier to decide on a common single price than to agree on a system of output quotas or to devise a complex structure of price premiums for a differentiated product. The advantage of the first method is swift effectiveness. Simplicity and convenience, however, are bought at a price: the members of the organization should be prepared to set aside any concern about the distribution of gains and leave it to the invisible hand of the market. The other methods bring the delicate issue of distribution into the open and agreement becomes very difficult to reach. These difficulties are well known and have paralysed many would-be cartels or brought about their early collapse.

In 1973, OPEC could safely ignore the distribution issue and was wise in doing so. As mentioned earlier, most producers were operating close to desired levels of capacity and the bulk of incremental demand had to be supplied by Saudi Arabia. None of the small producers (except perhaps Iraq) either could or had the desire to improve its short-term position by the supply of increased quantities; and Saudi Arabia was beginning to feel unhappy about the excessive demands placed by hungry oil consumers on her. The price increase was expected to benefit all producers because its effects on revenues could not be cancelled by any plausible decline in offtake. A typical Pareto situation was involved with every OPEC member becoming better off and none worse off after a bold price increase. There was no need to incur risks of disagreement and possible paralysis with an irrelevant concern for the distribution of gains.

At that time, OPEC had no reason to worry about the distributional effects of a distorted price structure for the different varieties of crude. It must be recalled here that any *administered* price structure always suffers from distortions because market information about the exact premium that equalizes the opportunity cost of using this or that type of crude is very imperfect. Further, administered prices are inevitably rigid. They may be subject to frequent and discrete revision but do not respond smoothly to changes in market conditions. In 1973, because of generalized excess demand, distortions in the price structure probably had little effect on the distribution of output among oil producers. None of the small producers was selling significantly below capacity because the price of its crude was too high in relation to that of other varieties. Pressures on capacity deprived buyers of the ability to respond to relative prices by purchasing more here and less there. They wanted, rather, to buy more from everywhere. The fact that all prices were too low blurred the significance of relative prices.

The critical question is whether the distribution issue could be ignored in all circumstances. OPEC did not immediately realize (nobody did for that matter) that the distribution issue will reassert itself in conditions of excess capacity through buyers' responses to distortions in the price structure. It is important to stress that the problem is not excess capacity (or decline in the aggregate demand for OPEC oil) as such. In the absence of distortions in the price structure, the initial distribution would probably have remained stable in the face of a general fall in demand. Every producer would have incurred a loss in output roughly proportional to his share of the market, and the solidarity of OPEC members would not be subjected to strains even if losses in output were very substantial. It is the combination of excess capacity and relative price distortions that creates problems.

These problems have characterized the petroleum market since mid-1974 and throughout 1975. Total monthly exports from OPEC began to decline steadily from May 1974 (31.8 mb/d) until April 1975 (25.8 mb/d). Stock replenishment and speculative purchases in the summer of 1975 (in anticipation of the September price rise) led to increases in offtake back to 30.5 mb/d in September. In the following month, however, exports hit a new low at some 25.2 mb/d. The interesting phenomenon observed during this period is that movements of exports from individual producers often diverged very markedly from this general pattern. The market witnessed a series of violent shifts, now against, now in favour of this or that producer. Libyan exports fell from 1.95 mb/d in May 1974 to 0.96 mb/d in November of that year (a 50 per cent decline to be compared with an aggregate fall in OPEC offtake of only 7 per cent between these two months). Later, Libyan exports climbed in large discrete steps from 1.14 mb/d in May 1975 to 1.52 mb/d and 2.10 mb/d in June and July respectively (OPEC total exports rose by 6.8 per cent between May and July 1975). Abu Dhabi exports fell from 1.22 mb/d in December 1974 to 0.75 mb/d in February 1975 (having peaked earlier on at 1.62 mb/d in July 1974) and then started to climb fast reaching 1.83 mb/d in July 1975. Qatar suffered a sharp drop in output between April and July 1975 (a 50 per cent decline); and Iraq enjoyed a steady growth in exports throughout the whole period considered (May 1974–October 1975) in spite of the decline of aggregate offtake from OPEC.

These phenomena can be easily explained. Oil producers entered the recession era with a price structure inherited from the days of the boom. Since OPEC was only concerned with the price of marker crude, decisions about differentials were left to individual members (changes in premiums are subject to some formalities but they are largely irrelevant). Meanwhile two major circumstances had changed. First, world recession not only led to a decline in the aggregate demand for petroleum but also altered the composition of demand for oil products, created excess capacity in refineries and desulphurization plants, and sent tanker freight rates tumbling down. These changes had repercussions on the demand conditions for different varieties of crude, increasing the possibilities of substituting one kind for another, and hence lowering the differentials that equalize their relative attractiveness to buyers. Secondly, the emergence of excess capacity in oil-producing countries enabled buyers to shift with considerable ease from one source to another whenever the price differential asked for one variety of crude was thought to be higher than the additional costs involved in using another. This discrepancy need not be large to elicit sizeable shifts in purchases from one source to another. Buyers have shown considerable sensitivity by responding swiftly to marginal discrepancies. In other words, demand for different varieties of petroleum has become almost perfectly elastic (over a long range) at a price related to that of the marker crude. The market differential is determined by the opportunity costs of substitution. These costs vary over time.

The seller's problem is to discover the correct value of this differential. If he makes the wrong guess and insists on too high a premium he prices himself out of the market. In the present circumstances of the oil industry the decline in exports – as we have seen – tends both to be steep and to occur very rapidly. But this reaction constitutes a strong signal calling for a downward adjustment of the administered premium. The seller may respond quickly but not sufficiently. It took Libya several months and a series of successive price reductions to approach the correct level. During this process the seller may overshoot reaching in the end a lower price than warranted. It seems that in mid-1975 both Libya and Abu Dhabi found themselves in this situation. Here again the market immediately indicated that the price was too low through a sharp rise in the level of offtake. Libya sold more than 2 mb/d in July and August 1975 and Abu Dhabi 1.8 mb/d in July. Two or three months earlier both had been unable to sell half these respective amounts.

All this may be inconvenient for the individual oil producer but need not be very worrying. A learning process is involved in the continual search for the correct price; and the market signals are so immediate and so strong that no seller need be trapped for too long in an unfavourable position.

This situation, however, has different implications for a particular oil producer – Saudi Arabia – and for OPEC as a group. Saudi Arabia constitutes a special case because it holds the reference price (that of the marker crude). As there is no differential to adjust it cannot itself alter the relative price of marker *vis-à-vis* other varieties but has to take the repercussions of changes effected by other producers. Its situation is analogous to that of the USA in the international monetary field under the pre-Smithsonian system. The USA could not alter the dollar exchange rate *vis-à-vis* any currency but all other countries could. Saudi oil exports are thus subject to fluctuations that result from changes in relative prices introduced by other producers. Other things being equal, Saudi exports rise when other producers price themselves out of the market and fall when they suck off demand by lowering their differentials too much. The only course of action open to Saudi Arabia if it wishes to regain control over the volume of its exports is to vary the marker price. But this is tantamount to dissolving OPEC. After all, the only significant function of the organization at present is to fix the reference price. This analysis reveals the way in which Saudi Arabia is the linchpin of OPEC. One could almost say without too much exaggeration that OPEC *is* Saudi Arabia.

So far, Saudi Arabia does not seem to be disturbed by the sharp movements in the volume of its oil exports (partly due to the actions of other producers and partly to the movements of aggregate demand for OPEC oil which it tends to shoulder to a much larger extent than other producers). This instability is not troublesome at present because its oil revenues exceed actual expenditures by a comfortable margin. But in a few years' time, as absorptive capacity and commitments to aid and external investment rise, the Saudis may begin to place greater value on the stability of revenues for planning purposes.

We may now turn to the implications of the situation described above for OPEC. There is no doubt that the strong shifts in offtake from one source to another and the clumsy process of price adjustment that has characterized the market since mid-1974 involve strains. It would be wrong, however, to exaggerate their immediate significance. Outside observers were too prompt to interpret repeated adjustments of price differentials as the beginning of a spiral that would drag down the price of marker crude. This interpretation misses an important point, namely that differentials are meant to be adjusted both up and down according to circumstances. What matters is not whether premiums are varied but whether producers take systematic advantage of this process for competitive undercutting. Judging from the behaviour of monthly exports in 1974–5 it would seem that Iraq is the only country that manipulates its price in a consistent manner. How else could one explain the slow but fairly steady rise of Iraqi exports in a contracting market? Both Libya and Abu Dhabi seem to have underpriced their crude in 1975. But their behaviour is of a different nature: an over-reaction to the shock created by a very substantial drop in export volumes. Both ended up with a higher offtake than their desired target. Libya would like to limit herself to 1.5 mb/d (instead of the 2.1 mb/d reached in July–August 1975) and Abu Dhabi is likely to become a conservationist with a preferred output level of 1.0–1.2 mb/d. It is true that in certain instances the line between legitimate adjustments and undercutting is difficult to draw; true that several producers have granted generous credit terms to companies, undoubtedly a form of discount; true that, if they were not bound by professional secrecy, company buyers could cite many deals that involve price concessions. All this is very untidy indeed and yet does not amount to very much. No amount of wishful thinking could liken it to cut-throat competition or deadly price war.

OPEC, nevertheless, would feel more comfortable in a tidier market. The issue of price differentials is receiving attention and experts have been commissioned to build models and make proposals. It is not clear whether the present intention is to attempt central determination of price differentials. Such an endeavour is too complex and is unlikely to succeed. To replace price administration by individual sellers with a centralized system would enhance rather than remove rigidities. The difficulty is not to devise formulae that determine *ex post* what the differential should have been. The real difficulty is inherent in the procedure that quotes premiums *ex ante*. In this procedure the individual seller has to form a judgement in advance on market conditions susceptible to rapid changes. The judgement can never be very accurate and we have seen that the market heavily penalizes mistakes. To replace the judgement of the individual seller by that of a collective machinery, even if backed by sophisticated (but how workable?) world energy models does not remove the difficulty. It is possible to argue that the individual oil producer, because he is close to his market and to the few companies that deal with him (in fact much bargaining and exchange of information does take place), is likely to make better decisions on prices than the collective machinery. There would still be a case, if the present system is retained, for improvements in the information, expertise, methods and techniques available to oil ministries for the determination of prices. OPEC could provide much more technical backing than it has done so far.

If the system is to be changed, I would be inclined to recommend a procedure in which differentials are not announced in advance but determined *ex post*, say every quarter, on the basis of actual data on costs, tanker freight rates and product prices prevailing in the preceding period. In other words buyers would pay their premiums in arrears and these premiums would closely reflect the realized advantage of having purchased this or that crude. The merit of such a procedure is that it could stabilize the distribution of OPEC exports among members. There would be no strong incentive for buyers to shift swiftly from this or that source as they do at present in response to misquotations. Though neither buyers nor sellers would know in advance what the exact premiums on current purchases were going to be (a minor inconvenience given that premiums represent a small percentage of the reference price), both would enjoy the certainty that no losses would be made. At present sellers suffer sometimes substantial loss in revenues as a result of misquotations; and though buyers are cushioned to some extent by their ability to withdraw some of their custom they are surely not in a position to stop all purchases from a country where oil is temporarily overpriced. This proposal does not involve bargaining over differentials. Some formula should be devised and applied consistently using recognized sources of information. There are undoubtedly some technical difficulties and the perfectionists will always object that the relative valuations of various types of crude at any given time differ from market to market and company to company. There is no need, however, for extreme sophistication because these differences are likely to be marginal. Clearly, these ideas require further discussion and elaboration. Whether they will elicit the interest of OPEC or oil experts remains to be seen.

I argued earlier that OPEC could afford to ignore the distributional issue when the market was buoyant and pressures on productive capacity were felt. In 1974 and 1975 significant excess capacity emerged and several producers faced unstable markets for their product – some of them because of false trading and Saudi Arabia because of its twin role as leader and buffer. Distribution is beginning to be perceived as a problem. But although offtake has been as low as 25 mb/d in certain months while total usable productive capacity is estimated at some 37 mb/d, OPEC has not dissolved through competitive undercutting. OPEC's strength is partly due to a physical factor – the concentrated distribution of productive capacity and oil reserves among members which gives so much to Saudi Arabia and leaves the other producers with little ability to break the market – and partly to a political economy factor – all members realize that they are ultimately better off both in terms of revenues and in terms of international recognition with, rather than without, OPEC. This latter argument also applies to Saudi Arabia, the linchpin of the organization and the member with the real power to keep it together or to break it.

If offtake from OPEC continues to decline, the strains arising from an erratic distribution of the reduction in total output among members could become dangerous. But OPEC need not collapse. There are several, yet untried, lines of defence. One is to replace the simple policy that restricts itself to the determination of the reference price by a policy that involves the whole price structure. There is some urgency here. First, because such a system cannot be designed and tested overnight; secondly, and irrespective of whether offtake declines, stagnates or begins to rise, Saudi Arabia may soon begin to favour greater stability in the volume of her exports. Another line of defence is to resort to production programming and quotas. Agreement on such a programme involves difficulties but they may be surmounted in an emergency. Resort to such a scheme would then turn OPEC for the first time in its history into a true cartel.

Whether OPEC's position will strengthen or weaken in the next five or six years is difficult to predict. The future trend of demand for OPEC oil is a crucial factor which depends on the scale, timing and duration of the expected (but much delayed) world economic recovery. The present level of demand falls between two critical limits, both within easy reach. If offtake declined to 20–22 mb/d and stagnated at or below that level, OPEC would face difficulties calling for the adoption of new measures. But offtake could as easily jump to 32–34 mb/d. Moderate growth in the world economy coinciding with favourable seasonal factors would be sufficient to send demand up to that level. In the summer of 1975, replenishment and speculative building up of stocks raised offtake by 5 mb/d in three months. Little is needed to restore OPEC to a position of great strength. An offtake of 32–34 mb/d implies the emergence of excess demand for several varieties of crude and pressures on the productive capacity of small oil-exporting countries: a familiar situation which could take the story back to where it first began with a round of price increases.

3 THE MARKER AND THE MARKET, THE HEAVY AND THE LIGHT (1978)*

Robert Mabro

The decision of Saudi Arabia earlier this year to restrict the share of 34 °API Arabian Light in its annual crude exports to 65 per cent has interesting implications for the world petroleum market, for the role of Arabian Light as marker (the reference for OPEC pricing) and for the relative values of various grades of heavy and light crude.

In the past five or six years, the export share of Arabian Light has varied between 70 and 80 per cent. That of 39 °API Berri, a light crude excluded from the restriction, was 7–8 per cent. Arabian Medium (31 °API) and Heavy (27 °API) accounted for the rest. Because Arabian Light is the incremental crude, its relative share in production, and hence in exports, tended to rise with the absolute level of output. The new Saudi policy may not involve a considerable change in the *average* export proportion of Light in years when output is low. But the change could have been large in a year of high output (say 1976) as the average export share of Light would have had to be reduced by fifteen percentage points to meet the 65/35 objective. The significant impact of the new Saudi policy on the export mix is at the *incremental margin*.

The interesting and unusual feature of the policy is its being cast in terms of oil export shares rather than levels. The latter is taken care of by the 8.5 mb/d limit announced in December 1977. This upper constraint on production is today much higher than actual output and hence non-binding. Conceptually the distinction between composition and volume of an aggregate can be absolute. In practice, attempts to modify through policy the proportions of various grades of crude in

---

* First published in *Middle East Economic Survey*, Supplement to Vol. XXI, No. 48, 18 September 1978.

production and exports are likely to entail changes in the level of the aggregate. There are situations in which the implementation of the policy (reducing the share of Arabian Light from, say, 75 to 65 per cent) would lead to a reduction in total Saudi oil exports, and others in which it would result in an increase. Much depends on the prices of both Arabian Light and Arabian Heavy relative to similar crudes of other origin and on the ease with which substitution can take place.

What are the implications of the policy for the composition of world petroleum exports, the market shares of various producers and the price structure of crude oils of different specifications?

A Market with Surplus Supplies

The implementation of the 65/35 policy means reduced supplies of Arabian Light and increased availabilities of Medium and/or Heavy for any given level of Saudi oil exports. But the final outcome will be different because the export level itself is likely to be varied in a set of adjustments involving producers of both competing and complementary crudes.

Let us assume, first, a situation of generalized excess supply in the world petroleum market. This is a fair representation of the conditions prevailing in the first half of 1978, when the policy was introduced. In such a situation any initial shortfall in supplies of Arabian Light can be easily compensated for by increased production of light crudes in, say, Iran, Iraq, Nigeria and elsewhere, simply because capacity is underutilized. It could also be compensated for by increased production in Saudi Arabia itself were it possible to dispose of the extra output of Heavy (a necessary accompaniment) without losses.[1] But this is where the difficulty lies. In a market with excess supplies, sudden and significant increases in supplies of Heavy

[1] A numerical example illustrates the point. Assume an offtake of 7 mb/d, 75 per cent of which is Arabian Light before the implementation of the policy. The application of the 65/35 ratio to 7 mb/d means that offtake of Arabian Light will drop to 4.55 mb/d from the initial level of 5.25 mb/d. If total offtake is then increased to 8.0 mb/d (an export volume which is roughly equivalent to the 8.5 mb/d allowable output) exports of Arabian Light will go up to 5.2 mb/d. In this example the full initial reductions in exports of Arabian Light will be compensated for by increased supplies of Arabian Light.

from Saudi Arabia would be resisted by other producers faced with the risk of large reductions in their own exports. They would first invoke minimum lifting obligations in contracts with offtakers and then begin to lower slightly their asking prices.

The outcome would depend on Saudi pricing policy on Heavy. If Saudi Arabia engaged in price competition on Heavy, its share of the market for this particular crude might increase. The more likely effect of price competition in a situation of excess supplies is a downward drift of the price structure and fairly violent swings, now in one direction, now in the other, in quantities exported by the competing producers. In the end, nobody gains much on quantity and all lose on prices.

If Saudi Arabia — as it has done so far — does not alter its asking price for Heavy, increases in the exports of Arabian Heavy will be almost impossible to achieve. The introduction of the 65/35 policy would initially entail a decline not only in Arabian Light but also in Saudi aggregate oil exports.

In the first case (price competition on Heavy) exports of Arabian Light are not reduced as much as in the second (price of Arabian Heavy left unchanged). Price differentials would tend to widen significantly for heavy crudes below the marker, much less for lighter varieties above the marker price. In the second case, the reverse would occur. Surpluses of Light outside Saudi Arabia would be more easily mopped up in that instance because of a greater reduction in the supply of Arabian Light, and prices for light crudes would harden.

In both cases price adjustments take place but they have different features. In both cases, quantities also adjust, always in favour of non-Saudi Light. But in one instance (price competition on Heavy) the Saudi 65/35 policy could displace some exports of Heavy from other producers (mainly Iran). Its application may be consistent with no change, or even an increase, in Saudi aggregate oil exports. In the other instance (price of Arabian Heavy kept unchanged) Saudi Arabia is the only producer that suffers from a reduction in the export volume of oil.

When Saudi Arabia, earlier this year, introduced the 65/35 policy, prices of light crudes were softening in the market. New supplies of Light from the North Sea were then displacing exports from Nigeria and elsewhere. Further, demand conditions for Light were unfavourable because of seasonal patterns (demand tends to switch towards Heavy in the winter and Light in the summer). Nigeria and some other producers of Light were continually reducing their asking price in order to prevent their exports from falling any further. Saudi Arabia did not alter its asking price for Arabian Heavy, an omission leading to an eventual reduction in its own exports of Light. Other producers of Light were thus helped as demand for their oil increased. They benefited from quantity rather than price increases. The market in 1978 was so weak that the impact of the Saudi policy did not raise the price of lighter varieties *vis-à-vis* the marker but it arrested the slide.

A Market with Tight Supplies

Consider now a different market situation characterized by tight supplies. We need not assume full utilization of productive capacity for all crudes, just for Light. This situation is not yet with us, but may occur sooner than expected. World demand for oil is growing; the rates of increase are low but positive. New supplies of Light from the North Sea, and increased supplies from old producers activated by the Saudi policy on the export mix will be absorbed sooner or later by the expanding system. While this absorption is taking place, Saudi output will increase towards the allowable maximum. The main resistance to that advance arises, as mentioned before, from the surplus of Heavy. Though gradually easing up over time (because of greater absorption of Heavy into the system through more sophisticated blending and modification to refineries), the difficulties involved in having to find an outlet for additional supplies of Arabian Heavy whenever it is necessary to increase exports of Light should not be underestimated.

In a tight market the Saudi policy on the export mix will make a significant difference to the availabilities of Light. The 65/35 ratio applied to an output level of 8.5 mb/d will reduce the export volume of Light by as much as 1.3 mb/d. In such a situation the final adjustments are different from those in the case of excess supplies analysed before. As soon as supplies get tighter, displacement effects will begin to lose their significance and the composition of the world export mix to shift, with Heavy increasing its share in relation to Light. The price structure will alter more significantly than in the previous case as demand for Light, interacting with tight supplies, opens up price differentials above the marker for the lighter varieties. Over time further adjustments will take place through increased substitution of Heavy for Light, but these long-term adjustments themselves, because they involve costly investment in cracking facilities for refining inferior grades of oil, will underpin a price structure with wider differentials in favour of Light.

If supplies become really tight, the opening-up of price differentials above the marker will be read as the first manifestation of market forces pulling the whole price structure upward. The marker will begin to fetch higher than official prices on the market. These are the sorts of circumstances that usually impel OPEC to raise the oil price.

Fetters on the Role of the Marker

The Saudi policy on the export mix has finer implications for the working of the petroleum market. The effects of the policy are complex because Arabian Light is the marker. Its price is determined by OPEC as the reference, independently of the rest of the price structure. All price differentials (or relative values) are allowed to move in response to market forces, within limits, on either side of the marker, which remains fixed between the relevant OPEC meetings. But the marker, on the production side, has become a *joint commodity*. An increase in the output of the marker involves a proportional increase in the output of heavier varieties of Saudi crude oil.

Complications arise because prices quoted by producers for any crude other than the marker are almost inevitably different from the prices buyers are prepared to pay for given quantities. In economic jargon this familiar situation is known as *false trading*. The differences between quoted and equilibrium prices may be very small. Adjustments take place both through the quantity responses (if the quoted price seems low, buyers take more than the sellers think they would) and price responses (sellers quote another price at the next round). In a dynamic market where circumstances change continually, false trading reappears as soon as, or even before, it is completely corrected by the induced set of adjustments.

The relevance of these remarks lies in the fact that the marker, which has so far been free from problems of false trading, will now be caught in them through the new production link with Heavy. Consider the following situations:

(a) The market is characterized by excess supplies and the Government price for Arabian Heavy is perceived as being a bit on the high side by Aramco. This would affect offtake of *both* Arabian Light and Arabian Heavy. Before the application of the 65/35 policy, offtake of Arabian Light would not have been perceptibly influenced by the overpricing of Heavy.

(b) There is some tightness in the supplies of Light on the world market and official prices for Arabian Heavy are perceived to be on the high side. Such a situation may lead to a slower pace of increase of Aramco output towards the allowable ceiling (now 8.5 mb/d) than in the previous state of the world, when the output of the marker could have been increased autonomously. The price differentials between the marker and lighter crude oils would also be wider. And a divergence between the official price of the marker, the OPEC reference that provides a strong backbone to the whole price structure, and the market price of a *free* barrel of marker crude, is likely to appear. The free barrel would fetch a premium simply because it would be acquired without the necessary accompaniment of half a barrel of overpriced crude.

(c) If the 65/35 proportion has to be adhered to irrespective of the direction in which the output of Heavy varies,[2] offtake of both Light and Heavy would tend to increase whenever the official asking price for Arabian Heavy is perceived as being low. A hidden divergence between the official price and the worth of an incremental barrel of marker crude to the offtaker would then occur.

---

[2] This does not seem to be the case at present. The policy, as generally interpreted, stipulates that 65 per cent is the *maximum*, not the *fixed*, export share of Arabian Light.

The market implications of the Saudi policy on export shares of Heavy and Light are now clearer. First, economic decisions about variations in offtake of the marker crude (so long as the allowable maximum is not reached) have now become a function of two sets of prices: the marker price and official prices for Arabian Medium and Heavy. If price differentials are administered skilfully, the Government will acquire an extra dial for 'fine tuning'. It can now signal a wish to restrict the output of Light, without interfering with the OPEC price, by overpricing Heavy. If it went further and fixed rigidly the 65/35 proportion, the Government would be able, when it so desired, to provide an additional incentive for lifting Light by underpricing Heavy (still without appearing to breach the OPEC price line). Of course, if price differentials are not skilfully administered, actual and intended signals will inevitably diverge and market responses will not correspond to the Government's objectives.

Secondly, explicit or implicit divergences between the official marker price and the market (or the offtaker's) valuation of a free barrel of Arabian Light will frequently occur. The task of all agents – whether producers, buyers or sellers – in interpreting the behaviour of the market will become that much more complicated. The interpretation of the market by agents involved in its operations is not an irrelevant academic exercise but influences vital decisions about transactions and hence prices.

Thus, some of the simplicity of the old OPEC system with the marker price fixed and the marker output free to vary (up to a non-binding upper limit) is gone. The marker price is still administratively fixed and output is still in principle free to vary; but joint production with Heavy increases the sensitivity of a system ruled by the marker to the price and market conditions of imperfect substitutes. Yet it would be mistaken to jump to the conclusion, as some impatient observers have already done, that Arabian Light should now be replaced by another crude in its role as the marker. True, the Saudi policy on export shares has reduced the range over which supply can vary. True, the link with Heavy introduces some rigidity. To say that Arabian Light is no longer as ideal a marker as it was may be correct. To raise, as we shall do below, the future problems of price determination when the marker becomes in scarce supply in the long term is perhaps legitimate. Yet it is difficult to identify another crude that enjoys the two properties that qualify Arabian Light for the role of the marker: (a) technical ease in varying production rates swiftly and substantially; and (b) economic ability or political willingness on the part of a major producer of that crude to accept the concomitant swings in oil revenues.

The Relative Scarcity of Light

All this leads to a more substantial issue. That Arabian Light has become a less than perfect marker through the effects of a policy decision does not mean that the policy is defective. In fact, the Saudi policy on the export mix recognizes that Arabian Light does not really possess the characteristics which make the ideal marker (a very high elasticity of supply) in the long run, and which, hitherto, most observers thought it had.

For the Saudi policy is about *long-term* relative scarcity of Light. Light crudes are perceived as being scarcer and more valuable in relation to Heavy than is indicated by the market today. Are these perceptions correct? It is difficult to be sure about future supplies of Light because predictions can easily be made worthless by all the unknowns of discoveries. But it is widely expected that long-term changes in the composition of demand for oil products will increase the attractiveness of Light. This is because the development of such alternative fuels to petroleum as coal and nuclear power will increasingly displace the heavier oil products.

If the perceptions about future market conditions for Light were correct – and prima facie, they seem to be correct – there would be a case for conserving Light. Saudi Arabia is thus following a sensible policy and other producers of Light (if at all possible, even the UK!) should also reduce their output until the present price structure begins to conform to perceptions about long-term relative scarcities.

If the perceptions are correct and if the scarcity of Light relative to Heavy makes itself felt in the medium term, then the oil price rises widely expected to take place in the second half of the 1980s may occur earlier and faster than predicted. A production pattern tilting towards Heavy while the demand pattern is tilting towards Light would widen the price differentials and trigger a general price increase while some crudes are still in excess supply on the market. The Saudi policy on the export mix will operate during the medium term in the same direction by reducing availabilities of those grades of crude in demand. The policy has real bite but the effects may only be felt in a few years.

Finally, if Light is in the longer run the scarcer crude, Saudi production policy, for good reasons, will become more and more concerned with optimum patterns of depletion. A system of price determination with the marker as a scarce commodity (rather than as the incremental source of supply) or with the marker output regulated by long-term objectives of policy (rather than allowed to act freely as the short-term buffer of the market) would necessarily be very different from the system which operates now. I do not think that changes will involve the emergence of a new marker; rather, that price administration will become more complex, involving the relative prices of a set of key crudes and by implication the whole structure of differentials. OPEC, perhaps through the new Ministerial Committee for long-term strategies, has an interest in an early consideration of these problems since it always pays to anticipate changes and prepare for them.

Conclusion

The purpose of this paper was to assess aspects of the Saudi policy which now determines the export mix of Heavy and Light. The analysis of the policy led us to consider the underlying motivation: perceptions about the long-term relative scarcity of Light. Interesting issues arise in this context, just mentioned here but worthy of further investigation. How far should producers conserve Light? Would oil prices rise sooner than expected? What is the future shape of the system of oil price administration? But it is fair to sum up with a short appraisal of the policy that provided themes for this paper.

The application of the 65/35 ratio to exports aims at restoring the balance in the relative depletion rates of the overexploited Light and the underdeveloped Heavy. As far as Light is concerned, this is essentially a long-term conservation policy.

In the short term, the policy also benefited some OPEC members badly hit by a reduction of their exports of Light displaced by new supplies from the North Sea. This important by-product may have been consciously sought by Saudi Arabia, but a temporary objective should not distract us too much from the more pervasive motivation which is conservation. One question is why Saudi Arabia did not follow the simplest method for conservation, namely to fix a maximum depletion rate for Light. The Saudi Government preferred to apply a ratio (rather than a ceiling on Light) thus involving both Heavy and Light in the policy. Two possible reasons explain this preference. First, a ceiling on the output of Light, say 5.5 mb/d, would have been interpreted internationally as as attempt to bring down the maximum allowable for *total* offtake. This would have been politically unacceptable. Further, by defining the policy in terms of a ratio the Saudi Government is seeking to develop the domestic production of Heavy, much neglected in the past, and to acquire market shares over a wide spectrum of crudes.

This is a brilliant policy. It fulfils, with a bit of a trade-off, two important production objectives, bypasses a political constraint, and provides relief to fellow OPEC partners (as it happens, to some who need it most). It helps to regulate output when needed without being too conspicuous about it. More significantly perhaps, the implementation of the new policy indicates that Saudi Arabia has at its disposal more than one way to intervene in the market. The composition of the export mix is yet another register, other than variations of total output, other than the administration of the marker price, on which to play. Observers who thought that by constraining output of the marker Saudi Arabia had endangered its leadership seem to misread it all. Leadership is enhanced, and has to become even more skilful, when the instruments of intervention increase in number. The continuing exercise of leadership, however, depends in part on the ability to respond with new answers to increasingly complex situations. Many such challenges lie ahead.

4 THE NATURE OF THE ENERGY PROBLEM (1981)*

Robert Mabro

Perceptions of future developments in energy keep changing over time as if in a continual state of flux. In the 1960s, optimistic views about future energy tended to prevail for the simple reason that a number of brighter features enlivened the picture and made up for the black spots. World demand for petroleum was growing steadily and at a high rate, and the development of large newly-discovered hydrocarbon resources enabled the industry to foster this expansion. Supplies were so plentiful that the real price of oil declined in the 1960s despite substantial increases in demand. The motto was growth. Oil was the 'king' fuel, cleaner and less cumbersome than coal which it displaced, cheaper and less objectionable than nuclear which it hindered. The balance of market and political power did not favour the oil-producing countries.

OPEC, established in 1960 as a defensive organization, remained weak for most of the decade. This weakness enabled the major oil companies to retain their dominant position upstream. In the 1960s, however, the situation was different downstream. The expansion of oil demand provided opportunities for the entry of new firms which began to compete successfully with the majors in the markets for petroleum products. Oil-consuming countries had good reasons to be complacent. Oil was plentiful and cheap; as such it was probably making some contribution to economic growth. The structure of the market ensured security of supplies at the crude end, and encouraged competition (and hence, low prices) at the product end.

---

* Lecture delivered at the Third Oxford Energy Seminar, 14 September 1981. Published as a Special Supplement to *Petroleum Intelligence Weekly*, September 28, 1981.

Changing Perceptions of Energy Issues

The rosy perceptions suddenly changed at the beginning of the 1970s. Some observers stated boldly that the high rates of production growth of the 1950s and the 1960s were not sustainable for very long. The geologists couched the argument in terms of expected rates of future discoveries of oil and current rates of depletion. The political economists were more concerned about the size and the location of the incremental productive capacity that would have to be installed to sustain the growth of world demand in the next ten or fifteen years. They reckoned that installed capacity in Saudi Arabia would have to rise from some 8 mb/d in 1972 to 16 mb/d in 1980 and wondered whether Saudi Arabia would be willing to accelerate the depletion of its resources at that rate. Predictions of a long-term energy problem were made on the strength of these and other arguments. Soon after, the OPEC price revolution of 1973 gave credence to the prediction. The features of the oil scene and of various economic trends changed too. The price of oil rocketed up on two occasions (1973 and 1979–80). Supplies no longer seemed plentiful; no longer did they seem secure. The motto became scarcity rather than growth.

Oil remained king, but the nature of its power changed. Oil ceased to assert itself through the pressure of sheer quantity – the gush which flooded world markets. It was now asserting itself through the magic of price – a price now administered on a stage with ritual, a price that is trebled or quadrupled by simple 'fiat', a price associated with images of riches in distant lands.

The old balance of power was upset. OPEC emerged as an international force. The major oil companies lost their dominant position upstream and the industry as a whole began to face the problems of stagnation downstream. In consuming countries the mood turned to pessimism, as adjustments to the new oil situation proved to be initially slow and always very painful.

A new set of perceptions seems to be emerging today as we enter the 1980s. Many observers are beginning to talk about the demise of oil. Some feel that, barring a very major accident, the oil supply/demand balance will remain slack for many years to come. The theme is no longer growth, no longer scarcity, but decline. It is true that today world demand for oil is shrinking. The high prices of oil, which in the 1970s mesmerized everybody on the stage, have quietly done some work behind the scenes. Prices do not have only magic; they produced some mundane economic effects referred to in jargon as conservation and substitution.

This summer (1981), the demand for oil was so low that it led to the emergence of significant excess supplies, despite the forced reduction of Iraqi and Iranian output due to the Gulf war. There is a glut. Nobody says how much of the current glut is due to seasonal factors, to low rates of economic activity and to inventory behaviour, but everybody seems to think that the glut is there to last. Those who feel most sanguine about it follow the track to the end and point out that a glut must lead to the erosion of prices, and that a falling price signifies the eventual demise of OPEC.

This brief survey of the changes in moods and perceptions immediately relating to changes in current features of the oil situation raises two important questions. The first is about the significance and reliability of the new perceptions for the 1980s. Do they present us with a plausible picture of future developments? Do they justify optimism, from the consuming countries' point of view, about these developments? The second question relates to the nature of the energy problem. Does the problem really exist and, if so, how should we attempt to define it? I propose to examine these two issues in turn.

Perceptions of the Problem and Outlook for the 1980s

We cannot accept readily and uncritically the emerging views about oil developments in the 1980s. A primary reason for caution is that we have been so consistently mistaken in the past. Our perceptions always tend to be partial, and hence misleading. To say that they are inevitably imperfect does not mean that our sight can never improve. An analysis of what went wrong with our past perceptions may help in this respect.

In the 1960s, perceptions focused on growth in oil, and growth there was. But other features of the oil scene did not receive the attention they deserve.

(a) Oil is a depletable resource.
(b) Towards the end of the decade, the rate of development of productive capacity upstream was too slow relative to the rate of incremental demand. (This may have been owing to lack of foresight on the part of the companies, to planning errors, or to a variety of political factors.)
(c) Oil-producing countries had aspirations and objectives which were then repressed, but which they were bound to express and implement as soon as the balance of power was redressed in their favour.

I am not saying that everybody missed these features of the oil situation; simply, that they did not sufficiently impress those who fashion the conventional wisdom and more particularly the relevant decision-makers. You may also ask whether better perceptions improve behaviour and policies. The answer is: generally, yes, except in situations of extreme helplessness.

In the 1970s perceptions focused on oil shortages, price rises and OPEC's power. The worries were about oil scarcity and insecurity of supplies. But these perceptions often involved certain misconceptions.

— The notion of scarcity was often misconstrued as a physical shortage, an absolute limitation on oil availabilities. Scarcity is better understood as an economic concept referring to a relative imbalance between supply and demand. Both the size and the sign of this imbalance can change through shifts in demand and supply brought about by price variations, by changes in the level of economic activity and by technical development. Even if the underlying physical limitation on oil availabilities remains constant, the size and the sign of this market imbalance can change over time. Finally the characteristics of the imbalance (whether shortage or glut) at any point in time are not, by themselves, an indicator of long-term tendencies. In short, a simplistic view about scarcity or abundance, shortages or glut will not do. We must give more than scant attention to the factors that determine these phenomena and continually change their characteristics. It is also essential to distinguish clearly between short and long term and to form some view on the relationship between current occurrences and future developments.

The nature of OPEC's power was also misunderstood. OPEC's power is generally perceived as its ability to raise the price of oil, as in 1973 and 1979–80. But both these price shocks were caused by political crises – the 1973 war and the Iranian Revolution – not by OPEC's own doing. Thus on both these occasions OPEC was responding to a strong lead from the market and moving in the direction of powerful economic forces. OPEC's power manifested itself, not in 1973, not in 1979–80, but during the period 1974–8 when the oil market was slack. This power manifested itself as an ability to hold the price line in adverse conditions. The glamour may be associated with tight markets and price rises but the acid test of power is a slack market when strong competitive waves batter the price front.

This analysis has important policy implications for both oil-consuming and oil-producing countries. An understanding on the part of consuming countries' governments that the real enemy is a tight market might lead them to take more seriously contingency plans – a common stock policy and an effective oil-sharing agreement – and to back them up with political will. A real understanding on the part of OPEC member countries that their power does not reside in their individual ability to raise prices (through surcharges, premiums, advance payments or the artificial introduction of a dual price marker) independently of each other when the market is tight, but in the ability to hold a unified price structure when the market is slack, may perhaps contribute to the resolution of the current impasse over the price structure. The mistaken belief about the nature of oil power has turned every Government Selling Price (GSP) into a political symbol. If a political symbol is needed, let it be the unique OPEC marker price.

The new perceptions that are now emerging at the beginning of the 1980s are also partial and could well be misleading. These perceptions focus on the decline in world oil demand. Taking opinions that are often expressed today at their face value would lead us to believe that the market may remain slack for most of the decade. This persistent state of depressed oil demand would postpone almost indefinitely the energy crunch. If we took that view, we might well be tempted to conclude that the energy problem will lose its significance and that the demise of an issue that weighed so heavily on the world throughout most of the 1970s will happen soon rather than late in the present decade.

This Decade's Possible Traps

We may be running the risk of falling into two traps. The first trap is that of a wrong forecast. A slack market is one in which demand falls short of the amounts that producers would like (and are technically able) to supply. The view that the oil market will remain slack in the 1980s depends on forecasts of demand and supply. Demand for oil is depressed today because the level of world economic activity is virtually stagnant, because conservation efforts are making an inroad, and because the supplies of non-oil energy are increasing. Demand for OPEC oil has declined by a larger amount than total oil demand because supplies from non-OPEC sources have increased and because companies are drawing down on inventories in order to force oil-producing countries to realign their prices.

Economic stagnation and conservation today combine to reduce demand. But economic stagnation and conservation cannot go hand in hand for a very long period. A long period of economic stagnation may lead to a fall in the 'real' price of oil. Conservation gains due to investment in energy-saving equipment survive; conservation due to consumers' restraint in response to a rise in the relative price of oil will not continue in the same way if the relative price of oil begins to decline. The incentive to invest in energy-saving devices will also be adversely affected by these changes in relative prices.

Economic stagnation, high interest rates and prospects of decline in the relative price of oil and of depressed demand for energy would discourage further investment in substitutes (other than coal).

Current forecasts are mistaken if they assume both that the rate of economic growth in the 1980s will be low, and that conservation and substitution will continue at current rates.

An alternative scenario is that the world economy will recover before the mid-1980s, if not earlier. Forecasters today attach a low probability to this scenario, but they may be wrong. Stagnation is causing unemployment problems and social tensions which Western democracies will not be able to tolerate for very long. Reversals in economic policy are to be expected, if not in 1982, then a year or two later. Demand for oil will grow again because the level of economic activity remains the strongest determinant. Economic growth not only increases demand for energy across the board, but reactivates energy-intensive sectors and industries; the very sectors that suffer most during a recession. Certain structural changes which account for the depressed state of demand for oil today will be reversed during a recovery.

One of the causes of decline in the demand for OPEC oil is the rise in non-OPEC supplies. The rate of increase in non-OPEC oil supplies has been high between 1977 and 1981. But this rate will not be maintained in the next few years. The major sources of growth were the North Sea and Mexico while Alaska was making up for the decline in the production in the lower forty-eight states. Output from the North Sea will not grow in the next four or five years at the rates of 1977–81. There is still room for growth in Mexico, but developments may be slow. Net exports of the Soviet bloc may still remain positive for a while but will probably decline. Net exports from Egypt will almost inevitably decline in the next three or four years; and the new producers in Africa and elsewhere are unlikely to have a significant quantitative impact on the market immediately.

If these factors are taken into consideration, it becomes difficult to be very sanguine about the balance of the market. Let us be warned also about the significance of the extraordinary drop in offtake from OPEC countries in July and August of this year. This drop cannot be entirely attributed to the decline in world oil consumption. It is partially due to the distortions in the price structure which induce buyers to withdraw from high-priced sources of supply. Companies are offtaking less then they need to meet consumption requirements and are able to do so because of the inventory cushion. This behaviour can be sustained for only a few months. By definition, inventory supplies are limited and have a very short life.

Optimism about supplies is based on a further factor: the resumption of exports from Iraq and Iran. My personal view is that Iraq will come back onto the market long before Iran, because the political situation in the latter is unlikely to settle soon. Additional supplies of 1.5 mb/d from Iraq can easily be accommodated by Saudi Arabia and other producing countries.

The Nature of the Energy Problem

Let us assume for the sake of argument that the oil market remains slack. Would that mean the end of the energy problem? We would be falling into the second trap, that of misconception, if we rushed to such conclusions. The energy problem is usually defined in terms of scarcity, and for that reason the oil glut creates the impression that the energy problem is losing its significance. Scarcity is but one aspect of the issue. It is a symptom which, in fact, manifests itself for very short periods on a few occasions. Oil shortages occurred for 10–12 weeks in late 1973 and for 6–8 weeks at most in 1979. Scarcity refers to a long-term trend, a decline in the reserves-to-production ratio which began in the early 1960s and which has continued unabated for some twenty years. The trend has been less steep in the past four years and will only level off in the 1980s if consumption remains depressed.

The energy problem persists under a variety of syndromes even when the oil market is slack. A glut due to recession conceals the scarcity symptom but does not signify the disappearance of the issue. What happens is that the energy problem becomes disguised as an economic crisis.

A continual slack in the oil market in the 1980s would still leave us with an energy problem under a different name. The energy world would be affected by very serious problems of misallocation of economic resources. We may have a glut, but both customers and producers would find that the apparent disappearance of the energy crunch is associated with very high costs.

Consuming countries may rejoice about the glut. They

should, however, reflect on the other features of the present energy situation, of which the glut is but one aspect. The average price of oil is $34 per barrel as against $13 at the end of 1978. Consuming countries and oil companies share a responsibility for this price upsurge through sins of omission. We know now that the tightness in the oil market in 1979–80 was not due to an imbalance between supplies and consumption requirements. The main causes of imbalance were:

— structural changes after the Iran disruption and the Nigerian nationalization of BP, which led to the withdrawal of the majors from the third-party market and forced Japanese and other companies to seek contracts directly from the producing countries;
— uncertainty about future developments in Iran which induce a very significant inventory build-up (from the second quarter of 1979 to the third quarter of 1980).

Sins of omission were: (a) the lack of an effective oil-sharing scheme which, if implemented, would have lessened the impact of structural changes in the market; and (b) the lack of a common stock policy. A lack of real understanding of OPEC production policies and of the important role played by stocks in creating temporary surpluses and shortages (inexcusable from sophisticated governments and oil companies) also partly explains faulty responses on the consuming nations' side.

Problems Will Remain in Different Guise

A glut associated with a high price of oil is the worst possible outcome, one which involves contradictory signals. The glut discourages both conservation and the necessary investments in alternative energy needed for a long-run resolution of the energy problem. The high price of oil encourages these measures, but the incentive may be nullified by uncertainty.

Consuming countries may be paralysed by fear of finding themselves 'hooked' in the future on expensive sources of energy when oil is abundant. If they relax their effort they may run the risk of finding themselves unprepared in the event of future crises. Uncertainty mars the responses and may produce very costly outcomes. The energy problem is still with the consuming countries, even though the name of the game may have changed.

Producing countries also face major problems of possible misallocation of their precious resource. If it is true that they have priced themselves out of the market of future years, they will incur considerable losses. They will have shortened the economic life of oil in relation to its physical life. But if they attempt to lengthen the economic life of their reserves by depleting them faster in an attempt to regain their former share of the energy market, they run the risk of very seriously undermining the oil price level. Their solidarity will be at risk. And this too involves enormous costs.

For the world at large, the question is whether the demise of oil is taking place too fast or whether the current situation is a temporary aberration, which should not distract us from a genuine scarcity problem in the long run.

I would like to submit that the nature of the energy problem should not be perceived simply in terms of shortages and gluts. Neither is the energy problem an issue of OPEC power leading to an artificial increase in the price of oil. The problem is with us and will remain with us for a long while whether there is glut or shortage, whether the oil price is pushed up or brought down.

The roots of the energy problem lie much deeper. They are in the inadequacy of the whole oil system. The system has flaws. It had flaws in the 1960s when it was dominated by the majors. It had flaws in the 1970s when the behaviour of producers and consumers and the interaction of OPEC and the market failed to produce correct signals and correct responses. It continues to be flawed.

This is perhaps a feature of the real world, a world of uncertainty, confused perceptions, divergent interests, and political constraints. We cannot replace the real world by ideal institutions. But we can constantly attempt to improve it. This requires, first, a more lucid and more profound understanding of the issue, and secondly, considerable political will.

If all concerned reflect on the costs, the damage and the disruption caused by the present system to the economies of all the parties involved, if all accept the view that the energy problem is still with us under a different guise, and that improvements are of paramount importance for the welfare of nations, the political will necessary for effective action may receive a welcome boost.

5 OPEC'S FUTURE PRICING ROLE MAY BE AT STAKE (1982)*

Robert Mabro

Will the price of oil hold at its present level, or will it come down to a lower value? If so, what will be tomorrow's price – $28 or $25, or a dismal $15 per barrel? These are the questions asked today, not only by the media, but by all those who are seriously engaged directly or indirectly in the energy business. Bets are being taken and reputations pledged on the outcome of short-term forecasts.

These are undoubtedly interesting questions. But the immediate concern with possible price changes is distracting attention from a more fundamental problem. What is at issue in the current oil crisis is the nature of the price regime under which petroleum prices are determined in international trade. The real issue is one of power. Will OPEC be forced to surrender its role of price administrator in the world petroleum market? And if that happens, who will inherit this role – a new agent yet to emerge, or the anonymous, powerful but uncontrollable forces of supply and demand, which cause erratic price movements on the market for spot transactions and short-term contracts.

World Price History

Let us briefly recapitulate the history of world oil in the past decades. Since World War II oil prices have been determined under two different regimes. In the 1950s and 1960s the price of oil in international trade was determined by the major oil companies. The industry was characterized by a high degree of

---

* Published as a Special Supplement to *Petroleum Intelligence Weekly*, April 19, 1982.

concentration and a high degree of integration. The companies, because of these characteristics, were able to dissociate the price of oil from movements in supply and demand, as supplies were carefully matched to anticipated demand. The integrated system was amenable to planning; and as planning achieved a balancing act, neither gluts nor shortages manifested themselves in the open. In such a situation it is perfectly easy to determine prices and prevent them from fluctuating. In fact, demand variations did occur all the time, but they were transferred to the producing countries who tended to accept variations in offtake fairly passively. Rises in demand led to increases in depletion rates; drops in demand to reductions in output. Companies were able to distribute these variations among various producers. The passivity of oil-exporting countries enabled capitalist companies to operate for many years a highly planned system. This was the golden age of administered prices.

A new price regime emerged in the 1970s. The industry divided into sellers and buyers of oil. The sellers, represented by OPEC, inherited from the companies the role of price administrator, but they did not take control of the whole system. The era of full integration and balanced planning was over. Supply and demand were now on separate sides of the divide; gluts (more precisely, excess supplies) and shortages (excess demand) could no longer be internalized. They began to manifest themselves openly. Planning and close integration gave way to the emergence of the market.

The price regime from 1973 until today involved a complex interaction between OPEC, a dominant institutional agent acting as price administrator, and powerful market forces. This is best characterized as a mixed regime. The interaction operated in two ways. First, OPEC was able to determine a reference price for oil (that of Arabian Light taken as the marker crude) while the market exercised a strong influence on the pattern of price differentials for the large number of crude varieties. Secondly, OPEC was able to hold its reference price fixed, at least in nominal terms, in periods of slack demand, when an unchecked market would normally have led to a price collapse. These occurred most markedly during the recession of 1975 and during 1977–8. But OPEC tended to follow the upward pull on prices exercised by a tight market, most notably during the major crisis of 1979–80.

Future Pricing Mechanisms

Thus, oil price movements in the period 1973–82 did not resemble those of the earlier period (the 1950s and the 1960s) when regulation by the companies left prices virtually constant. Nor did they resemble the price movements of conventional primary commodities which involve significant ups and downs. The oil price remained fixed in periods of excess supply and exploded in times of excess demand.

The question that ought to concern everybody today – producing countries both within and outside OPEC, companies and consumers – is whether the current 'oil demand crisis' will lead to the emergence of a new price regime. The implications of a change (or indeed of a continuation of the present regime) are far-reaching for all parties in the game.

The range of price regimes includes, at one extreme, complete price administration; at the other extreme, price determination through the exclusive operations of the market. In between, the price regime would continue to involve both OPEC and the market variously, in the relative degree of influence exercised by these two forces.

Pure price administration is virtually impossible. It would require either an agreement between producers and consumers on a unified price strategy, or a reintegration of the industry under a single controlling power. The former is unlikely; and the latter is inconceivable

OPEC's Future Pricing Role

The question therefore boils down to the following: will OPEC continue to play a part in the oil price regime, or will the market completely take over? To put the issue in this way reveals very clearly what is at stake for OPEC in the present crisis. It also helps us to understand and predict OPEC's behaviour and responses.

Most oil commentators got it wrong in the past months (and continue to get it wrong) when they convinced themselves, and tried to convince the public, that OPEC, and more particularly Saudi Arabia, will automatically react to the glut and the price collapse on the spot market by lowering the price of the marker crude. The issue for OPEC, and indeed for Saudi Arabia, is not one of a simple and inconsequential price adjustment. Failure to hold is to surrender, or at best to go a long way down the road that leads to the surrender of the power over oil prices.

Every OPEC member understands very clearly what is at stake: the moderates as well as the militants; Saudi Arabia, which is generally perceived as the linchpin of the system, as well as Nigeria which everybody, perhaps with a large dose of exaggeration, believes to be the weakest link in the chain; the rich Gulf producers as well as the countries with large populations and significant revenue needs, such as Indonesia.

They all know that their ability to administer the price of oil has yielded considerable financial benefits and important political rewards. An ultimate surrender of this role to a blind market would deprive them of these gains in the future.

They are told by those who make no secret of their wish to destroy OPEC that consuming countries should appropriate the oil rent by imposition of an import duty or an excise tax. To lower the price of oil in such conditions is tantamount to offering a free gift of income to the industrialized world. Furthermore, a rise in import duties removes the only incentive to lower prices that may exist, which is to induce some immediate revival of oil demand. Paradoxically, those who want to break OPEC nicely reinforce the resolve of its members to stick together and maintain their cohesion.

In the short term OPEC also realizes that it will have to defend any reference price it chooses in present market circumstances through production cuts. If production cuts are unavoidable, one might as well defend the present price and not suffer compound loss of revenue arising from lower prices *and* a lower output.

More fundamentally, it should be recalled that, since its creation twenty-two years ago, OPEC's identity has been uniquely related to the defence of the price of oil. OPEC was formed in 1960 to check any further reduction in the posted price. Throughout its history OPEC's preoccupations, actions and achievements have concerned the price of oil. It is difficult to conceive why so many observers of the industry, and so many oilmen – who ought to have gained some understanding of OPEC through long years of acquaintance – are so prompt in assuming that OPEC will renounce its very *raison d'être* at the sound of the first gunshots.

Finally, OPEC countries have achieved a measure of political power on the international scene through their oil power, manifested by their role in matters of price. Before 1973, most OPEC countries were indistinguishable from the rest of the Third World in that they were virtually ignored on the international scene.

In 1973 they suddenly began to enjoy international recognition. Oil power enabled some of them to establish regional political leadership. It enhanced in some cases the security of regimes. It gave weight to their presence in international forums and helped them on occasion to promote broader political objectives outside the world of oil.

Pricing Control in a Soft Market

OPEC's behaviour in the present oil situation, as manifested by the recent Vienna decisions, can only be assessed in terms of this logic of power. To retain control over price in a slack market is the real test of strength. This control, when demand is weak, can only be exercised through production cuts – hence the speed with which oil ministers in Vienna agreed to a production schedule which involves heavy sacrifices for many. The strength of their resolve is evident from the fact that no time was wasted in trying to fine tune the distribution of relative burdens. The determination to hold prices must be made abundantly clear when a weak market induces everybody to doubt – hence the unambiguous statements by Sheikh Yamani, both in Doha on 5 March and in Vienna on 19 March, that Saudi Arabia is committed to the $34 reference price.

Any different stand would have signalled the ultimate surrender by OPEC of this pricing role to the market. The mechanism is simple: a price cut generates expectations of further price cuts because the market remains slack in the short term and the seller has exposed his weakness. (This is precisely what happened in the North Sea when BNOC reduced its price by $4 at the end of February. The companies wanted to keep the door open for further cuts and successfully insisted that BNOC should renounce the three-month price freeze.) An OPEC price cut would probably have been followed by another BNOC or Mexican price cut. The price spiral would have driven everybody down throughout the second quarter and perhaps well into the third quarter From then on OPEC would have had little choice but to follow the market down, flat, then up or perhaps down again. This is precisely what happens to peanuts, cocoa, copper and tea. The same would happen for oil. The consequences for OPEC would be considerable. To fail over price is to lose the power to determine one's share of the oil rent. The identity and *raison d'être* of OPEC would begin to fade, and little would remain of the elements of political power acquired in the past twenty years.

Saudi Determination

I have developed at length simple points about OPEC which are self-evident to its members and to those, alas a small minority, who have made the effort to understand OPEC as it is. Judging from the bulk of what is being written and said, they are not self-evident to a majority of observers. Many have decided that OPEC is on the run and will not even engage in battle. Many conclude on the basis of poor evidence that Saudi Arabia is determined to break the price of oil. A clear concept of the nature, goals and interests of OPEC would have instilled at least some qualifications in these analyses which ignore how much OPEC has at stake. And the key to interpretation of Saudi Arabia's behaviour is in the notion of leadership. I think that I was first to coin in 1975, tongue in cheek, the aphorism which is now a common cliché, that 'OPEC is Saudi Arabia'. Clichés become terribly devalued, and though everybody repeats them, nobody cares to discover what they mean. The fundamental point, however, is that Saudi Arabia identifies its own role within OPEC with OPEC's very role as price administrator. The essence of this role is to prevent the price from falling when the market pushes it down, and also to prevent it from shooting up sky high when the market leads a price explosion.

Saudi Arabia was indeed determined to put a brake on the price rises of 1979–80, and later to allow a readjustment in real terms through a prolonged price freeze. And Saudi Arabia is consistent in this role today, while the market is so weak, when it expresses its determination to hold the price line. To imagine that its aim is always to break the price irrespective of market conditions and of the imperatives of its role misses the point completely.

To say that OPEC has good reason to attempt by extra-ordinary means to hold the price (a production programme is indeed an extraordinary measure) does not necessarily imply that the battle is won. So far, we have assessed OPEC's strength on one side of the equation. On OPEC's side the incentives to hold are considerable, and the resolve is firm. One should ask however two further related questions: what is OPEC up against, and are the means employed adequate?

Market Features

Three features of the world petroleum market define the adverse conditions facing OPEC. The first is a marked decline in world oil consumption, begun in 1979 and continuing ever since. Most forecasters expect consumption in 1982 to be again below the 1981 level, but nobody is willing to say by how much. I am prepared, for the sake of argument, to accept the most pessimistic figure and would put world oil consumption in 1982 at 44 mb/d, 2 per cent below the 1981 level.

The second adverse feature is the inventory drawdown. The main difference between these two features is that consumption may remain low for a long while, but the inventory cycle will inevitably reverse itself at some time in the third quarter. It is impossible to produce meaningful stock figures because those who think they know do not tell the truth, and those who do not know make all sorts of guesses. My gut feeling about stocks is that they were drawn down at the rate of 4 mb/d in the fourth quarter; that consumer stocks are pretty well depleted; that commercially disposable stocks are in the range of 500 million barrels, and that they are very unevenly distributed in the industry. Some of the Aramco partners have a lot, Shell has probably less and BP even less. Smaller US companies are not all in the same boat: some managed to run down their stocks pretty drastically, others are still encumbered. The Japanese, the French and perhaps the Italians are well stocked up. An uneven distribution means that the sustainable rate of de-stocking is lower than may be inferred from the aggregate volume of available stocks.

No Complacency

Assume consumption as low as 44 mb/d, non-OPEC produc-tion and Soviet net exports of 23 mb/d and average stock drawdown of 4 mb/d in the first quarter, 2 mb/d in the second and third quarters, and a modest inventory build-up of 1 mb/d in the fourth quarter. This implies a call on OPEC oil of 19.25 mb/d. Because of seasonal fluctuations in consumption and the quarterly pattern of inventories, it is easy to infer that the 17.5 mb/d ceiling introduced by OPEC at Vienna (to which one should add 900,000 b/d of NGLs) might just about do the trick in the second and third quarters, but the ceiling would seem to be tight in the fourth quarter. The conclusion is that there is no room for complacency on OPEC's part in the next three or four months. Yet the output adjustment required may be small and could be very effective if Saudi Arabia sheds, as soon as the need arises, some 500,000 or 750,000 b/d. This is easy, because the Vienna arrangement has left Saudi Arabia with enough production to act effectively and credibly as a second line of defence for the price.

The third feature of the oil industry that complicates OPEC's price role is the recent emergence of significant non-OPEC producers. They pose a more permanent problem than the stock cycle, and perhaps than the decline in demand. These producers are outside the price-adminstered system and yet benefit from it. Being outside enables them to maintain the volume of their exports by shedding prices. But so long as the OPEC price peg holds they can get away with relatively small price reductions which do not eat up very large chunks of revenues.

Non-OPEC Influences

But the price behaviour of non-OPEC producers in slack markets transmits its pressures to OPEC producers. There is a clear transmission chain from the North Sea to Nigeria, then to the other African producers. The next link may eventually carry the pressures to Abu Dhabi, Qatar and Indonesia and so on, until the core producers of the Gulf are ultimately reached.

The non-OPEC producers have little incentive to behave differently so long as OPEC holds, but their very behaviour strains the system under which they shield themselves. It is not difficult to imagine a situation where they may succeed in breaking the peg. This is a game in which all producers stand to lose, and the question is whether they are able to perceive the danger in time and to do something about it.

Paradoxically, oil companies find themselves in the same equivocal situation. For example, those who operate in the North Sea want a low UK–Norwegian price for crude oil in order to shift the locus of taxation from the ring-fenced wells to the downstream market where corporation tax does not bite very hard; they also want to improve their refinery margins. The enormous pressure put on BNOC by the big North Sea operators elicited in February a generous response in terms of a lower price. But the same companies would be appalled by a disorderly collapse of the crude price structure, which could be the ultimate result of these North Sea developments in which they have a hand.

To my mind there is no conspiracy, just schizophrenia. Non-OPEC producers want to enjoy both the ability to play the market and the protection of an OPEC price assurance for which they pay no premiums. The oil company wants both a low price for the crude it acquires and a higher general crude price level that prevents a free fall for product prices. Nobody can have it both ways. Sooner or later everybody will have a rude reawakening.

Conclusion

I am not willing to predict which kind of price regime will emerge in the 1980s. I fear that, if the market wins the contest, the international oil industry will have to cope with a long and difficult period of adaptation for which it is not prepared. Price movements of the type normally associated with primary commodities' would involve very costly attempts to hedge through stocks, costly errors in planning the complex logistics of the industry and a disruptive investment cycle. All producers would lose, the non-OPEC producers with large marginal costs of production more than OPEC producers with low marginal costs.

What is certain is that OPEC's resolve to hold the price will have to be strengthened fairly soon by a new long-term strategy involving non-OPEC producers as a major concern. The 1978 strategy plan was designed with reference to the consumers. In my judgement, however regrettably, this is now a secondary priority.

To sum up; the significance of the present oil crisis is not related to the outcome on the price level but to the outcome on the pricing regime. Implications of various pricing systems have only been touched upon here but the analysis of structural changes and of agents' behaviour may provide a starting-point for further investigation of fundamental issues.

6 STATEMENT OF SAUDI POLICY (1982)*

Sheikh Ahmed Zaki Yamani

Maybe you want to know my views about the present situation, and about the future. Probably I am not as wise as those who say 'we don't know'. I don't claim that I know, but I think I have a clear picture in my mind which might differ from the scenarios adopted by so many. Usually when we make a forecast about the future, the present situation reflects itself in that forecast. When there is a surplus in the market, you tend to see the future in that light; and when there is a shortage, it is difficult to talk about a surplus in the future without facing a barrage of disbelief. I remember in 1979, in Caracas, I was talking to representatives of the media about a surplus that would be with us in 1980 or not later than 1981, and I said that the OPEC countries would be fighting among themselves and that the price of oil would face a very serious threat and might even collapse. Those representatives of the media went to one of my colleagues – another oil minister – reporting my views. He said to them, and he was polite: 'Yamani is joking.' Then they went to another colleague – the Iranian oil minister – and told him about my views, and he said 'Yamani is out of his mind.'

I am not going to tell you that there will be an immediate shortage in the supply of oil, otherwise you will say that I am out of my mind. But this would have happened if the efforts of some major consumers in the last 7–8 months to force down the price of oil had succeeded. If, for example, the price of oil had gone down to $28 per barrel or well below that level, I would then say with confidence that there would be a shortage in the supply of oil and energy in the future – probably even by the end of this decade. But the shortage, if it has to happen,

* This is the full text of the statement of the Saudi Oil Minister to the Oxford Energy Seminar, September 1982.

might take place in the 1990s; and I don't think the present situation of over-supply will continue indefinitely, or, as we read in some of the leading newspapers, that the over-supply will be with us for ever.

Now if we sit down and try to analyse the reason for the present over-supply situation, I think we have four major factors. Number one is the recession. I cannot tell you whether we will have a recovery or will continue with this recession. Nor can I tell you, if we have a recovery, what type of a recovery we will have. But I really find it difficult to envisage that the OECD members – mainly the USA and the major industrialized countries – can continue with a recession for a long period of time. Politically this is a very hard path. Once we get out of this recession, consumption will definitely increase. The industrial use of energy is depressed and it will change immediately.

The second factor is conservation. I think a great deal has been achieved in this area, but it is very hard to foresee much more effort in the area of conservation. As a matter of fact I am afraid that countries like the USA have already started to go into reverse. Looking at the statistics you see that those Americans who in 1979 and 1980 wanted to buy small cars are now going back to their old habits in opting for larger cars. Insulation is already in place, but I do not think in the coming winter the thermostat will stay as it was at a lower level. What I am trying to say is that we are noticing a new trend which does not reflect the shortage in the supply of oil and the sharp increases in the price of oil that took place in 1979 and 1980. To what extent this trend will continue I do not know, but there are strong indications that this is the trend unless we have a different price in 1983 or 1984.

Substitution is the third factor, and definitely with the sharp increases in the price of oil that took place in 1979 and 1980, a huge amount of money was invested in substitution. But the major competitor for oil is coal. As we all know, coal played a major role in 1979, 1980 and 1981 when the gap between the price of fuel oil and the price of coal was so huge that it became attractive to companies to shift from fuel oil to coal, and this is what happened. But that gap is narrowing down now, and the plan envisaged by the IEA to increase the consumption of coal on a yearly basis by an equivalent of 1 mb/d of crude oil is no longer a plan that can realistically be realized. The gap is narrowing a great deal in Japan, though it will take some time in the USA. But if the price of fuel oil continues to be depressed, or at least frozen at the present level, until the end of 1983, then we will see a reverse of the present situation; we will see companies coming back to fuel oil by 1984. It is very difficult really to handle coal and to burn coal, and the problem of pollution is a serious threat to our world.

The fourth factor relates to stocks, and here we have a strange situation. As we all know, stocks play a role for any commodity: when there is a surplus, you buy for your stock to replenish it; and when there is a shortage, you draw from your stock. But what has been happening in the oil industry is exactly the opposite. When we had a shortage because of the Iranian Revolution in 1979, companies started to buy heavily to stock up; and when we had a surplus in 1981 and 1982, those same companies started drawing heavily from their inventories. That is, of course, not a healthy situation, but it is a fact. Right now, with all the differences in views about the level of stocks, I think we have already approached a vulnerable level. Let's say something happens in the Gulf – and it might happen and it won't be a surprise. The Iraqis have started bombing tankers at Kharg Island. If the oil exports from Iran come down to zero or just above zero, I don't think the Iranians will keep quiet for long – they said as much very clearly. And if the Iranians start bombing tankers in the Gulf calling on any port – Ras Tanura or Ahmadi for example – if the flow of 10 mb/d of crude from that area to the world markets is halted, even for two to three weeks before the major powers interfere to stop that, the price of oil will go to something like $40 per barrel as above for Arabian Light and consumers will be obliged to draw from their strategic reserves. This is a very vulnerable situation.

In the light of these factors, we can together try to look into the future. The immediate future indicates that there will be an increase in demand, at least because of the fourth factor. Companies will start replenishing their inventories; and with the onset of winter, consumption will go up. So we will have an increase in consumption because of the winter, and increased demand owing to the replenishment of the stocks. At the same time, the halt to destocking will add to the demand side of the equation. Coming into 1983, hopefully there will be a little economic recovery; and if this happens, we will have an increase in consumption. However, there might at the same time be an over-compensation on the supply side if the war between Iran and Iraq comes to an end and the two nations start to pump large volumes of incremental oil supplies onto world markets. But that is a big 'if'. For one thing, unfortunately, we can see no sign as yet of any imminent possibility of a peaceful settlement. And, even if there is a settlement, it will take the two nations some time to start exporting at a level consistent with their financial requirements. We know that the present situation in the Iranian oilfields does not allow the Iranian Government to increase production. We have heard that the maximum sustained capacity right now is between 2.2 mb/d and 2.7 mb/d. If they want to increase it, then they will have to open their doors to foreign expertise to come and help with gas reinjection and oilfield maintenance work. And this does not sound very likely for the time being.

As for the Iraqis, they have two outlets, one to the Gulf and the other to the Mediterranean. The Gulf terminals have been shut down since the outbreak of the war with Iran in September 1980, and on the Mediterranean side the pipeline across Syria has been closed owing to the political situation between Iraq and Syria, which leaves only the Turkish pipeline with a capacity of 650,000 b/d. But the Syrian line could be reopened as a result of initiatives at the Fez Summit Conference – not immediately tomorrow but perhaps sooner than expected – and then the Iraqis could increase their oil exports. If the Syrians are willing to give up storage space and generally co-operate politically and on the technical level, the capacity of that line could exceed 1 mb/d. Then the Iraqis would be able to export a bit under 2 mb/d from the Mediterranean – though that of course, is being very optimistic. As regards the Gulf terminals, it would take maybe seven or eight months to clear the area after the end of the war. Then the Iraqis could start exporting some oil from Basrah using the SBM method, and this would be increased gradually until the previous level was reached.

This, of course, would take us to 1984 and 1985, but when we deal with politics we cannot see our way very clearly and therefore any increases in the level of production in Iran and Iraq should not be reckoned as an immediate prospect. Now, supposing we see an increase in consumption in 1983 owing to a world recovery and then again in 1984 because of that recovery and because of a decline in the consumption of coal, by 1985 I do not see this huge surplus existing – it will gradually diminish. Then again on the supply side, we all know that some of our fellow members in OPEC will gradually stop being exporters after 1985 and will completely disappear as exporters by 1990. This will take away some oil from the market. Take also other countries, like Saudi Arabia for example: we had a plan to expand our maximum sustained capacity to 12 mb/d or a little bit more, but we stopped that plan. It is not only this: if we stop investing money to maintain the present sustained capacity, that level will gradually come down until we invest to bring it up again. The oil is there, the reserves are not touched, but the capacity to bring it up and pump it is gradually coming down. At the same time, I do not see additional supplies coming from areas outside of OPEC. I mean I do not see another Alaska, Mexico or North Sea on the horizon. And investments in exploration, which reached a peak in 1980 and 1981, are being cut back drastically – it is enough to take a look at the number of wells drilled in the USA in 1980 or 1981 as compared with 1982. It is a very sharp drop and this is a world-wide picture.

What I am trying to tell you today is that I do not share the opinion of those who think that the present situation of over-supply will definitely stay with us for the remaining period of this decade and probably the coming decade. I have noticed how we tend to reflect the present situation and inject it into any forecast, and this became clear in the course of the two years when we were studying the long-term strategy for OPEC. Early in 1978 – which was a time of surplus – we thought that we would have an over-supply, then we would reach a period of a balanced supply/demand situation in the early 1980s, and by the second half of the 1980s we would have a shortage in the supply of oil. Some time in mid-1978 we said we did not think that we would ever face a shortage in the supply of oil – but the shortage in the supply of oil was with us by the end of 1978 because of a political event. In 1979, we thought that we would never see an over-supply situation. This is all in writing, and this was done by eminent consultants whose services we engaged – names that we respect and usually agree with. So, in 1979, they agreed that there would never be a surplus in the supply of oil. And therefore when I said at the end of 1979 that there would be a surplus in the supply of oil, someone said that I was out of my mind. So I think we should not be really so relaxed right now and think that we will never have a shortage in oil supply.

A great deal will depend on the price policy. If we, for instance, think that we will be in a position to increase our prices in 1983 – and we hear some noises from some of our colleagues in OPEC calling for that – then definitely we will continue with this surplus for a longer period of time. But if we freeze the price of oil until the end of 1983 and probably for part of 1984, then we will definitely encourage demand for oil and reduce consumption of coal; and we will reach a balanced supply/demand situation sooner than is expected by others. This brings us to a crucial question: is it better to reduce the price of oil in money terms, as a Brazilian speaker urged at this Seminar, or to freeze it in money terms and thereby reduce it in real terms? I think that it would be extremely harmful to reduce the price of oil in money terms as was envisaged by the major consumers when they started their campaign against OPEC earlier this year to force us to reduce the price of oil. It is my strong belief that, if that had happened, the result would have been very harmful in the medium term. We have already seen how so many investors who put huge amounts of money into schemes for alternative sources of energy have been scrapping or withdrawing from these projects. If we reduce the price of oil to a level of, say, $28 per barrel, it will subsequently fall to a lower level because there will be competition from countries like Libya and Iran and those companies that are giving heavy discounts in the market, and this will bring it down further to $24 per barrel or below. Of course, the immediate result would be an immediate shift from coal to oil that would put a stop to any investment in exploration – probably some of the oilfields in the North Sea would become marginal or maybe even not profitable. So that is very harmful. Of course, it would definitely help the economy and boost a recovery, but this is not a problem to be compared with the main problem – the energy supply for the end of the 1980s and the 1990s. I would prefer to have a balanced situation and leave this century without too many difficulties than to have an immediate recovery – which could anyway be brought about merely by reducing the rate of interest in the USA.

7 THE CHANGING NATURE OF THE OIL MARKET AND OPEC POLICIES (1982)*

Robert Mabro

The characteristics of the world energy scene have changed radically in a very short period of time. In 1979–80 the major features of the oil situation were a concern about security of supplies and a rapid escalation of petroleum prices. New features depict today's situation. First, there is a marked decline in world oil demand and a much greater reduction in demand for OPEC oil. Secondly, the concern about prices no longer relates to their high level or to prospects of future rises but to distortions in the price structure continually aggravated by competitive undercutting by some producing countries. Thirdly, the structure of the world petroleum market has changed in a significant way and is likely to continue to change. This latter aspect has not yet received the attention it deserves though its implications for producing countries, the industry and oil consumers are of considerable interest.

My purpose in this paper is twofold: first, to describe and analyse these new features of the petroleum situation, and, secondly, to assess their significance for OPEC's behaviour and OPEC's policies.

The New Features of the Petroleum Situation

(a) Demand. I shall be brief on demand as this topic has been well covered elsewhere. Two remarks are worth making on this subject. The first involves a simple but often overlooked distinction between consumption and inventory demand. The present drop in total oil demand is sharper than the underlying trend for oil consumption because of a significant reversal in

* Lecture delivered at the Fourth Oxford Energy Seminar, 30 August 1982, and published as a Supplement to *Middle East Economic Survey*, Vol. XXV, No. 49, 20 September 1982.

inventory behaviour between 1979–80 and 1981–2. In 1979–80 stocks were being built up world-wide at a high rate. In 1981–2 stocks are being drawn down. Estimates of this swing in inventory demand vary from source to source. The lowest figure I have come across is 2 mb/d (1 mb/d average build-up followed by 1 mb/d drawdown). These averages calculated over periods of twelve to eighteen months conceal very sharp short-term inventory movements of 3–5 mb/d.

Whether a significant inventory build-up will take place in the winter of 1982 following the long period of stock depletion which has been upsetting the oil market since mid-1981 is a point of debate. Attitudes about stocks within the oil industry are undergoing some changes. Nobody seems to believe that present supply uncertainties warrant a precautionary stock cushion; the view taken being that a shortfall caused, say, by a political accident in one area would be immediately compensated for by increased supplies elsewhere. The industry is thus likely to keep the level of inventories held for precautionary motives at the minimum level compatible with mandatory requirements.

Some demand analysts in the industry have recently formed the view that the seasonal movements in oil requirements will no longer be as marked as in the past. One reason is that winter demand does not involve as large a component of fuel oil as in the past, since most of the substitution against oil has taken place against this particular product. Another reason is the greater flexibility now built into refineries, which facilitates a quick response to variation in the demand for a product mix. This suggests that lower stocks are required now than in the past to smooth seasonal fluctuations in demand.

If these arguments are correct, we should not expect a big upsurge in inventory demand this winter, but rather an end to the drawdown as the industry reaches stock levels that are thought to be optimal. From then on, changes in inventories will play a minor role and the oil demand trend will tend to converge with the oil consumption trend.

All things considered, this may not be a bad development. Movements in inventory demand, the ups as well as the downs, have often destabilized the market. Further, the interpretation of oil demand data would become much easier if inventory changes were marginal and could be safely ignored. However, there are too many 'ifs' in this analysis and the situation depicted here may not materialize.

The second point worth making about oil demand relates to the causes of the decline. There is a wide consensus about the nature of these causes – recession, conservation and substitution – but no agreement about their relative quantitative importance. Research done on this subject has not yet produced conclusive and widely accepted results. Yet, we would like to know whether conservation or recession is the most important factor behind the reduction in oil demand. A different way of putting the question is to ask how much of the decline is a permanent change and how much is reversible should an economic recovery take place or should energy prices fall relative to other prices. Much depends on the correct answers to these questions. Without them, forecasts and analyses of the demand outlook for the coming years are pretty meaningless exercises. No serious assessment of the future responses of producers can be made without firm views about the determinants of oil demand trends. The IEA, which will shortly publish its new *World Energy Outlook*, will probably take a position on the relative weights of structural and conjunctural factors in the decline of energy demand. Many experts and less learned observers will no doubt use the report to jump to conclusions about such varied but important issues as OPEC's behaviour, government policy in consuming countries and the future shape of the oil industry. And yet they will be unwise to do so because the IEA's findings on demand, though backed by sophisticated models, are probably as tentative as anything else we have obtained so far from other authorities.

(*b*) *Price Structure.* The oil price structure has been affected by serious distortions since the beginning of 1979. The price realignment achieved at the OPEC Geneva meeting of October 1981 removed the most glaring flaws but new distortions obtained soon after. In 1979–81 the price structure was defective in two major respects: (a) there were two different prices for the marker crude, an actual price at which Arabian Light was officially sold and a deemed marker price which served as a reference for other OPEC crudes; (b) the price differentials for light crudes overstated their value relative to the marker. These distortions eventually had an adverse effect on the OPEC supply pattern, as some countries suffered big losses in export sales while others were induced to produce higher volumes than those traditionally specified by their output allowables.

Soon after the Geneva price realignment new distortions appeared. They were different in nature. Non-OPEC countries began to fix their GSPs below the equivalent OPEC price. They were followed by one or two OPEC countries who sought to revive a very depressed demand for their oil, either through a formal lowering of official prices, or through disguised discounts. This state of affairs means that:

(a) Non-OPEC producers have not suffered any reduction in export volumes despite the world demand shortfall.
(b) OPEC has to carry the whole brunt of the reduction in demand.
(c) OPEC is in danger of being unsetttled from within as dissatisfaction about volumes and market shares spreads among members.

Other distortions affect oil-importing countries and are caused by exchange rate fluctuations. The appreciation of the dollar effectively raises the price of oil to Europe and Japan, and defeats the purpose of any OPEC price freeze. A depreciation of the dollar *vis-à-vis* other currencies has the opposite impact on Europe and Japan.

Price distortions have other effects. They unsettle the industry because some companies find that their profits are being squeezed while other companies enjoy windfall gains. They discriminate between consumers, between those with access to the cheaper crudes and those who happen to be committed to the relatively more expensive sources. They discriminate between importing countries depending on the behaviour of their exchange rates relative to the US dollar.

Price distortions are a feature of market instability. Unless producers take measures to align their prices (and, in the present situation, this implies not only a price alignment within OPEC, but also a willingness on the part of non-OPEC countries to hold the OPEC reference price) the market will take over and will tend to do the job for them. In conditions of glut, market forces pull prices down towards the lowest bid. This is the inevitable outcome of competition among suppliers. Market forces, if they eventually succeed in removing distortions, will level down the oil price structure to a cost floor set by the marginal fields. In the petroleum market these forces have recently become more powerful as we shall argue below.

(*c*) *Structural Changes.* During the 1970s most people's attention was fixed on the oil price shocks of 1973 and 1979. These were important phenomena indeed, deserving careful analysis and appraisal. Other phenomena which have marked oil developments in recent years have elicited much less comment. I propose to describe them under the heading of 'structural changes'. These changes have weakened both vertical and horizontal links which integrated the industry world-wide in previous decades, and they have widened the narrow area in which competitive forces have free play. In short, the role of the market has been enhanced at the expense of the regulatory power exercised by institutions – the major oil companies of yesteryear and the OPEC of today.

These changes may be summarized as follows. In the 1970s, oil-producing countries retrieved full sovereignty over their most valued natural resource – petroleum. Governments, through a ministerial agency or a national oil company, became responsible for all economic decisions on oil, from investment to production and marketing. The concession system broke down. This meant that upstream oil ceased to be part of the integrated structure of the major corporations, at least in the OPEC countries. There is now an interface between producers and offtakers which is identical in most respects to the normal seller/buyer relationship that characterizes any market. The previous host government/concessionaire couple, which involved little more than fiscal negotiations about taxes per barrel, has given way to a commercial relationship between autonomous agents engaging in normal trade transactions. The producer is a genuine seller of oil, free to define his output policy, his supply price and the terms of the selling contract. The oil company is a buyer who can accept or refuse to buy what is on offer, but can no longer decide how much to produce in this or that country in the OPEC region. (There are minor exceptions which do not affect the argument.)

Having regained their sovereignty over oil resources and having become autonomous producers/sellers, most OPEC countries have diversified their sales outlets. Until a few years ago the eight major companies lifted 80–90 per cent of OPEC oil exports. The number of lifters has now increased manyfold to some 150. A typical OPEC country has between twenty and forty customers, including previous concessionaires, US independents, European and Japanese companies, Third World companies, refiners, traders and governments. The high degree of concentration that characterized the oil trade upstream, on the buying side, has been substantially reduced. This means greater competition between buyers in tight markets; also a reduced commitment by the buyers to their supply sources when the market is slack.

Another feature of change is the disappearance of long-term oil supply contracts between companies. Until the mid-1970s crude oil used to flow within the integrated structure of the majors or between crude-long and crude-short companies. There was a 'third-party market' in which some of the majors supplied US independents, Japanese refiners and European companies, among others, under long-term contracts. These stable arrangements extended in effect the integration of the oil market world-wide to those parts of the industry that did not belong to the majors.

The structural changes described above – namely the reduction of the majors' share in offtake and the considerable increase in the number of buyers dealing directly with producing countries – have led to the virtual disappearance of long-term contracts in inter-company crude oil trade. The dominance of the majors over offtake from OPEC countries, and the confidence that this dominance would continue for ever, underpinned the old system and made it possible for some majors to commit themselves to the third-party market through long-term arrangements. This is now impossible. Most inter-company trade is in the form of short-term transactions. Naturally the number of transactions and the frequency with which they are made has increased (even though the volume traded per contract is much smaller). In this sector of the oil business an active and responsive market has replaced the heavily institutionalized 'third-party' system. This is an important change.

The large increase in the number of companies operating outside the old integrated channels has enlarged the scope of the spot market. One function of the spot market is to enable companies to correct in the last resort a mismatch between supplies and requirements. Supplies never correspond exactly to requirements, but adjustments can be made in a variety of ways through inventory changes, redirection of tankers, changes in the refinery input mix, to name a few. In the past most of these adjustments were made internally, because a very large, international and vertically integrated concern has infinite opportunities to correct imbalances within its own system. Recourse to the spot market was very rare indeed, a last resort operation which had little 'market' significance.

Today, the scope for internal adjustments has been reduced, because companies are smaller and more numerous, and because their primary suppliers of crude are one or two producing countries, not an international major with world-wide access to a large number of sources. Hence the increase in short-term inter-company transactions, also the increased recourse to the spot market.

As the spot market grows in size and importance it acquires new functions. In the past the transactions were so rare that spot prices had little economic meaning. At present spot prices relating to actual transactions are recorded every day. The spot market reveals both price levels and price tendencies. It indicates imbalances in the supply/demand balance. It invites arbitrage by intermediaries and speculators. It provides opportunities for trading for the sake of trading. All this is changing attitudes within the oil industry. Supply is no longer viewed *exclusively* as a planning function, but as an activity which combines planning and trading in a more intimate way.

A developed 'spot market' which relates backward to an active short-term 'contract market' tends to encourage the establishment of a forward link with a 'futures market'. Recent developments in New York and London suggest that dealings in futures may soon become an interesting (though not very significant) feature of the world petroleum market.

I noted that the degree of industrial concentration has been reduced on the company side. The degree of concentration is also declining on the producing country side. Recent years have seen the emergence of a number of non-OPEC exporters. The UK, Mexico and Norway are the most important, but others – Egypt, Angola, Oman, etc. – are also playing a substantial role.

The non-OPEC exporter behaves, typically, as a newcomer mainly concerned with penetrating the market and securing a share for himself. The newcomer is concerned with volume, not with price administration which he is happy to leave to the club of old-timers – in our case OPEC. In a tight market he will, of course, take advantage of rising prices. He is neither lumbered with the ponderous institutional procedures which may delay the response of the price administrator, nor is he inhibited by some feeling of responsibility for price stability, precisely because he is not a price administrator. In a slack market he will undercut the administered price in order to maintain his export volumes.

Producing countries are now divided into two groups. There is an OPEC group committed to holding prices on a firm peg, and a non-OPEC group which is willing to sell at prices below the peg in order to maximize volumes. The strategy of non-OPEC producers is beneficial to them only because OPEC is holding the peg firmly fixed. There is no doubt, however, that their policies threaten OPEC's ability to hold the price line. The strategy is risky. It strains the very system that provides them with a shield. Nobody knows how far one can go before bringing about a price collapse. As non-OPEC countries act independently of each other, none of them can assess the total effect of individual actions. They should only be reminded of a simple economic truth: that competition in a slack market ultimately brings prices down. Consumers naturally welcome such an outcome. It is odd that producers should behave for the sake of short-term gains in ways that endanger their long-term interests.

Another feature of change is oil price deregulation and the abolition of import restrictons in the USA. US suppliers and consumers are no longer shielded from price movements in the international oil market. The US market is very big, and has now become very responsive. In short, the area in which market forces operate fairly freely has been considerably enlarged. There is less segmentation – in the international trade for crude oil – than in the past; therefore more room for flexible economic reactions and quicker transmission world-wide of both signals and responses.

To sum up, the world petroleum market today involves sovereign producers and a large number of companies as autonomous sellers and buyers. Demand and supply are no longer brought into balance internally in the vertically inte-grated system of the majors. Demand and supply now fall on two different sides of the market and have to be brought into balance in the open, that is in the market-place. This means that excess demand or excess supplies have now become visible phenomena, eliciting market responses. In the old system there were no apparent shortages or gluts despite continual varia-tions in demand. The disequilibria were corrected internally by varying output rates and inventory levels within the major companies.

There is now a wide interface between producers, buyers and, inevitably, intermediaries. The degree of concentration has decreased on the buying side of the international crude market, as has the degree of concentration on the oil-producing side. The number of market transactions has considerably increased, and a larger proportion than in the past are on short-term contract or on a spot basis. Finally, the immense US oil market has become linked to the rest of the world receiving and transmitting signals and responses. The outcome of all these changes is that the balance between institutional regulation and market forces that prevailed under different systems until the late 1970s has now altered. The institutional power of OPEC, and for that matter of the oil majors, is still strong, but market forces are acquiring strength and the field in which they operate is becoming wider.

The Challenge to OPEC

Depressed demand, price distortions and increased competi-tion define today's challenge. OPEC conceives its role as a sovereign administrator of the price of its members' natural resource. Historically, this role has become identified with an ability to hold the reference price of oil constant in current dollars when the petroleum market is slack. Prices rise in any case when the market is tight, and though OPEC takes both the blame and the credit for the price explosions the truth of the matter is that these phenomena have been market-induced rather than engineered. In today's conditions the challenge is to hold the price because this is the only possible way open to OPEC to prove that it remains a sovereign price administrator. A formal price reduction – whether desirable or not is another question – would be widely interpreted as a surrender of the pricing role even if the reduction was decreed freely and in an agreed and sovereign manner. Paradoxically, OPEC is constrained in its freedom to change prices by the perceptions of the outside world. To raise prices in the present economic conditions of the world would be widely interpreted as an unacceptable and highly inimical action; to reduce them would be widely greeted by OPEC's adversaries as a sign of collapse.

OPEC faced a major crisis in the first quarter of 1982. OPEC's production fell to around 17 mb/d and some members – Nigeria, Kuwait, Libya among others – suffered reductions in export volumes of 60–70 per cent from peak levels. Everybody expected Saudi Arabia to lower the marker price of Arabian Light. Self-appointed experts went as far as affirming that the new marker price would be $28–30. The news media were so taken in by these predictions as to give them priority for the headlines over an official statement made in Doha on 6 March 1982 by Sheikh Yamani who solemnly declared that Saudi Arabia would hold the price line. One would have thought that Sheikh Yamani is a more authoritative source on Saudi Arabia's and OPEC's intentions than some third-rate oil analysts of New York stockbroking firms.

When market agents refuse to believe that OPEC, come what may, is determined to hold prices, it is pretty useless to talk about this resolve. The message has to be conveyed in a different language, a language that the economic agents operating on the oil market understand.

Unfortunately, this language is that of production programmes and restraints. With few exceptions everybody has been saying for the past ten years that OPEC administers prices by curtailing output which was never true. OPEC held prices fixed in a slack market by sticking to them without indulging in competitive undercutting. Individual members accepted the penalty of a demand-determined reduction in the volume of their exports. A cartel curtails production in order to raise prices; OPEC fixes prices and copes willingly with variations in demand.

In March 1982 OPEC had no other option but to adopt a production policy in order to signal to sceptical agents its resolve about prices. The policy was adopted with remarkable swiftness at an extraordinary meeting of the Conference of Oil Minsters in Vienna on 18 March. The market understood the signal; and though some companies tried to test OPEC's resolve by exerting further pressures on Nigeria, the message eventually sunk in.

The Vienna programme involving output ceilings and individual production quotas was a good emergency measure, but does not fulfil the requirements of a satisfactory policy beyond the very short term.

The problem may be stated as follows. The declared objective of the OPEC output policy is to stabilize the price of oil and the instrument used is a fixed production ceiling. But a fundamental feature of the petroleum market is continual variations, almost day-to-day variations, in the volume of demand. As demand freely fluctuates it will rarely be equal to the fixed output ceiling. Any occasional correspondence between demand and the ceiling is in the nature of a fluke event. Normally, two situations will arise.

(a) Demand is below the ceiling. This happened in late March and early April 1982. Clearly the ceiling is redundant if demand is below its level. In such a situation the ceiling does not operate *directly* on prices. Yet, the OPEC price held in the period following the Vienna meeting, though demand fell just below 16 mb/d while the output ceiling was set at 17.5 mb/d. This illustrates my earlier assertion that prices hold simply because OPEC members stick to their fixed prices, not because they interfere with production.

(b) Demand is above the ceiling. In such a case two different courses of action are possible. Producing countries may decide to respect the ceilings and their individual allocations. The immediate impact would be a reduction of stocks; but if demand remains above the ceiling and is not met by producers, prices will eventually harden and prices will begin to rise. This means that the policy will *not* achieve its stated objective which is to stabilize prices. Of course, the ceiling could be revised upward. But such a revision is bound to occur after a time-lag. As nobody seems able to predict correctly demand today even from quarter to quarter, the revision may either be insufficient and fail to achieve its purpose, or turn out to be too generous making the new ceiling redundant as in case (a). The other course of action is to ignore the ceiling and meet the higher level of demand. Prices would then remain stable but the production policy would come into disrepute unless formally repudiated. Much harm is done to the credibility of a policy-maker who adopts measures that are openly flouted. Nobody should want such a thing to happen in a market where agents' actions have important psychological effects on other agents' expectations and behaviour.

What actually happened in the second and third quarters of 1982 did not correspond exactly to any of these theoretical cases. Demand was met when it rose above the OPEC ceiling of 17.5 mb/d, but the output increase was associated with a shift in the distribution of offtake among members. Some were able to sell more than their allocation while others found themselves selling less. Later, demand fell below the ceiling and the actual distribution of offtake diverged even further from the agreed allocation programme. Some of those who managed to exceed their quotas continued to do so while others found themselves selling even less.

This is a messy situation. What appears to be a failure of the output allocation policy is more fundamentally a change in the attitude of some OPEC members towards price discipline. Crude of similar quality is being offered by different producers at different prices; and it is alleged –

evidently with good reason – that one or two producers are discounting their official prices.

The solution to this problem cannot be sought successfully through a revision of ceilings and allocations. The key is in a return to price discipline. OPEC should rediscover the secret of its past successes – the real achievement of its twenty-two year history which is for OPEC to define the reference price of oil and for each member to stick with absolute determination to a GSP reflecting a correct differential with the marker.

The initial psychological impact on market expectations of the ceiling/allocation policy is no longer felt today. The views and attitudes of market agents are now being strongly influenced by the expectations of competitive undercutting outside and, to some extent, within OPEC. Unless producers are seen, visibly and credibly, to return to price discipline, their ability to administer prices in a sovereign manner will be in serious jeopardy. I have no ready remedy for this problem, which depends on the political will of the various actors. Assuming that this political will emerges in the future, one could suggest that the best technical method to sort out difficulties is through the restoration of a correct price structure of differentials rather than a rigid output quota system. True, the price structure and the allocation of market shares are two sides of the same coin. But a policy relating to price differentials has the advantage of accommodating demand variations. Demand changes are an important degree of freedom for the system. The disadvantage of the quota system is that it either constrains demand or turns out to be redundant. In this case, price changes provide the degree of freedom for the system. But this contradicts OPEC's objective which is to administer prices.

In the old days, when the shortfall in demand for OPEC oil never exceeded 10 or 15 per cent of allowable output, a price policy relating exclusively to differentials was a sufficient condition for OPEC's success in preventing a price collapse during the slack. The situation today is different in two major respects:

(a) The reduction in OPEC's output is very significant.
(b) The role played by OPEC as residual supplier is becoming increasingly unacceptable to this group of producers.

The burden of having to absorb demand reductions and to make room for increases in non-OPEC supplies is becoming intolerably heavy on OPEC. When demand for OPEC oil is very low, buyers are able, if they so wish, to exert enormous pressures on individual producers by reducing their nominations for offtake from one of them in order to induce a price cut. There is enough excess capacity everywhere to enable these buyers to compensate for any withdrawal from one source by additional supplies from another.

It is essential therefore for OPEC producers to have a safety net. There are well-known problems with direct financial subsidies from the rest of the organization to those members that come under pressure. My proposal is to have a system of output floors. The individual floor for each member would have to be negotiated. With some modification the floors could be defined in the same way as the ceilings were agreed in Vienna. The individual floors could add up to 16 or 17 mb/d in a first trial.

OPEC would then commit itself to defend these floors collectively. When a member found that his production was falling below the floor, others would immediately return to their own production floor (and if this was not enough they would each reduce their production pro rata below their floor).

The impact of such a policy, if and when implemented, would be immediate. Buyers would be forced back to the producer they had deserted earlier on. Prices might harden a bit but need not be allowed to explode because output would be increased again in response to demand as soon as the victimized producer re-established his former position. The merits of the policy are as follows:

— The floor does not constrain upward demand variations.
— The policy needs to be implemented sucessfully only once. Once this is done buyers will be careful to avoid shifting their custom around.
— The policy, which is in the nature of a safety net to be used in exceptional circumstances, enables OPEC's solidarity to express itself in a positive way should an occasional emergency arise. An output allocation programme with ceilings and quotas has to be continually applied. It

continually causes argument and bad blood. It strains rather than reinforces solidarity.

— Finally, this policy may enable OPEC to protect itself from the worst feature of the 'residual supplier' role, the risk of seeing output falling down below any pre-set limit. The 'output floor' policy will signal to the world that OPEC is not prepared to act as a residual supplier in an open-ended way. There is a minimum amount that it wished to produce and this amount is defined by the sum total of output floors.

But I would like to emphasize that there is no magic solution. The first prerequisite always remains the political will to hold prices. The second prerequisite is an oil price structure in equilibrium with differentials set at the correct level and regularly revised on the basis of technical criteria and in the light of changing market circumstances. The safety net of an 'output floor' policy would be an additional safeguard to be used in an emergency. But as nobody knows well in advance when the emergency will arise, it is prudent to design a policy and secure agreement upon it in readiness for any possible crisis.

8   OIL PRICES IN 1983: A CRITICAL YEAR (1982)*

Research Group on Petroleum Exporters' Policies

Introduction

The current conditions of the world petroleum market present oil-exporting countries in general, and OPEC in particular, with a difficult challenge. At the root of OPEC's difficulties is the low level of demand for oil which is likely to last for another year and possibly longer.

It is clear that the organization will not be able to maintain its cohesion at such low levels of demand if it continues on its present course. Both external and internal pressures are currently placing severe strains on OPEC. External threats come in particular from other large exporters, notably Mexico and the UK, whose pricing policies have a direct impact on OPEC. Internally, pressures arise from the determination of some member countries to maintain and raise their current levels of production by indulging in various forms of price cutting.

There is now a renewed danger that the price of oil will collapse. While demand may pick up seasonally over the winter and temporarily alleviate some of the pressures, there is a clear possibility that demand may again drop so low in the second quarter of 1983 that a price war may break out as producers compete for a larger share of a shrinking market. Indeed, certain producers who have seen their share of output within the organization drop drastically over the past year may

* This is the full text of a study prepared and issued by 'The Research Group on Petroleum Exporters' Policies', and first published as a Supplement to *Middle East Economic Survey*, Vol. XXVI, No. 8, 6 December 1982. This is an independent group established in October 1982 to examine and analyse policy issues facing petroleum exporting countries. The members of the group involved in preparing this report were Nordine Aït-Laoussine, Ali Jaidah, Robert Mabro, Francisco R. Parra, Ian Seymour and Ibrahim Shihata.

feel compelled to initiate a substantial cut in official OPEC prices.

The purpose of the present paper is to analyse the problems facing the producing nations, to examine the likely adverse consequences of a price collapse, and to suggest how it may be avoided.

The Objectives of Oil-exporting Countries

Since late 1973, OPEC has been able to administer the reference price of crude oil in international trade and, in so doing, has secured considerable material benefits for member countries. The main objective of OPEC – whether or not explicitly stated in its constitutional instruments – is to regulate and determine crude petroleum prices.

OPEC's actions on prices have been of two types depending on the state of the oil market. When markets happened to be tight, OPEC responded by raising prices – either suddenly as in late 1973, or in steps over a period of time as in 1979–81. However, there was a major and generally unnoticed difference between the two episodes. In December 1973 the OPEC oil ministers took note of the plausible future prices of substitutes in determining the new oil price level, while in 1979–81 official price rises followed the movement of the spot market with a time-lag. In 1979–81 OPEC's pricing behaviour was strongly influenced by short-term signals, and did not relate clearly to long-term factors such as the price of competing substitutes.

Whenever markets are slack, OPEC responds by holding the price line. This happened in 1975, occurred again in 1977–8, and is happening today. The ability to hold the price in slack markets is the least conspicuous but probably the most remarkable achievement of OPEC. Such an achievement should not be taken for granted, considering the usual performance of primary commodities whose prices tend to collapse to very low levels indeed whenever demand declines.

The ability to administer prices in slack markets critically depends on market shares. Until recently, OPEC enjoyed a very large share of world petroleum exports and controlled a significant proportion of world oil output, if not of world energy supplies. But these shares have begun to shrink significantly.

This is a novel situation which may now lead OPEC to consider that the implementation of its main objective – the administration of the oil price – has become dependent on a new but important objective: to regain and then to protect a large share of the relevant energy markets. The oil situation has ceased to be as favourable to OPEC as it was in the past; and market power, which used to be taken for granted as a solid fact, must now become a goal for present and future strategies.

It is important also to recognize that individual OPEC member countries often have their own revenue objectives in addition to the collective goals of price administration and aggregate market shares to which they adhere. The revenue requirements of oil exporters have increased considerably because of new patterns of expenditure adopted immediately after the oil price rises of the 1970s. Governments may feel bound to maintain these levels of spending by a variety of economic and political commitments, but it should be realized that overspending is no longer compatible with the objective of defending the oil price structure.

The willingness of OPEC member countries to co-operate is therefore likely to be affected when a conflict arises between their individual 'revenue' goals and OPEC's collective objectives of price administration and market power. This is the familiar conflict which arises when the pursuit of long-term benefits is constrained by the urge to satisfy short-term needs.

To be sure, OPEC member countries have learnt through twenty years of companionship and common experience that 'hanging together' and 'holding the price line', especially when the market is slack, can and do yield immense benefits to all of them. None of them really wants to rock the boat. All would be truly appalled if competitive price-cutting actions brought about a dramatic price collapse.

If this is so, how can the behaviour of those who indulge in competitive price cutting be explained? There are two possible interpretations. The countries that break the price line *either* must feel that their revenue constraint is so intolerable that they cannot afford to be concerned with long-term gains and objectives, *or* must secretly hope that OPEC will manage to survive the harm done to its market power by their pursuit of short-term revenues.

It is possible already to draw two conclusions of some practical importance from this analysis. The first, recognizing that some OPEC member countries are prompted into competitive behaviour by genuine distress, suggests the need for an OPEC 'safety net'. The most vulnerable members must be protected from the effects of the intolerable fall in revenues by some device – financial or otherwise – put in place by the rest of OPEC. This would strengthen the organization and increase its chances of implementing successfully its main objectives.

The second, recognizing that some OPEC member countries indulge in competitive behaviour in the belief that other members will repair the damage done, suggests the need for improved communication between members on their respective positions. All should gain a full appreciation of what each of them is prepared or not prepared to do, of the burden it can be expected to carry, and of the limits beyond which it cannot reasonably be expected to go.

Those countries that are holding to the official price level – absorbing all demand shocks and all losses in export volume induced by the competitive behaviour of their fellow members and of non-OPEC producers – cannot be expected to provide continuously an open-ended commitment to act *alone* as the swing suppliers. And countries that find special economic circumstances requiring them to seek an increase in revenue must be able to rely on the sympathetic understanding of their fellow members, so long as they ask for reasonable concessions on volumes and refrain from engaging in competition on prices.

The responsibility of administering the OPEC oil price is a collective one; a responsibility which is difficult to assume at the best of times but which is better exercised when member countries acquire a deep appreciation of their respective capabilities.

The Problems Facing OPEC

OPEC's main objectives, namely the administration of crude oil prices and the protection of a dominant market share, are today under serious threat. This statement defines as succinctly as possible the nature of the problem facing the organization. This problem cannot be construed as an accident; most of us believe that it is the result of long and complex developments in which all the economic agents involved in the energy market, OPEC included, have played a role and for which they carry a responsibility.

Several features of the current petroleum situation explain the threat to OPEC's role as price administrator. Though many of these features are familiar it may be useful to review them briefly.

(*a*) *The Decline in World Oil Demand.* The decline in world petroleum demand has been very significant in the past three years. Several factors, in combination, have been the cause.

First, the slow-down in world economic activity is having a significant impact on energy demand not only in the industrialized world but also in developing countries. The resulting energy demand reduction includes the effects of structural changes, some of which are cyclical and some of which are permanent. The recession is hitting the energy-intensive industries more severely than other sectors, while fundamental technological developments are shifting the industrial structure towards new (less energy-intensive) products.

Secondly, consumers' responses to higher energy prices have affected both the demand for and the supply of energy in general and oil in particular. Higher oil prices (provided they are passed through) induce:

— conservation in the use of petroleum;
— substitution of other fuels for oil;
— development of improved energy-using technologies and management;
— increased effort in the search for and development of indigenous hydrocarbon reserves.

Thirdly, governments of industrialized countries reacted to the oil price changes of 1973 by promoting policies designed to limit their dependence on imported oil. The IEA was set up for this purpose among others; and Economic Summits held in the late 1970s never failed to define energy objectives including very precise import targets.

The combined effect of these factors has been a dramatic drop in energy and oil demand. The overall energy intensity of major consumer economies (units of energy consumed per unit of GDP) has dropped noticeably (see Table 8.1). The decrease in oil intensities is much more striking and, indeed in nearly all cases, accounts for all of the drop in energy intensities as a result of substitution by other fuels.

These figures show that between 1978 and 1981 the amount of energy used in the OECD area as a whole to produce a unit of GDP fell by an average of 8 per cent while the oil component of that unit of energy fell by 24 per cent. Considering the magnitude of these changes in energy and oil intensities, it is unlikely that a future economic recovery will cause an increase in oil demand commensurate with the rates of economic growth.

(*b*) *Non-OPEC Exporters.* Apart from the fall in world oil demand, OPEC now faces the aggressive competition of a new group of petroleum exporters. Four or five years ago non-OPEC oil exports amounted to a small proportion of total trade in crude. Today, the proportion is much higher, and the number of exporters has increased.

These non-OPEC exporters are behaving as typical new-comers in a market previously dominated by a few major suppliers. Their first priority is to secure for themselves a share of

Table 8.1: Energy and Oil Intensities.
Percentage Change. 1981 over
1978.

Country	Energy	Oil
Canada	−3	−12
USA	−9	−26
Japan	−14	−26
France	−2	−15
West Germany	−7	−28
Italy	−4	−8
UK	−4	−21
Average OECD	−8	−24

the world market, which they tend to do by maximizing the *volume* of their export sales. This policy is facilitated by two factors:

— the favourable treatment given by the new oil-producing countries to companies operating under an equity or a buy-back arrangement on their territories;
— the fact that OPEC provides a guarantee against the risk of revenue loss through its commitment to uphold prices.

This means that oil companies have good economic reasons (over and above any political ones) to satisfy demand requirements from non-OPEC suppliers before they turn to OPEC; and that non-OPEC countries can safely maximize both output and revenues by offering their oil at prices set just below the OPEC prices.

The policy pursued by non-OPEC countries is perfectly rational from their point of view so long as they prove correct in their assumption that OPEC, come what may, will hold the price line. Yet, in a slack market competition weakens OPEC's ability to uphold the oil price as competitive habits spread from non-OPEC producers to OPEC member countries.

(*c*) *Structural Changes.* The structure of the world petroleum market has changed significantly in recent years. There has been a simultaneous decline in the degree of concentration on both the buying and the selling sides of the market. This has led to a large increase in the number of transactions and the development of markets for short contracts and spot purchases with an emphasis on quick and immediately profitable deals. Further, US policy has changed the structure of the market. Deregulation of oil prices and the removal of import controls in the USA have linked the large US oil market more closely to the rest of the world. All these changes have enlarged the size of the area in which market forces operate and have weakened the grip of the price administrator.

(*d*) *Inventory Movements.* Inventory behaviour played a very important role in destabilizing the market in the period 1979–82. Inventories were built up to unprecedented levels during the Iranian crisis, in the initial stages as a precautionary move in response to supply uncertainties, and later for speculative purposes as lower-tier prices were expected to rise in adjustment to the higher-tier prices. The inventory build-up of 1979–81 created additional demand over and above real consumption and thus contributed to the oil price explosion.

A reverse inventory movement aggravated the slack market of late 1981 and 1982. A slack market induces expectations of falling prices. The natural response is to draw down inventories, which further slackens the market and reinforces the expectations of falling prices. Pressure is then put on producers to reduce their official prices; in effect they are being asked to confirm the verdict that buyers have proffered against them. The impact of the 1982 inventory drawdown – in effect an additional source of supply in competition with OPEC – would have been much less severe had OPEC managed to moderate the phenomenal build-up of the preceding years induced by the multi-tier price system.

(*e*) *Uncertainty about OPEC.* OPEC has contributed to the destabilization of the world petroleum market to its own detriment. Too much uncertainty has surrounded OPEC policy: first, during the period 1979–81 when member countries seemed to act independently of each other in response to short-term market inducements and with an obvious lack of coherent pricing policy; secondly, in the period starting in May/June 1982 when some members began to flout the Vienna production agreement and to discredit both the output programme and the agreed price structure.

No analysis of OPEC's current crisis would be complete without some reference to the political cleavage within the organization, which has brought about the prevailing impasse in communications among some member countries. This political rift was greatly exacerbated by the outbreak of the Gulf war between two founder member countries, Iraq and Iran. Moreover, the economic conflict between price maintainers and volume maximizers in OPEC coincides with and is reinforced by that political divide. This has an obvious bearing on the threat of a price cut. Furthermore, such a political rift is bound to interfere with the workings and the decision-making of an organization which depends so much for its success on the goodwill and the *esprit de corps* of its members. It is hoped that common economic interests will override the present political differences.

OPEC as a Swing Producer

Thus far, OPEC has accepted the role of residual supplier, increasing its output when world demand for oil rises and absorbing the whole drop when demand falls and when competitive suppliers raise their production.

The high growth rates of demand for OPEC oil experienced during the 1960s and early 1970s threatened member countries with premature depletion of their oil reserves. With the continuation of this trend, production would have reached levels by the mid-1980s which could only have been sustained for a few years. It was only after the price increases of the 1970s and early 1980s that this trend of fast depletion of reserves was arrested. However, owing to the suddenness of the oil price increases and the unexpectedly prolonged and severe economic recession, the fall in world demand for OPEC oil has become so sharp that it is threatening the cohesion of the organization. Thus, OPEC crude oil production declined from 31 mb/d in 1979 to 19 mb/d in 1982 (partly estimated). It is worth looking at the orders of magnitude of the components of this decrease (see Table 8.2).

The decrease in the demand for OPEC oil is due to both short-term conjunctural and long-term structural factors. Clearly, the inventory drawdown cannot be repeated without an intervening build-up. Equally, the potential for further substitution for OPEC oil over the next five years – by non-OPEC oil and by non-oil sources of energy – is significantly different from the five-year potential which existed in 1977. Estimates of future substitution can be made with a fair degree of confidence with a range of possibilities not too wide to lack predictive value.

The greatest difficulty comes in determining how much of the drop in total energy demand was caused by: (a) short-term economic recession, and (b) long-term structural change in the economies of industrial countries, including permanent conservation measures. Each of these will have a different impact over time.

Table 8.2: Components of the Reduction in OPEC Crude Oil
Production. 1979–82.

	mb/d	%
Drop in World Energy Demand[1]	3.5	29
Substitution by Non-Oil Sources of Energy	3	25
Substitution by Non-OPEC[2] Liquid Hydrocarbons	2	17
Inventory Building in 1979 plus Drawdown in 1982	3.5	29
Total Decrease, 1979–82	12.0	100

Notes: 1. Excluding the centrally planned economies (CPEs).
  2. Including CPEs exports and all NGLs.

If one believes that recession is the main cause of the drop in consumption, that demand for OPEC oil will eventually pick up in response to an economic recovery, and that the problem of the late 1980s could well be that of excess demand rather than supply gluts, it follows that OPEC need not embark on any course of action for the medium term. This view implies that OPEC faces *only* a short-term problem, and that all efforts should be concentrated on surviving the obstacles and stresses generated by a temporary crisis.

If, on the contrary, one believes that much of the demand decline is irreversible (that structural changes, government policy and consumers' responses to higher prices are permanent demand-reducing features of the economy), it follows that petroleum exporting countries should search for positive measures to reverse the trend. They cannot rest on the comfortable assurance that the medium term will look after itself.

Though our purpose is to concentrate on OPEC's short-term difficulties, some brief consideration of long-term policies may be in order. The central long-term issue is to gain a full understanding of the determinants of oil demand, and particularly of the demand for OPEC oil. Without such an understanding it is virtually impossible to decide whether a reduction of oil prices in real terms, as is often advocated, would have a significant impact on energy consumption behaviour. Lower petroleum prices, however, would certainly slow down the development of substitutes for oil (especially coal), and they might reduce the rate of exploration and development of oilfields in the high-cost areas outside the OPEC region. Other things being equal, these effects would necessarily increase the demand for OPEC oil. This could be stimulated further by other means such as conscious efforts to contribute to renewed world economic growth, particularly in the Third World, through expanded oil credit facilities, other aid efforts and the financing of energy projects.

Whatever the position taken – whether one believes that the current drop in demand is a short-term or a long-term phenomenon – it is necessary to face immediate crises first. Long-term policies designed to reverse the future demand trend may not help OPEC to surmount successfully the obstacles that lie along its path in 1983 and 1984. Such policies usually have long gestation lags. Their effects are slow to materialize, and they may even worsen the short-term situation before permanent improvements are achieved.

These are not reasons for discarding long-term pricing policies. On the contrary, once these are identified, they should be designed and implemented as soon as possible. But the proviso is that these long-term policies must be supplemented by a strategy capable of dealing first with the impending emergency, and they must even give way to this strategy should a conflict of priorities or objectives arise. Because of its seriousness the immediate crisis is the one that requires urgent remedies.

The Short-term Outlook for OPEC Oil Demand

There is at present a consensus among forecasters that world petroleum demand (excluding that of CPEs) during 1983 will be little changed from 1982 levels (around 45 mb/d). The

resulting demand for OPEC oil, as drawn up by various
forecasters, is shown in Table 8.3 on a quarterly basis.

It is clear that while OPEC may be able to live with the levels
of production forecast for the first quarter of 1983 (20–21
mb/d), the demand for OPEC oil foreseen for the second and
third quarters (18–19 mb/d) would impose serious strains on
the organization's cohesion.

Early in 1982, OPEC was able to meet the challenge of
demand falling to critical levels. The spirit of strong internal

Table 8.3: Forecasts of 1983 Oil Demand. Million Barrels per Day.

Source	OPEC Production[1]	Other Supplies[2]	Total Demand[3]
Major Oil Company A			
1Q	20.5	26.8	47.3
2Q	19.0	24.9	43.9
3Q	19.0	24.9	43.9
4Q	21.5	26.2	45.7
Year	20.0	25.7	45.7
Major Oil Company B			
1Q	20.5	27.2	47.7
2Q	18.7	25.0	43.7
3Q	18.9	25.0	43.9
4Q	20.9	25.9	46.8
Year	19.8	25.8	45.6
OPEC Country			
1Q	21.2	26.3	47.5
2Q	19.0	24.6	43.6
3Q	n.a.	n.a.	n.a.
4Q	n.a.	n.a.	n.a.
Year	20.2	24.9	45.1
IEA			
1Q	21.7	25.4	47.1
2Q	17.9	25.7	43.3
3Q	17.8	25.9	43.7
4Q	21.0	26.2	47.2
Year	20.9	24.4	45.3

Consultant			
1Q	21.3	24.9	46.2
2Q	19.1	24.1	43.2
3Q	19.3	24.2	43.5
4Q	22.1	25.0	47.1
Year	20.5	24.5	45.0
OPEC Source			
1Q	20.0	26.9	46.9
2Q	18.9	24.2	43.1
3Q	19.0	24.1	43.1
4Q	20.2	26.8	47.0
Year	19.5	25.5	45.0

Notes: 1. Crude oil only.
   2. Includes CPE net exports, processing gains, stock changes and all OPEC NGLs.
   3. Excluding CPEs and SPR build-up.

solidarity, compromise and determination to 'hang together' that prevailed among member countries enabled OPEC to maintain its cohesion and, for a few months, the organization succeeded in restoring order to the market and the pricing structure. However, its ability to resist the severe market pressures next spring is likely to be hindered by the following:

(a) The financial difficulties of some member countries will make it difficult for them to exercise the necessary restraint that is in their long-term interest.
(b) Non-OPEC competitive supplies, coming in at lower prices and in increasing volumes at a time when the production capability of the two founder member countries at war may be less severely constrained, will intensify intra-OPEC competition.
(c) The resistance of some member countries to upward adjustments of their differentials needed to re-establish an orderly official price structure may increase.

   The lack of discipline on the part of OPEC member countries determined to maintain or raise their output at the expense of fellow members manifests itself through substantial price concessions. These concessions take the following principal forms:

(a) Outright price discounts.
(b) Extended credit terms, worth approximately 35 cents per barrel for each additional thirty-day period.
(c) Processing deals under which products obtained from the crude refined are sold at whatever price it takes to move them. The netbacks (revenue from the sale of products minus refining and freight costs) achieved by the supplier currently yield a value significantly lower than the official crude prices.
(d) Barter deals with the value of imported goods artificially inflated resulting in an effective crude price below official levels.
(e) Package deals under which crude oil is sold at the full official government price, but tied in with refined products and/or NGLs that are priced much below going market prices. The total value of the package implies a discount on the crude.
(f) Sales made at the official government price, but on a c.i.f. basis, with the seller absorbing part or all of the freight.
(g) Generous fiscal terms for companies holding equity production in some countries so that profit levels can be maintained on offtake booked at official government prices.

As a result, OPEC today is divided into a core, defined by its commitment to the administration of prices, and a competitive fringe whose behaviour is indistinguishable in practice from that of non-OPEC producers. The size of the core shrinks as the market slackens further and further, and if the process goes on for some time, the few countries remaining in the core will eventually find that price administration entails intolerable costs.

The Short-term Consequences of a Price Decrease

Oil prices could fall if discounting spread to those member countries that so far have not engaged in this practice. While official prices would continue to be quoted at present levels, no sales would be made at them. Discounts would become progressively larger under the pressure of numerous buyers searching for the best bargain.

This kind of competitive discounting has no theoretical floor above the marginal cost of production and in practice would be unlikely to stop until so much damage had been done to the economies of a sufficient number of the financially weakest member countries that they would be impelled to agree to some system of price maintenance and production quotas. This process might take from six months to one year, and it is quite possible that much of the damage would be irreparable. If this price war scenario of competitive discounting resulted in a price decrease of several dollars per barrel before an agreement on production quotas could be reached, it is not at all clear that the organization would, or could, restore the full amount of the decrease.

Another possibility is that those OPEC member countries who have held their official prices fixed may decide on a substantial cut, as implied in the warning issued in mid-October by the oil ministers of the Gulf Cooperation Council in Salalah (Oman). Such price cuts might be accompanied by a pledge to review them in the event that discounting from the new level was not initiated and that agreed production quotas were observed. In neither case would a price cut solve OPEC's short-term problems. The principal short-term consequences of such a price decrease for exporters would be the following:

(a) A direct loss of per barrel revenue, without any offsetting overall gain in volume because of short-term price inelasticities. Each dollar per barrel price cut, if extended over a period of a year, would mean a loss in total revenue to OPEC of about \$7.5 billion. This could in turn have serious economic and social repercussions.

(b) Most member countries (especially those indulging in price discounting) and some other exporters, notably Mexico, would run into serious balance-of-payments difficulties, aggravated in some cases by current obligations to service a large external debt. They would in addition suffer a loss of borrowing power.

(c) Discounting would probably resume almost immediately, but from the lower price level, as member countries would be tempted to maintain and even increase their volume share in a market which would not be expanding over the short term. The price decrease would thus encourage rather than discourage further discounting, because it would increase the incentive for any individual member to seek greater sales volume in order to offset revenue losses.

(d) In the short term, there would be a further depletion of inventories (if the current low level permits) as buyers held off their purchases for as long as possible, anticipating even lower prices.

(e) Under this assumption, OPEC's power could be further eroded, thus threatening its effectiveness and the community of the national interests it has represented. This would make any step to re-establish OPEC's control over the situation more difficult because of the breakdown in communication.

The price decrease would also have adverse consequences for oil-importing countries despite the short-term gains in their balance of payments. Among the principal long-term consequences are:

(a) A further drop in the development of alternative sources of energy, the effect of which would only become apparent in the long term.

(b) A decrease in oil and gas exploration, both in industrial and in developing countries.

(c) An increase in oil demand over the long term, which would again put pressure on supplies, causing a repetition of the cycle of sharp oil price increases. A decade of conservation efforts would thus have been wasted in exchange for a relatively short-term gain.

(d) A halt to further expansion of the coal industry and trade as heavy fuel oil again became competitive with coal c.i.f. Japan and Western Europe as well as some locations along the US East Coast.

Avoiding a Price Collapse

As noted above, there is a possibility that certain OPEC member countries may initiate a substantial decrease in the level of official prices before or during the first quarter of 1983 in response to the competitive action of other oil-exporting countries. In this respect the Salalah statement needs to be taken seriously, given the present market conditions. If not, it may very well bring about a collapse in prices.

How can this be avoided?

At present, the residual suppliers within OPEC feel that they have been put in an unsustainable position by the actions of other producers, both inside and outside the organization. The problem is perceived by them as one of inappropriate price differentials, discounting and violation of production quotas.

In our view, too much emphasis has been placed by some member countries on the problem of price differentials when a more serious problem is the current discounting. In the case of African producers, differentials may be between $1.00 and $2.00 per barrel below their appropriate level, whereas discounts in the Gulf and from the African producers range from $3.00 to $4.00 per barrel. We estimate that at official government prices, the weighted average price for all OPEC crudes would be $34.10 per barrel if all price differentials were adjusted to realistic levels. We also estimate that the current actual going price for all OPEC crudes is $32.80. Of the difference of $1.30, $0.85 is due to discounts granted by certain member countries (excluding the effect of discounts resulting from the sale of products at prices below crude netback value) and the balance of $0.45 is attributable to lower than appropriate differentials. In other words, the problem of discounting is about twice as important as the problem of differentials in the overall picture.

The problem of production quotas is also of central importance, since price cannot be maintained when agreed quotas are not being observed by individual member countries. The Gulf producers have attempted individually and collectively to make it clear that they cannot continue for much longer to bear the main burden of being residual supplier to the world; that other producers, both inside and outside OPEC, must play a role;

that OPEC members must stop discounting and observe production quotas; and that outside producers, particularly Mexico, Norway and the UK, must at the very least realign their prices on the marker crude and exercise some temporary restraint on output. In any event, it is clear that, if the major exporters outside the OPEC area remain passive, they will contribute materially to a turn of events from which they would suffer substantial economic loss.

We believe that OPEC can manage the situation if agreement is reached among *all* members – including Saudi Arabia and Iran – on new production quotas to cover the situation that is likely to arise in 1983. The expected total demand of 20 mb/d could indeed be accommodated through a quota system along the lines of that considered during the last meeting of OPEC's Ministerial Monitoring Committee.[1] This quota system would, however, require downward adjustment to cater for the anticipated seasonal demand drop in the second and third quarters of 1983, which could be as much as 2–3 mb/d for OPEC as a whole. The second and third quarter quotas could be similar to those agreed upon in Vienna in March 1982, subject to appropriate adjustments, particularly with respect to the special cases of Iran and Iraq. However, any quota system must be periodically reviewed, perhaps on a monthly basis, in the light of changing market conditions and developments in the Gulf war.

Agreement on production quotas for the short term is, however, unlikely to be reached, or, if reached, unlikely to be successful unless the alternative is made clear. Any agreement should be based on the understanding that those who respect its provisions should have the right to require observance of OPEC's decisions. Such observance requirements should be

---

[1] We understand that the fifth meeting of the Ministerial Committee held in Abu Dhabi on 20 September 1982 considered the following distribution for an overall OPEC crude oil output of 20.325 mb/d (all figures in 1,000 b/d):

Algeria	750	Libya	1,200
Ecuador	200	Nigeria	1,500
Gabon	175	Qatar	350
Indonesia	1,500	Saudi Arabia	6,650
Iran	2,500	UAE	1,250
Iraq	1,200	Venezuela	1,900
Kuwait	1,150		

backed by an option for disciplined members to resort, if necessary, to price decreases with a view to deterring other members who violate the agreement. However, such disciplinary measures need not necessarily be implemented in practice. Experience shows that a threat could have a credible deterrent effect if it were to specify clearly in advance:

(a) the amount of the price decrease envisaged;
(b) the date on which the price decrease would be introduced;
(c) the period over which the new price would apply before coming under review;
(d) an indication of a second round of measures to be applied if the first round proved insufficient.

In strategic terms, the issue has to be seen as deterrence rather than attrition. Deterrence requires enormous diplomatic skills. Governments have their pride and their domestic political constituencies to watch – hence the advantages of persuasion and quiet diplomacy.

To be realistic, respect for agreements on quotas and prices cannot be ensured through deterrence alone. OPEC countries should be able to agree on a mechanism to compensate those among them who may be adversely affected by unforeseen developments. The compensation could then take the form of readjustment of quotas or of direct financial support.

Conclusion

To sum up, OPEC today faces difficulties that threaten its cohesion and its ability to defend the price of oil. Much is at stake for member countries: the very considerable economic benefits that have accrued to them over the past ten years as well as their political status on the international scene.

Today's difficulties are not entirely due to chance and accidents. OPEC is responsible for part of them, as it sometimes failed to anticipate impending problems and to design well in advance the appropriate policy responses. For example OPEC has tended to be complacent about the impact on oil demand of *sudden* price rises and of *uncertainty* about its intentions and policies. OPEC has also tended to ignore certain important phenomena such as the emergence of non-OPEC exporters and has not yet established with them those special relationships that foster mutual interests.

Member countries have never been in greater need of a cohesive and strong OPEC. Yet their very actions can lead to a damaging drift into price undercutting – or worse, to a price collapse. The situation could worsen in the spring of 1983 when a further drop in demand for OPEC oil is widely expected.

There is no merit in postponing action. OPEC will in fact suffer much damage if the outcome of the next OPEC Conference of Oil Ministers – expected to be held this December – is a lack of decision and the maintenance of the status quo.

OPEC needs to define two sets of actions, the first designed to *cope* with the current emergency and the second to *change* the conditions of the petroleum market in the long term.

The short-term crisis which may upset oil producers in 1983 is manageable, but it may not be managed successfully if current attitudes continue to prevail. The restoration of price discipline and the adoption of a new quota system are musts, and the approach to restoring this discipline is gentle but firm insistence that, otherwise, some members would bring about a significant price cut in a swift and sharp manner, despite the economic losses that they would suffer from such an action. There is no point in hoping that the slow price erosion induced by competitive behaviour would force the recalcitrant members to change their behaviour. All member countries should join in the adoption of the quota system, and attentive consideration should be given to the needs of members facing genuine economic difficulties.

OPEC's long-term objective is an increase in its share of the relevant energy markets; OPEC's cohesion will always be under threat unless demand for its oil rises to a higher level. The study of measures required to revive demand is a most urgent task. These include the definition of new pricing principles to guide policy in the long term and the establishment of constructive relationships with non-OPEC producers. Meanwhile, every effort should be made to avoid price wars in which all OPEC members stand to lose.

9 OPEC IN A LONGER-TERM PERSPECTIVE (1984)*

Alirio A. Parra

In my remarks today I would like to consider briefly some of the main factors that are encouraging OPEC to continue playing a constructive, coherent and leading role in world energy matters over the next decades. In the shorter run, the organization has made considerable progress already in working towards more orderly world oil markets. Moreover, it has demonstrated its capacity for enhancing and broadening areas of effective co-operation with the non-OPEC producers. In the longer run, it must lend support to and encourage a market structure that will give permanence and strength to its present-day efforts. In addition, a wider area of understanding should be promoted between the organization and the industrialized importers that would involve security and predictability in energy matters for both parties.

The years 1979–82 ushered in a period of turmoil and strain in world oil markets. The industry witnessed violent increases and decreases in crude and product prices and a steep decline in demand. For OPEC this period represented a dramatic and devastating drop in the real revenues of its member countries. And for all participants in the market, planning horizons were reduced to almost complete uncertainty. In addition, two other factors became more evident which were to have, and to a certain extent still have, a potentially depressive effect on prices, although to different degrees. The first of these was the 'overhang' of shut-in production capacities. This unused potential, which is declining, may last into the 1990s. The question arises as to whether a substantial reduction in spare capacity, through lack of correct forecasts, will again disrupt orderly developments in the market, especially on the upside. The second factor refers to the breakdown of the integrated

* Lecture delivered at the Sixth Oxford Energy Seminar, September 1984. Published in *OPEC Review*, Vol. VIII, No. 4, Winter 1984.

networks of the industry, which has already exacerbated market reactions.

The years of confusion and disorder brought reaction and a measure of correction, not necessarily permanent, of this situation. Under market conditions bordering on chaos, OPEC to a large degree succeeded in re-establishing some order. The historic London Agreement of March 1983 represented a turning-point and brought a measure of stability to the market-place. It set a production ceiling on a realistic basis and distributed national quotas. Although price discipline was a strong feature of this Agreement it did not entirely solve the problem of the differential values of crude oils which once again are coming to the surface. The 1983 Agreement explicitly recognized the role of the 'swing producer' within OPEC as a short-term balancing mechanism between supply and demand. By moving volume onto the market-place, often through third parties, the swing producer effectively can set a ceiling to world-wide prices while a floor can normally be guaranteed by shutting in production.

The period of turmoil has gradually subsided. In its place a new but tenuous and as yet unconsolidated equilibrium in the market-place now appears to be evolving. Price fluctuations have been dampened for the first time in a decade. Demand has finally revived, but the recovery is slow. Supply pressures from some non-OPEC producers are still present, although any destabilizing influences that they may have caused in the past are declining gradually. Within OPEC some tensions still persist but these should diminish as demand grows. Supply constraints are by no means perfect and room will sooner or later have to be made for the 'repressed' production from Iran and Iraq. In other words, what has been achieved is a situation of relatively fragile stability which, given the right conditions and time, can grow in strength and duration.

A better understanding of the recent changes in demand will be revealed only as the world economy consolidates its return to a normal path of economic growth. The energy developments of the past decade have provided a striking insight into a feature that will have to be reckoned with through the 1980s and beyond: this is the situation of OPEC as the residual supplier of the world energy economy.

Conservation efforts coupled with world recession have reduced the total demand for energy. Energy output ratios have decreased; that is price rises have had a negative impact on energy consumption. According to some observers, the swings in demand that have occurred in the last decade or so have been lower than expected. In the first instance, energy savings were realized as a result of the lower utilization of capital plant and equipment or, in other words, through lower output. Wide replacement of existing plant with more efficient energy-utilizing equipment has taken place in the industrial and other demand sectors. But by no means all the capital stock has been turned over. With the prospect of lower or at least stable real energy prices for the next several years further additions to energy efficiency are now beginning to recede. There is a lagged effect, however, from past investment decisions of perhaps as much as five years. Sustained world economic recovery will be reflected in growing energy consumption. As energy demand rises, the demand for oil should eventually rise at a higher rate. On a yearly basis, these increases could average out to more than 1 mb/d, most of which will come from OPEC. The implications of OPEC's role as a supplier of last resort are important. In this context the organization has the opportunity to play a decisive role in managing prices and supply to achieve reasonable stability over a term horizon.

The message is quite simple: OPEC in a longer-term perspective will be compelled to strive for the continuing stabilization of world oil markets. The organization has gained in sophistication and knowledge of the market. It is to OPEC's credit that it was able to react so quickly and effectively to the recent weakening of 'spot' prices.

OPEC will no doubt continue to seek stability mainly through the administration of prices and the orderly development of markets in the years to come. It will exercise restraint in production but be responsive to market forces. At the same time, stable prices should not be construed as necessarily meaning stable nominal prices frozen at today's levels. A price freeze need not always be the best way to achieve reasonable stability.

The role of managing supplies and administering prices may

become more complex in the future. Demand will not match potential availabilities for some years. New supplies from within OPEC itself will have to be accommodated and the effect of resource refineries better understood. Among the preconditions for setting the scene for a more predictable outlook for oil within the longer-term energy scene is the strengthening of ties with other important producers and exporters of oil.

The first demonstration of converging interests between OPEC and non-OPEC producers became apparent in early 1983, coincident with the signing of the London Agreement. Relations with non-OPEC producers are vital if attempts to restore equilibrium and order are to be successful. In the past, most of these countries were in vigorous competition with OPEC as they carved out a share of the world market, often through the pricing mechanism. Some of them are now reaching peak production and may no longer be a threat from the point of view of future market shares. It is essential, however, that during fluctuations of a short-term nature they should exercise normal restraint and adhere to established term prices.

Many of the larger non-OPEC oil exporters now realize that all ultimately lose from price discounting activities and that the total export market should be shared at a stable price by all exporters. The argument that price cutting eventually may lower revenues without increasing total sales should be persuasive. A loose system of administered prices has very definite attractions to producers reaching maturity and hoping to develop remaining higher-cost resources.

The partial collapse of the market in 1983, just as North Sea production was moving towards a peak and government revenue requirements were rising, had a profound effect on the attitude of the UK towards OPEC. Indeed this may have marked the turning-point in the way the country was to see its own role within the international energy economy. The new approach of the UK has been flexible and prudent, but is progressively becoming more visible. The recent letter of the UK authorities urging the industry to maintain stability of oil prices in the common interest is a remarkable document and clearly reflects the convergence of national interests with those of other important producers and exporters. It goes on to warn that if prices were to decline in the North Sea then competitive price reductions elsewhere could lead to a collapse of the world oil economy. It in effect reflects the growing view becoming more common among non-OPEC producers that fluctuations that are clearly of a short-term or temporary nature should not be allowed unduly to disrupt the longer-term stability of the industry itself. The firmness of attitudes in the North Sea and elsewhere should be a lesson to some OPEC producers themselves.

The Buchanan-Smith letter falls far short of 'interfering' with normal production and disposal of oil from the North Sea. Neither was this its intention. Fortunately, however, it coincided with a cut-back in North Sea production, planned on an operational basis, to allow for the summer maintenance of some of the producing platforms.

The case of Norway is not identical to that of the UK. Norway has preferred to develop its oil resources more slowly than those found in the UK sector of the North Sea. Substantial but only gradual increases in production are therefore most probable in the next decade or so from the deeper and more costly, although prolific, areas of the Norwegian continental shelf and beyond. As production increases, Norway will move into a more important role in the international oil scene. Therefore the arguments and actions in favour of price stability and supply management may be becoming more attractive to policy-makers in that country.

Mexico was the first non-OPEC producer to perceive that it must act in concert if it was to maintain the unit value of its oil exports, and the role of Mexico has been important in this sense. It is the only non-OPEC producer that has set production targets below its total productive capacity. Quite recently it reaffirmed its intention not to increase exports beyond 1.5 mb/d unless there was clear evidence of an expansion of world demand. Although not a member of OPEC – and the question has not been raised – Mexico acts very much like a quasi-member country.

It seems quite probable that the present understandings will broaden to a point where non-OPEC producers will play a more active role in ensuring that market fluctuations are kept within controllable limits in the future. The years of sharp volume growth of these producers are drawing to a close. The newcomers have been accommodated in the market-place. A dialogue has been opened up and extended to cover some half a dozen producers of varying degrees of importance. In practice, all producers are entering a flexible and informal relationship at the policy level. However, frequent contacts on technical and information exchange levels would also do much to maintain and extend these understandings.

The world cannot do without OPEC oil, but on the other hand member countries cannot do without export markets. It is within these limits, rather narrowly defined, that a mutuality of interests arises between producers and importers. But while there exist sufficient supplies of oil and policies on alternative sources of energy are coming to fruition, the urgency for dialogue on the part of the industrialized importers is simply not present. Dialogue is viewed by them as necessary in the longer rather than the shorter term. In effect, the problem of relations with industrialized net importers is complex and goes outside the field of energy politics. It would be well to remember also that the policies of 'energy protectionism' of many industrialized countries are still tuned towards reducing dependence, not so much on oil as on OPEC oil. In this, they have been singularly successful. The security problems are aggravated when demand for OPEC oil is made to fluctuate more than is necessary by misguided policies, thereby creating uncertainty as to market size instead of identifying the role of imported oil in the years to come.

The degree of co-operation between producer and industrialized consumer groups will depend to a large extent on the identification of 'overlapping' interests, if these in fact exist. As a first step, a common perception of the longer-term energy and oil market would allow us to reach a greater understanding of our own positions. It is necessary for consumers and producers to know a considerable amount more about each others' long-term energy plans and aspirations. In addition, it is as essential for the consumer to avoid future price shocks as for the producer to understand the rules under which oil markets will develop.

Naturally, consumers are faced with a set of options and

choices that are often different from those of the producing countries. For example, stability for the consumer is one choice but it is by no means the only one. It may well be that the consumer would prefer to accept the present *de facto* equilibrium price rather than face unpredictable fluctuations of both prices and available volumes.

The years of transition should be used to best advantage to forge new understandings and relations in the energy field between industrialized net importers and the main producing countries in the world. In the longer run, there is surely a basis for co-operation and co-ordination which has gone largely unrecognized because of the lower priorities accorded to energy issues at this time. For example, no mechanism presently exists to prevent price shocks; nor are there long-term strategies that would encourage fresh investments to prevent declines in capacity output in the producing countries.

The expectation of slow growth in demand for oil and continuing excess production capacity is entirely logical and feasible. Such a scenario implies inherent instability. This situation is exacerbated by the breakdown of the old integrated networks. Only OPEC's supply restraint and price stabilization programmes stand between order and chaos in a marketplace never accustomed to the total free play of forces. In effect, the instability of the market has been unnecessarily amplified by important changes in industrial structure in the total set of relationships within which buyers and sellers operate. Whatever its disadvantages, the old integrated industrial structure with relatively few participants gave considerable stability to world-wide supply and demand movements in a potentially volatile market of global proportions.

The role of the actors has undergone changes not yet completed and has left a vacuum not yet filled. The present market structure, whereby there is little buyer commitment to supply sources at times of surplus and extreme competition when supplies tighten, not only serves to exaggerate price and volume changes but also lends itself to the manipulation of inventories. It is obvious that a policy framework aimed at reducing the volatility of the market in structural terms is required. It is an area where OPEC attitudes or policies are not yet visible but which at some date must be taken up and considered systematically.

A realignment of the roles of market participants is required for a new and more stable equilibrium to develop and persist in the long run. The scope for internal adjustments has been reduced, whereas previously the integrated system had infinite opportunities to correct imbalances. The possibility of mismatching between supply and demand is now permanently present. In the absence of the ability to correct imbalances rapidly, one recourse is the spot market. But the spot market is really not in a position to play the role of matchmaker over any significant time period. It is poorly organized, badly coordinated and totally incapable of looking ahead. It often magnifies change rather than balancing situations, and the advent of the futures market has increased the size of the swings.

In the longer run some degree of reintegration appears to be desirable if a limit is to be placed on the more volatile aspects of market forces over any term horizon. The traditional majors are concerned with balancing their own systems. Some are acquiring reserves to match their potential outlets. But none has retained its former power: there is a sad lack of opportunity to gain access to fresh reserves.

It has become apparent that the 'state-owned' majors cannot isolate themselves from market realities but indeed may be more exposed to the uncertainties of a changing environment than many of the traditional integrated companies. As with the traditional majors, they need to improve the balances of their own systems in order to minimize risks and optimize long-term gains. To protect their long-term position it is becoming necessary for them to develop strategies of greater involvement in the chain of processes that integrate the international market. For the state-owned majors the concept of internationalization involves the integration of strategies of different kinds, some of which are totally unfamiliar to these corporations.

The possibility of becoming a downstream mover in the international market holds attractions and involves risks for a state-owned corporation. It seeks essentially the same objectives as the private international majors and must face similar strategic issues. Downstream involvement for the producer may strengthen stability and ensure steady and predictable outlets in a slow-growing and competitive market. In an industry subject to cyclical change the security and diversity of markets are as important as the security and diversity of supply. Downstream arrangements make for more sensible and viable long-term relationships between the market actors. In an orderly integrated operation, downstream rewards can be considerable over a term period while, in a fragmented market, price risks tend to move upstream.

In summary, the new state-owned majors will become more thoroughly internationalized and integrated into the total petroleum industry context, giving OPEC members an interest not only in crude oil profits but also in industry rewards and risks at all levels. The market decisions of OPEC members must therefore seek to ensure the minimization of market movements. In the shorter-term view, supply restraint and firm price policies are essential. Over a sufficiently long planning horizon, internationalization and integration of state-owned corporations should give structural strength to the objective of 'reasonable' stability. OPEC itself should also increase its emphasis on long-term planning and the establishment of firm links on a policy level with all producers and consumers. The means of achieving these objectives are varied but can be summed up in one concept: long-term relationships.

10   OIL MARKET STABILITY: TIME FOR ACTION?
(1985)*

Ali Jaidah

As on previous occasions I would like to take this opportunity
to review the current petroleum situation and to describe its
salient features. An analysis of the main forces operating in the
petroleum market and of the likely future trends in world oil
supply and demand will enable us to define the major
problems facing oil-exporting countries in general and OPEC
in particular. These problems are important because they
involve the stability of world oil prices. As you know, any
serious threat to the stability of the world petroleum market
can have very wide repercussions. Significant reductions in the
oil revenues of exporting countries, whether they are due to a
decline in demand, to a decline in prices or to both, have
adverse effects on their economies. The oil-exporting countries
of the Third World (not all of them member countries of
OPEC) suffer from sharp falls in revenues because they become
less able to finance development plans and social expenditures
for the welfare of their citizens. Some of these countries, such as
Mexico, Venezuela, Nigeria, etc., have a large international
debt. A fall in revenues leads to difficulties in the servicing of
this debt. A serious international banking and financial crisis
could occur if these difficulties became so intolerable as to
cause a country to default.

Oil-exporting countries in the industrialized and in the
Communist world will also suffer from an oil price crisis. The
Soviet Union owes a very large proportion of its foreign
exchange earnings to oil and gas exports; and you all know that
the Soviet Union is very dependent on these precious earnings
for its imports of wheat, capital goods and technology. In the
UK, oil makes significant contributions to Government

---

* Lecture delivered at the Seventh Oxford Energy Seminar, September 1985.

revenues and to the balance of payments. These contributions represent a sizeable percentage of the total Government budget and of export earnings and they are extremely significant compared with the PSBR and the current-account surplus. There is no doubt that an oil price crisis may cause problems for the pound, push interest rates up, and increase unemployment.

Neither the prospect of a continuing fall in the demand for oil nor that of a sharp price decline is good news for the petroleum industry. On the one hand, a shrinking market forces the industry to retrench; plant, equipment and labour become redundant and some companies either lose their independence through mergers or go into liquidation. On the other hand, a significant price decline causes other problems as it lowers the value of oil reserves and affects the profitability of their expensive ventures in high-cost oil-producing regions.

I also personally believe that an unstable oil market does not serve the interests of oil-consuming countries. Market instability fosters expectations of price falls and these in turn inhibit investments in the energy sector. Such a situation would not cause immediate problems because of the existence of a large surplus of oil capacity but would prepare the ground for an energy supply crisis in the 1990s. As you know the lead-in times of energy investment projects are very long, and a failure to plan adequately for future needs ten or fifteen years ahead of time causes serious long-term problems.

Recent oil history abundantly proves the point. The oil price explosion of the 1970s was partly due to insufficient investment in the late 1960s as high-cost energy development was discouraged by low prices. The very sharp and very destabilizing adjustments caused by these low prices have in turn caused the surplus of the 1980s.

I do not need to dwell much longer on the significance of oil market stability nor to stress any further that all parties in the international energy scene have a solid and fundamental interest in ensuring this stability.

Let us now turn to the analysis of the current situation and of likely future trends; this will enable us to identify the forces and factors that threaten the stability of the oil market and to assess the exact nature of this threat.

The first and perhaps the most important feature of the current petroleum situation is the behaviour of oil demand. To say that world oil consumption has been stagnant in recent years will cause no surprise. The worrying facts, however, are that consumption is expected to remain depressed and that all forecasts about demand are constantly being revised downward. Oil companies and independent experts are almost unanimous in the view that demand is not expected to increase in 1986 and will be devoid of meaningful growth in the next two or three years.

The second feature of the oil supply/demand picture is that non-OPEC production may continue to increase. The consensus is that the rate of growth of non-OPEC output in the second half of the 1980s will be much lower than in past years but many experts believe that this rate of growth will remain positive. Oil production in non-OPEC countries will probably fail to increase in the UK and in the Soviet Union but some growth is expected to obtain in Norway, China, Colombia, West Africa and in many small oil-producing countries which usually escape our attention because they are not in the limelight of the international market. The small contributions that these countries make to world oil supplies add up to significant numbers when they are all taken into account.

The combination of stagnant demand and increases in non-OPEC supplies causes a reduction in the demand for OPEC oil. I understand that oil companies are generally agreed in their forecast that the demand for OPEC oil will be in the 15.5–16.0 mb/d range in 1986 and in the 15.5–16.5 mb/d range in 1987. These annual output estimates conceal seasonal variations. It is possible, for example, that the demand for OPEC oil may average 15.5 mb/d in 1985 but rise to 17.0 mb/d in the fourth quarter of the year. But these seasonal increases should not distract our attention from the declining trends which are likely to reassert themselves in 1986–7.

There is no doubt that OPEC will face a period of belt tightening and experience increasing difficulties in its effort to stabilize prices if these forecasts turn out to be correct. This leads me to the third feature of the present world oil situation, namely the OPEC dilemma in the face of lower demand and downward pressures on oil prices.

In a lecture delivered to the Society of Petroleum Engineers in Bahrain earlier this year, I expressed the issue as follows:

> Their dilemma is *either* to accept a drastic reduction in their market shares and in their revenues in order to defend the oil price level, *or* to compete for market shares and face the risks of a price collapse which will also curtail their revenues.

So far OPEC has done its best to prevent oil prices from falling in a rapid and disorderly manner, and though official oil prices are lower today than in March 1983 the decline has been very gentle and its effects have been partly mitigated by improvements in the exchange value of the dollar. These results on the price front have been achieved by OPEC member countries at a very high cost in terms of export volumes.

It is wrong to believe that OPEC members can follow indefinitely the same policy and continue to accept further and further declines in their production and in their market shares. In fact even if OPEC countries decided that it was in their best interest to do their utmost to defend the price, we should not forget that OPEC's leverage on the market has become very weak because its share of world oil exports has considerably declined. OPEC now accounts for only one-third of total non-Communist world oil production while five years ago, it supplied two-thirds of the same total. This lower share makes it very difficult for OPEC to regulate oil prices.

Officials in non-OPEC countries often take the view, at least in public statements, that OPEC has such a considerable interest in defending the price of oil that it will continue to do so irrespective of the output sacrifice. At a recent oil conference organized by the *Financial Times* in London, the Deputy Oil Minister of Norway expressed this view and drew the conclusion that Norway will therefore continue to produce oil at full capacity and to increase this capacity in the next few years in accordance with current investment plans.

This Norwegian statement is important because it expresses very candidly and very accurately the policy of non-OPEC exporters and the premisses on which the policy rests. I can only repeat what I have said on past occasions to the audience of this Seminar, namely that non-OPEC governments are wrong in their belief that OPEC can provide a perpetual insurance policy on the stability of oil prices and that the non-OPEC countries can enjoy the benefits of this insurance without paying their share of the premium of the policy.

Relentless output maximization by non-OPEC countries in a period of stagnant demand has destabilized the market and has strained OPEC's ability to perform its price administration role to the limit. The non-OPEC countries have reaped considerable short-term benefits from this policy but pursuing it to the brink entails risks of very substantial long-term losses.

I would like to stress again that a fall in the demand for OPEC oil to levels below 17–18 mb/d puts considerable strain on the organization. Many oil experts are always groping for the magical number – say 16.0 or 15.0 or 14.0 mb/d – below which OPEC would immediately and suddenly disintegrate. There is no such number. My point is that there is a fairly wide danger zone. As OPEC output begins to sink into that zone the difficulties increase and the risks of a policy failure rise accordingly. It is also important to add that the risks involved in being in this danger zone are also a function of expectations. The situation is more risky when producers believe that they will be stuck in the danger zone for a long time than when they expect the output decline to be temporary and short-lived.

Today's situation is particularly worrying because OPEC's production is low *and* because recent forecasts are failing to predict even a modest recovery in demand in the immediate future.

The fourth interesting feature of the current oil situation is the role played by non-OPEC crudes such as Brent and WTI in the process of price formation.

The development of spot and forward markets for Brent in London and of a futures market for WTI in New York has introduced new factors into the determination of oil prices. These forces and factors interact with OPEC in a complex way which has not yet been well analysed and fully understood.

The importance of the Brent and NYMEX markets derives from two main factors: (a) the volume of transactions and (b) the speed with which information about prices is transmitted around the world.

The volume of transactions is a very high multiple of the volume of physical crude. It is said that the 'daisy chain' in the

Brent market has between ten and twenty links; in other words every barrel of Brent blend is sold and bought up to twenty times. On the NYMEX the number of daily futures contracts for WTI is an even larger multiple of WTI production and this multiplier seems to be rising all the time. Brent blend output is less than 1 mb/d; WTI production is of the same order of magnitude; but the weight of these two crudes on the market is equivalent to 30 or 40 mb/d because of the rapid turnover of paper contracts in the market.

Price information is transmitted instantaneously in the case of NYMEX and fairly swiftly in the case of Brent. This information elicits reactions on the part of traders who then decide to buy or sell and their quick responses move prices up and down almost immediately.

Prices fluctuate constantly throughout the day and of course from day to day. In this volatile world very small factors cause rapid price movements: markets react to rumours, snippets of news, gossip and other trivia. Markets also have their idols. Everybody watches the weekly API statistics published in the USA on Tuesdays, and oil prices then move up or down depending on whether these statistics show a decrease or an increase in stocks from the levels expected by the market.

There is no doubt in my mind that the operations of these markets are destabilizing. When the Brent or the WTI price comes down, for reasons which may have nothing to do with the underlying supply/demand situations, pressure is brought to bear on oil-exporting countries to lower their prices and offer discounts. These pressures are not only applied to OPEC members but also to such countries as Mexico or Egypt who do not belong to OPEC.

It is important to realize that a drop in North Sea or WTI prices does not signify that the supplies of these crudes are plentiful and that any buyer could obtain from these volatile markets all the quantities he requires. As mentioned earlier, the liquid base of these markets is very small. Furthermore WTI is not even an international crude. It cannot be exported from the USA, and cannot even be transported economically from the Gulf of Texas to the Eastern Seaboard.

The fifth feature of the world oil scene worth commenting upon is the role of Saudi Arabia. The actions and policies of this major exporting country have a direct psychological impact on the market. Saudi Arabia, together with other OPEC countries, has absorbed the reduction in world oil demand through a drop in its output. Because Saudi Arabia was initially a very large producer, the absolute decrease of its oil production has been very significant. Accordingly the direct role played by Saudi Arabia in the stabilization of oil prices has been and still is very important.

Oil companies and oil traders recognize the significance of this role and are always on the look-out for signs of possible changes in Saudi trading policies. Rumour and speculation about both real and imaginary Saudi action influence expectations about future price movements and influence trading behaviour. The psychology of the market is such that anything relating to Saudi Arabia gets out of proportion.

Although Saudi Arabia's commitment to defend oil prices has been amply demonstrated by the very large reduction in its output, many commentators turn their backs on this evidence and continually misinterpret Saudi Arabia's policies and objectives. In such a climate any policy that Saudi Arabia wants to implement can elicit exaggerated and unwarranted responses from the market.

This short description of the main features of the current oil situation leads us naturally to a discussion of its possible outcomes. It is becoming increasingly evident that the present fragile stability is under serious threat unless one or several parameters of the situation change.

One relevant parameter is the behaviour of demand. It is difficult, however, to argue that the forecasts are wildly wrong and that there will be a significant upsurge in the demand for OPEC oil in 1986–7.

Another relevant parameter is the behaviour of non-OPEC exporters. Their output maximization strategies have contributed to the crisis, pushing OPEC into this 'danger zone' that I mentioned to you earlier on. The short-sightedness of this policy is detrimental to the countries concerned, not only because of its effects on the market, but also because some of these countries are over-depleting their own reserves without consideration for their own long-term supplies. For example, oil production in Egypt increased by 18 per cent in 1984 despite a lack of significant discoveries or re-evaluation of reserves. Similarly one may question the wisdom of the UK output policy which seems to ignore totally long-term depletion objectives. A change in the behaviour of non-OPEC exporters could contribute to the stabilization of the market.

A third important parameter is the OPEC strategy. Until now OPEC has pursued a strategy of price determination underpinned by a system of production quotas. There has been a noticeable absence of innovation in the OPEC approach to oil policy; here again, the adoption of novel strategies could help in the resolution of the present crisis.

Let us now consider three scenarios involving these parameters.

A first scenario involves co-operation between major OPEC exporters and a few major non-OPEC countries. The number of exporting countries with potential influence on the market is small. The key non-OPEC countries are the UK, the USSR and Mexico. Within OPEC only five or six countries have the financial strength and the productive capacity required for effective action.

Co-operation means a common production programme, a price strategy and a policy to regulate supplies on the spot market. Co-operation is in the best interest of all oil-exporting countries. A rational analysis of the dangers involved in the present situation must persuade all those who have the power to act to get together. The objective of a common market-stabilization programme, if it is well conceived, is to improve the state of the world economy, and as such should not be frowned upon as an objectionable attempt to serve narrow producers' interests. It seems to me that now is the time for action. To delay any further until a serious crisis takes place can only entail considerable losses for all concerned. Is it not more rational to avert such crises and avoid the disruption and the losses?

The second scenario is one in which OPEC musters the political will to adopt some novel strategy. There is no shortage of ideas on what can be done. OPEC for example could explore ways of co-ordinating the marketing policies of its members. A promising approach, suggested at the recent Vienna conference, is for OPEC to sell all its oil export volumes exclusively through long-term contracts. The rationale of this strategy is to turn OPEC's role as a residual supplier from being a source of weakness into being a source of strength. The weakness has manifested itself in a continual reduction in the volume of OPEC's output. But there is another side to the coin.

The world needs every drop of oil supplied by OPEC, however small this amount has now become. This is because non-OPEC suppliers have no spare capacity. If OPEC succeeds in getting its act together it could supply this residual amount at a stable term price. The long-term contracts will ensure stability of volumes and revenues for the member countries. Of course this strategy involves a quota system and some co-ordination to ensure that the contracts signed by each country correspond to its quota. Contrary to many inter-pretations of the scheme, sovereignty is not at issue because OPEC has already accepted, since 1982, the principle of production quotas. Co-ordination of trading arrangements can leave countries free to choose their customers and to apportion their quota between these customers.

The third scenario is one in which nothing changes. Demand for oil remains low. Non-OPEC producers refuse to see the light and they continue to maximize their output oblivious of the damaging consequences that this policy inflicts on them. OPEC's production remains in the danger zone and OPEC continues to tinker with its conventional strategy. In such a scenario oil prices will continue to drift downwards. Market-determined prices will continue to gain in importance. Crude oil price realizations will become the key to price deter-mination and official prices, even if they survive, will be no more than irrelevant labels.

Such a price drift would continue until prices fell to a level perceived as unacceptable by the main oil-exporting countries both within and outside OPEC. At that point there would probably be a new attempt at stabilizing the market. It would then be very difficult to push prices up to their former levels and the best that could be achieved would be to prevent a further fall. In such a scenario exporting countries would suffer considerable economic losses, and as I argued earlier, other parties would also suffer.

I do not want to end on a very pessimistic note. I believe that the current situation is serious but that there are solutions to the problem. The real difficulties lie in the area of political will and political perceptions. It is to be hoped, however, that a rational understanding of the present crisis, backed by the efforts of quiet and intelligent diplomacy, will persuade the relevant actors of the urgency of action aimed at protecting their very considerable interests.

11 THE ROLE OF OPEC IN MARKET STABILIZATION (1985)*

Fadhil Al Chalabi

The present instability in the world oil market is the result of long-term structural changes initiated during the 1970s in the wake of successive oil price increases together with policy measures by the industrialized countries. Those changes are not expected to be reversed by short-term factors, such as variations in the level of world economic activity. The prime cause of the crisis in the oil market is the falling trend of world demand for oil since 1979 which is unlikely to be reversed in the near future. It is also the result of the growth in energy supplies, oil and non-oil, in the world outside OPEC that began in the 1970s. Although it is unlikely that this latter trend will continue in the future, investments that have already been made during the past few years will probably add new capacities to world energy supplies.

The industrialized countries have achieved tremendous success in increasing the efficiency of fuel utilization through conservation of energy and improvements in technology so that, with the same level of economic activity, the consumption of energy and especially oil has been reduced dramatically. Economic growth nowadays requires much less oil consumption than the historical pattern. The income elasticity of demand for oil has been reduced drastically in the same manner as the reduction in the oil intensity per unit of GNP. Whereas the GNP in the OECD countries has kept growing on average since 1979, albeit at a low level, oil consumption has fallen sharply. Between 1979 and 1984, oil consumption in the OECD area dropped by about 7 mb/d. It is estimated that

* Outline of a paper delivered at the Seventh International Colloquium on Petroleum Economics, Laval University, Quebec, 6–8 November 1985, published in *Middle East Economic Survey*, 25 November 1985.

about half of this fall was due to conservation measures and increased efficiency in fuel utilization.

The oil price increases of the 1970s have also changed comparative energy costs in favour of certain other available sources of energy, especially coal and nuclear power, which have displaced oil in many sectors, above all in the generation of electricity. Social and environmental problems of those sources of energy have been overshadowed by the impact of the oil price shocks of the 1970s. During the period under consideration it is estimated that more than 3 mb/d of oil have been displaced by these sources of energy.

However, the most important source of the present oil crisis lies in the ever increasing supplies of oil from outside OPEC. The OPEC price increases in the 1970s tipped the balance in favour of expensive oil outside OPEC which would not otherwise have been developed. Between 1974 and 1984 over 7 mb/d of new capacity has come on stream in non-OPEC areas – the North Sea, Mexico, Egypt, Malaysia, etc. Besides these new oil-exporting areas, additional production capacity has been developed in some countries to meet, partially at least, domestic energy requirements which otherwise would have been filled by imported oil (the case of India, Brazil and others).

In a shrinking market, new oil producer/exporters have to undercut the price in order to get a higher share. Hence, through price reductions and other advantages offered to the buyers, the new oil has been systematically displacing OPEC oil in the world market. Net exports from the Socialist bloc to the rest of the world have also increased since 1973. Like the other exporters, the USSR has been very aggressive in undercutting OPEC's price with a view to moving the maximum volume of oil in the world market.

As a result of the developments which took place on both the demand and supply sides, the share of OPEC oil in the world market has been reduced dramatically. From a level of 31 mb/d reached in 1979, OPEC's production during 1985 is estimated to have dropped to 15.5 mb/d. Whereas OPEC oil accounted for about two-thirds of world oil supplies outside the centrally planned economies (CPEs) in 1973–4, its share now amounts to only about 40 per cent.

This retreat of OPEC oil in the world market was the natural consequence of its price policies and, above all, its willingness to assume the role of the world's residual supplier of energy. Since OPEC took over the pricing of oil in 1973, its pricing policy has been based on fixing the price at a certain level below which no member country would sell its oil, while letting the volume of its sales be determined by the market. This simply meant that, in meeting their energy requirements, consumers would resort first to the relatively cheaper energy supplies, oil and non-oil, from outside OPEC before taking OPEC oil which is rigidly priced at a comparatively higher level. Consequently, OPEC oil served to fill the shrinking gap between world demand and non-OPEC world supplies. OPEC was thus able to defend the price level it fixed, and secure relative stability in the world oil market, but only at the expense of reducing its market share by allowing world demand for its oil to decline drastically. Never in its history did OPEC consider defending its share in the world market.

Until 1981–2 OPEC was still able to control the market and administer the price from a position of strength, even though world demand for its oil was on the decline. Playing the role of the world's swing producer did not affect OPEC's position as price administrator in the market, when world demand for its oil was still higher than a certain level corresponding to its minimum financial needs. For example, with OPEC production of over 23 mb/d in 1981, OPEC did not find any difficulty in administering the price and in leading the market and setting its pace, simply because this level of production, together with the then prevailing price, provided OPEC with sufficient financial resources to enable it to maintain the price by further reducing production.

It was only when world demand for OPEC oil had fallen well below this level that the problem of market stabilization began to pose itself acutely. OPEC has to resort to production programming by setting a ceiling for its total production and stipulating quotas for individual member countries as the only means of stabilizing a market which has become inherently unstable. Thus, in 1982 OPEC for the first time fixed a ceiling of 17.5 mb/d for its total production. This ceiling was reconfirmed in 1983, but then reduced in 1984 to 16 mb/d. It was only through these programmed cut-backs in production that OPEC was able to avert a collapse in the world price structure.

This fall in OPEC's production not only entailed a drastic decline in oil revenues (between 1981 and 1984 OPEC's overall revenues declined from over $280 billion to less than $130 billion), but also adversely affected OPEC's capacity to administer the price and control the market. Confronted with the aggressive policies of non-OPEC producers to maximize their sales at the expense of OPEC and the increasing financial pressures from within OPEC, the organization's member countries had to face mounting difficulties in defending the price level. Producers were under such great pressure to increase their sales that a real threat to the price structure began looming dangerously.

This new situation of over-supply together with the marketing behaviour of non-OPEC exporters, especially the North Sea, led to another series of structural changes in the oil market itself towards more disintegration and greater strength of the buyer/refiners' position to the detriment of the producers. Contrary to the old pattern of the world industry, where a few buyers entered into long-term contractual relationships with a few sellers for the purchase of crude oil to be used in the buyers' downstream systems, thus providing a high degree of stability in the buyer/seller relationship, the present market is characterized by disintegration. The bulk of the oil, 80–90 per cent, is being sold in a volatile spot market with daily variations in prices, where a large number of buyers, traders and middlemen have emerged in the market for the purchase of crude oil, which is not necessarily to be used directly in downstream operations, but is destined to change hands many times before finally being utilized in the refinery. The stable long-term buyer/seller relationship has given way to speculative short-term purchases in a market which has become over-sensitive, even to rumours.

In spite of all these developments, OPEC has been able to cushion the market and to defend the price structure by counteracting the aggressive policies of non-OPEC producers of undercutting OPEC's prices. Obviously, OPEC would not have been able to stabilize the market without its role as residual supplier in a shrinking market, which it continued to play at great sacrifice. No matter what is said about the weakness of the OPEC price structure and the non-adherence of its member countries to its price decisions, OPEC is still the only force in the market maintaining the price structure by cutting back production and forgoing revenues which are essential in implementing member countries' development programmes.

However, OPEC has reached a limit in holding the price, beyond which it is no longer possible to continue. Non-OPEC producers seem to be oblivious of the fact that the present situation could easily lead to a price collapse, if they continue with their policy of undercutting OPEC's price in order to maximize their sales at the expense of OPEC. In spite of many warnings expressed by OPEC spokesmen about the gravity of the present situation and the continual appeals for a reasonable degree of co-operation between OPEC and non-OPEC producers in sharing the market, non-OPEC producers are still adhering to the same strategy that led to the present serious situation.

In the long run those countries have self-interest in co-operating with OPEC to avert a price collapse, given their weak position concerning the limited volume of their reserves and the high cost of their production as compared with OPEC's. Apart from Mexico, oil reserves in all those countries have a very short life-span, while production is running at full capacity. Against this very high rate of reserve depletion, the cost of discovering new reserves in those countries is the highest in the world. This is in contrast with OPEC where the life-span of member countries' reserves is very long and the cost of production very low, while the cost of discovering new oil to replace depleted resources is the lowest in the world. This simply means that, in the event of a price collapse, non-OPEC countries will have to deplete their limited resources at low prices and face the problem of raising huge capital to find new expensive oil to replace the depleted reserves.

In the short term, however, those producers outside OPEC do not seem to see clearly their interest in co-operating and sharing the market with OPEC. Their immediate aim is to maximize their sales at any price, benefiting from OPEC's continuous adherence to its role of residual supplier. In fact those countries believe that OPEC has no other choice but to continue with its policy of defending the price through cutting back production, a policy which secures for the non-OPEC exporters high revenues in the short run and provides at the same time a guarantee for their future investments to find new oil. Therefore, unless those countries face real difficulties in their pursuit of maximizing both volume and price, and unless OPEC changes its stance *vis-à-vis* the role of residual supplier, it is unlikely that they will be ready to co-operate with OPEC in stabilizing the market on a fair basis.

OPEC will, of course, continue to make every effort to stabilize the market and prevent a price collapse. However, the process of replacing OPEC oil in world supply by other producers should be stopped. If there is no co-operation from the other producer/sellers, this could mean that OPEC may cease to play the role of residual supplier. With the very low production levels and the increasing financial difficulties for its member countries, the concept of OPEC as the residual supplier is already breaking down. Perhaps a possible alternative would be that OPEC should set for itself a minimum production level and market share that could be defended in order to optimize the relationship between OPEC's financial requirements for development and world market stability. This would ultimately mean that, contrary to its past policy of rigid price defence at the expense of volume, OPEC may consider the possibility of shifting to defending a minimum market share in addition to the price. This may mean that OPEC will abandon its role as the world's swing producer of oil.

For such a shift to be achieved smoothly and healthily, it is absolutely necessary that a last endeavour be made for negotiations with the other producers – mainly the North Sea, the Soviet Union, Mexico, Egypt, Oman and Malaysia – in order to reach an acceptable formula of market sharing that would guarantee for OPEC a minimum production level without, however, jeopardizing the position of the non-OPEC producers and with a view, at the same time, to securing a stable market and solid price structure.

In conclusion, it should be stressed that oil market stability is no longer the sole responsibility of OPEC. The major structural changes in the world oil market and the world energy scene in general are such that closer co-operation should be sought between OPEC and non-OPEC producers to co-shoulder the burden of that stability. A dialogue towards closer co-operation between producing and consuming nations is also necessary to achieve the objective of long-term stability in the supply and cost of oil for a sustained growth of the world economy.

PART II

THE OIL CONSUMERS' VIEWS: SECURITY AND FREE TRADE

12   MARKET STABILITY AND MARKET SECURITY (1982)*

Edward R. Fried

For the past few years, off and on, I have been working on the problem of what should be done to improve energy security in the oil-importing countries. I have understood the problem to have two aspects: first, what financial investments and political commitments should the industrial countries undertake to limit damage from an oil supply interruption; and, secondly, what could be done to increase energy investment in the oil-importing developing countries so as to reduce their oil cost burden, shore up their financial viability and improve their economic prospects. I will not be addressing the second aspect in my remarks today. But I will touch on still another element of this general subject, one that has not heretofore been seen as a burning issue: what constitutes energy security for the oil-exporting countries? As a general matter, it is fair to say that the subject of energy security, in any of its ramifications, is going out of style these days. Unfortunately, I fear it will return to centre-stage.

Energy security planning for the industrial countries centres on the International Energy Agency, which has the major responsibility for co-ordinating their energy policies in a crisis. When the IEA was established in 1975, oil-exporting countries, to say nothing of some of its designers, saw the Agency as a means of generating consumer market power to counter the spectacular display of exporter market power. That notion dies hard.

The real-life existence of the IEA was never confrontational in character. In point of fact, it could not be; effective emergency responses to an oil supply shortfall have to include the implicit co-operation of exporters, at least those exporters who

* Lecture delivered at the Fourth Oxford Energy Seminar, September 1982.

are prepared to use any surplus capacity to help offset the shortfall in supply. Without that co-operation, let alone counter-action, the problems of dealing with a supply shortfall would multiply.

This is not to gloss over the confrontational aspects of oil markets. There is inherently a strong element of conflict between the interests of exporters and importers in how oil markets perform; for good reason, these have monopolized attention in the past ten years. There are also important areas of overlapping interests, which receive little attention.

My purpose today is to show, on the basis of the experience of the past decade, why markets are moving away from the first and towards the second phase. As a consequence of those turbulent years, the oil world, indeed the economic world, may be near an important divide, characterized by a common concern about market security on the part of exporters as well as importers. I propose, also to explore some policy implications of that proposition.

As a first point, it is necessary simply to restate the critical relation between rapidly rising oil prices and economic growth. Ten years of upheaval in oil markets have run in parallel with a dreary transformation of the world economy – from self-confidence to self-doubt, from sustained, rapid growth to stop-and-go, low growth. The correspondence of these two trends is no coincidence. Without attempting to argue that point now, I will assert that the oil price shocks of 1973–4 and 1979–80 were major causes of the sharp turn for the worse in the world's economic performance.

Other factors certainly were at work. This was particularly true in the early 1970s when a boom in non-fuel commodities, a breakout of grain prices and a synchronized expansion that strained capacity made the world economy unusually vulnerable to new shocks. Each of these factors was destabilizing, but each corrected itself fairly soon. The oil price shocks, however, were much larger in size to begin with and proved to be more indigestible.

Since 1973, OECD economic growth has averaged only half as much as in the preceding decade, inflation has doubled, and unemployment as a percentage of the labour force has also doubled. In the oil-importing developing countries, the average rate of economic expansion has dropped by one-third – recently by more. Today's bleak economic outlook testifies to how much time it takes to adjust to oil price shocks. To repeat, only a share of this comparative misfortune is attributable to oil, but that share is certainly large.

To say that is independent of the question of whether the present real price of oil is too high, or too low, or just right in the sense of what is necessary to facilitate an orderly energy transition. The answer to that question is no longer self-evident, one way or the other, which is also part of the story. What I want to stress now is that what happens to the price of oil critically affects the performance of the world economy, and with it, the future course of oil markets.

A second point is that the battle over oil rents, waged through the medium of two supply interruptions and two price shocks, turned out to be very heavily a negative-sum game. Importers lost very much more than exporters gained. Furthermore, exporters, although benefiting handsomely, gained considerably less in real economic advance than would have been expected, and they had to accept greatly increased uncertainty about future markets into the bargain. In both cases, the reason was the same: the inefficiencies that seem to be inherent in adjusting to sudden, quantum changes in fortune, good or bad.

In the case of importers, the arithmetic is fairly straightforward, using for these purposes the events of 1979–80 and their aftermath. Initially the increase in oil prices over the two years meant a transfer of resources of $240 billion per annum in nominal terms from importers to exporters, of which some $200 billion was paid by industrial countries and $40 billion by oil-importing developing countries. Up to this point, income losses by importers had their counterpart in income gains by exporters. This is a characteristic phenomenon of a commodity boom: the element that is unique is the size and speed of the transfer, which in fact led to the ominous ramifications described earlier. Over the next two years, these incremental transfer costs declined in real terms by one-third, because of the reductions in import volume and prices, which themselves were the result, direct and indirect, of the initial oil price shock.

In addition, importers suffered huge income losses for which there were no counterpart gains by exporters. OECD estimates, which at present are the most systematic measure available, indicate that the economic disruption costs of the oil price shock will reduce OECD output by some $400–500 billion (1981 dollars) below what it otherwise would have been.

Such disruption losses stem from limitations in the capacity of industrial economies to adjust smoothly to very large external shocks, such as quantum jumps in the price of oil. Other prices do not fall when oil prices rise, wages tend to be rigid as labour seeks to avoid the real income losses stemming from rising energy prices, sudden large distortions in international payment balances influence trade and monetary policies, and widespread uncertainty and apprehension adversely affect investment and consumption. On top of all this are the feedback effects of similar developments in other countries.

Even then, these losses are understated. No allowance is made for the accelerated obsolescence and reduced utilization rates of the energy-intensive capital stock, which represents efficient energy adjustment but probably reduces productivity.

Less work has been done on estimates of comparable losses in output for oil-importing developing countries. A plausible assumption is that oil price shock indigestion is responsible for about half the deterioration in their recent economic performance, suggesting total disruption costs of $50–75 billion (1981 dollars), before trend economic growth is restored. Again these costs to importers represent income losses for which there are no counterpart gains to oil exporters.

For exporters, adjusting to good fortune involved no pain, but the final box score looks as though it will contain some grave disappointments. The decline in incremental revenues has already been mentioned. Even more serious is the tendency for sudden, large receipts of revenue to lead to boom and waste. This need not be true, nor *is* it always true. Still, a review of what has been happening in oil-exporting countries in the wake of the price jump of 1979–80 is replete with instances of new or larger subsidies to consumption, costly overemphasis on capital intensive investments, the misallocation of resources attributable to inherently overvalued exchange rates, and a general disposition to do too much, too quickly. When funds look as though they are not a constraint, too much is undertaken. When they again become a constraint, retrenchment is not cheap.

One of the mysteries that needs careful examination is why the average rate of economic growth of oil-exporting countries as a group in the past ten years is lower than it was in the period 1960–73. This startling fact emerges from the data appearing in the 1982 *World Development Report*. It draws further credence from the extraordinary difficulties now confronting a number of oil-exporting countries.

How could this be possible? The phenomena mentioned earlier are certainly a part of the explanation. The feedback effects of lacklustre performance in the rest of the world may be another part, but probably a small one. A general implication is that a sudden burst of new revenue followed by cutbacks is far less of a boon than gradual, sustained additions to revenue, which have greater promise of effective use. The point is critical for everyone: must it not be brought to bear on oil strategies?

A third point has to do with the question of the future course of oil markets. A consensus answer to that question no longer exists. The very strong decline in demand, thus far, in response to the 1979–80 price jumps, has been something of a surprise. How durable will it be? The weakness of economic recovery is also a surprise. How long will it persist and does it portend a distinctly lower long-term growth path for the world? You are aware of other variables: for example, new discoveries, the capacity for fuel-switching, technological breakthrough, and the role of nuclear power.

In the face of these uncertainties, a wide range of oil futures becomes possible. A plausible case can be made that the real long-run price of oil will either rise significantly, or moderately, or not at all. I personally believe a gradual rise is in the offing. Yet, it can also be argued, reasonably, that a producer strategy designed to maximize long-run revenues would lead to lower oil prices than those existing today.

These uncertainties strongly suggest that the battle over oil rents is just about over, certainly the phase in which very large new gains or losses can be anticipated. They also explain why resource-rich exporters concerned about long-term revenue maximization would have a different approach to market pricing strategy than those countries whose exportable supply is soon to run out.

This leads directly to the fourth point: are future oil shocks possible, and, if they occur, will they produce any winners, or will everyone be a loser?

Supply interruptions are surely possible, if not probable, over the course of the decade. That presumption stems directly from the unusual concentration of oil resources in the Middle East, the existence of chronic political tension there, and the fragility of oil supply lines. As in the past, such interruptions are likely to be temporary and reversible. Even so, a large short-fall coming at a time when the market has begun to tighten raises the danger of a replay of the melancholy events of the past.

But there is more to the story than that. A third oil price shock will certainly have all the costly consequences of its predecessors, and perhaps more. Another world recession coming with economic and financial institutions not fully recovered from the economic disasters of the past decade will be that much more long-lasting and damaging.

A third oil price shock will also set in motion another wave of structural adjustments, leading to a further decline in the relative use of energy in economic output and to a wholesale substitution of other primary energy fuels, including synthetic fuels, for conventional oil. These adjustments will require huge investments, which inevitably will be made, although at great cost to current world output and consumption. Once in place, or substantially in progress, these investments will be protected, notwithstanding a subsequent decline in the price of oil. Shaken to its roots a third time, the oil-importing world will probably bear the cost, large as it will be, of protecting itself against a fourth price shock. Oil markets, thereafter, will be dominated by a chronic overhang of excess productive capacity.

Does this not suggest, rather conclusively, that there will be few, if any, winners from a third oil price shock? Oil importers clearly will lose a great deal, once again; in the end, so will oil exporters. If so, what could be done by both importers and exporters to reduce the economic damage from a supply interruption, that is, to avoid another episode of markets getting out of hand?

One frequently mentioned possibility is a producer–consumer agreement to assure a reasonably stable price path for oil. Such agreements exist for a very few commodities, with mixed results. An agreement covering oil would dwarf any of these other agreements in scale and would contain characteristics that are unique, to say the least.

When the oil market looks to be uncontrollable on the upside, many importers suddenly see great merit in a producer–consumer agreement, and almost convince themselves that it is the only long-term solution to the oil problem. When markets turn slack, the many operational difficulties in making an oil agreement work, or, more accurately, in obtaining price security from an agreement, suddenly become very vivid. I have not seen many comments from exporters on this subject, but I suspect their attitudes, in reverse, are not too different.

Perhaps a producer–consumer agreement directed towards stabilizing the price of oil will be possible some day. I am sceptical. Discussions about what price stability means, whether it makes sense, and how it could be achieved could go on for years. I can recall that it took more than ten years to negotiate an international stabilization agreement for cocoa, and even then a major producer, the Ivory Coast, and a major consumer, the USA, decided against participation.

In any event, trying to make stable prices a permanent feature of the oil landscape goes well beyond what is necessary for the market security problem I have addressed. We should expect gradual changes in oil prices, up or down, in response to shifts in underlying factors. Price shocks are an entirely different matter. Defences against them could be strengthened by informal understandings between importers and exporters about complementary action in an emergency, or even by closer analysis of what is at stake.

To be specific, the major defensive action importers can take is to release emergency stocks onto the market to offset in whole or in part the effects of a sudden interruption of normal channels of supply. The IEA system, among other measures, provides for carrying emergency stocks for use in this kind of situation. The problem is that present IEA requirements for holding emergency stocks are not high enough, and the usability of these stocks is open to serious question. These requirements should be increased and the additions should take the form of government-held, rather than industry-held, reserves, whose use in an emergency would be unambiguous. The USA, Japan, and West Germany have been moving in this direction. Other industrial countries should follow suit so as to increase the prospects and the capacity for co-ordinated defensive action.

At times, exporters contend that the building of consumer stocks is a threat to their market interests and a transparent attempt to weaken OPEC's market power. This allegation should be candidly faced.

Stocks held by industry in excess of the amount needed to satisfy IEA emergency requirements have fluctuated widely over the past few years. Their build-up contributed to the price jump of 1979–80; their subeequent drawdown is contributing to the slackness of current markets. There was nothing conspiratorial about such tactical moves in inventory strategy, neither in 1979–80 nor in 1981–2. The build-up was a response to uncertainty of supply and expectations of further increase in price; the drawdown is a response to high carrying costs, declining demand and weak prices. Arguably, the strategy may not have been ideal for public purposes, but what meets the eye in commercial motivation is all that is there.

On the other hand, mandatory stocks, whether held by industry or by governments, are locked in for use in an emergency, not for use as a buffer stock to influence day-to-day operation of the markets. Parenthetically, however, the building of these government stocks now is offsetting part of the drawdown of industry stocks and therefore serving to prop up a slack market. The real purpose of government stocks, however, is market security. Their use will depend on an intergovernmental decision, which will not be taken lightly. To my mind, the danger lies in the opposite direction; governments will be over-cautious in coming to that decision, worried about holding these stocks until the shortfall becomes even more severe. If so, it may become a case of too little, too late, with the price shock already upon us.

Emergency stocks held by importers should be seen as the counterpart to the existence of surplus capacity in some of the major exporting countries. Both should be used to reduce the economic damage from a sudden oil supply interruption. Each should complement the other. Use of emergency stocks by importers will facilitate operation of the IEA sharing system. Increases of production by those exporters not affected by the causes of the shortfall could be directed in whole or in part to importing countries that have been most heavily caught short. As I mentioned earlier, some exporters acted in this way in 1979 and 1980, to their ultimate benefit and to the common benefit. Would it be possible to create greater assurance that such surplus capacity will exist in the future and will be used?

Such actions by importers and exporters would offset supply shortfalls and allay panic in markets. Both would improve market security in the critical sense of restraining the tendency of the market to overshoot in this type of situation and therefore of avoiding a third price shock.

If avoiding such price shocks is a common concern of importers and exporters, as I have argued it is, there should be a closer interchange between them about market prospects, the operation of emergency systems, and how they could be strengthened. Regular meetings on a technical level between the Secretariats of OPEC and the IEA would be a good beginning. There should be no mystery about what each group will try to do, or could do, in an emergency. On the contrary, a regular programme of confidence building measures could in itself be a factor in reducing the danger of market panic and, therefore, of the price shock that both sides should be seeking to prevent.

I believe the danger of such a price shock continues to be the largest single threat on the international economic horizon. It is not an imminent threat. A combination of temporary and structural factors has produced an unusually large amount of excess capacity which provides a margin of safety for the next few years.

That margin of safety will gradually diminish and could well disappear entirely over the course of this decade. On the other hand, a sudden interruption of oil supply will be a continuing risk. Time is available for both importers and exporters to improve the security of the oil market. The experience of the past ten years is convincing evidence that it would be in their common interest to do so. As insurance, the premiums would be small in comparison to the costs that would be avoided. Not using this opportunity could inflict damaging economic and political losses on the world. Sadly, they would be unnecessary losses.

13 ENERGY TRADE: PROBLEMS AND PROSPECTS (1985)*

E. Allan Wendt

I want to talk today about a business in which we all have a stake, a more than $300 billion enterprise that has tripled in constant dollars since 1973. I am not referring to the energy sector as a whole, which is many times larger. I am referring to a small but key part of the energy business: energy trade. Trade in oil, natural gas, coal, electricity and uranium amounts to over 20 per cent of total world trade. Every country in the world today imports or exports energy in one form or another, and the continued healthy growth of the world economy depends on our ability to maintain and expand energy trade.

Trade issues today are controversial. Increasingly, we are seeing efforts to protect national industries by one means or another. Such efforts are not new. I would like to recall Adam Smith's view, expressed more than 200 years ago. He said:

> Each nation has been made to look with an invidious eye upon the prosperity of all the nations with which it trades, and to consider their gain as its own loss. Commerce, which ought naturally to be, among nations, as among individuals, a bond of union and friendship, has become the most fertile source of discord and animosity.

My aim is to demonstrate how we can contribute to establishing that bond of union and friendship and avoid the discord and animosity that have all too often characterized energy trade.

I would like to begin by examining in some detail the growth and changing patterns of energy trade since 1973. I will then turn to future prospects and, in particular, how energy trade

* Lecture delivered at the Seventh Oxford Energy Seminar, September 1985, also published by the United States Department of State, Bureau of Public Affairs Office of Public Communication.

can grow and prosper if it is freed from the constraints currently imposed on it.

Growth and Changing Patterns in Energy Trade

The spectacular growth of energy trade is dominated, at first sight, by oil: oil trade increased from about $100 billion in 1973 to about $275 billion a decade later (in constant 1983 dollars). As a percentage of total world trade, crude oil and product trade has grown markedly – from about 10 per cent to almost 20 per cent. But this growth in dollar terms hides a reduction in volume terms. As a consequence of the oil price increases of 1973–4 and 1979–80, crude oil trade volume is down – from 30 mb/d in 1973 to 21 mb/d in 1983.

The pattern of oil trade has also shifted sharply in response to the price increases. OPEC oil exports, which in 1973 represented 92 per cent of total world crude oil exports, had declined by 1983 to less than 70 per cent and the total volume was approximately halved. With the sharp rise in North Sea production, OECD oil exports have more than doubled in volume, increasing from 3.7 per cent (1.1 mb/d) of the total in 1973 to 12.5 per cent (2.6 mb/d) in 1983. Non-OPEC, non-OECD oil exports (excluding those from Eastern Europe and the Soviet Union) have increased even more sharply, from 4 per cent (1.2 mb/d) of global oil exports in 1973 to 18.7 per cent (3.9 mb/d) in 1983.

Thus, the sources of oil exports have shifted dramatically from OPEC to non-OPEC oil producers. To put it more sharply, oil exports have shifted away from those who seek to control prices and production towards those willing to produce in response to market forces. OPEC's effort to maintain prices above long-term production costs has caused it to lose market share.

As spectacular as the more than threefold growth in the value of the oil trade is, the growth of the natural gas trade is even more striking. Natural gas trade in 1973 was worth about $3.5 billion (in 1983 dollars). By 1983, it had grown to around $30 billion. Volumes increased by 75 per cent between 1973 and 1983. The market share of natural gas as a fraction of energy trade has increased from about 3 per cent in 1973 to about 10 per cent in 1983. The producers who benefited most from the growth in natural gas trade were those in a position to supply the growing West European and Japanese markets: Norway, the Soviet Union, Algeria and Indonesia.

Growth in two other energy sectors – coal and electricity – has been more moderate, and they comprise less than 10 per cent of total energy trade. While coal trade increased considerably in constant dollars from 1973 to 1983, it has stagnated in recent years and has declined as a percentage of total energy trade. Electricity trade, which roughly doubled in constant dollar terms from 1973 to 1983, still represents only about 1 per cent of total energy trade.

What are the constraints today on energy trade? Where is it being artificially restricted by government policies, and how might it develop if the constraints were removed?

OPEC Limitations on Oil Production

Certainly, the most significant of the constraints on energy trade today is the OPEC limitation on oil production. OPEC today is producing around 14 mb/d. As much as 10 mb/d of oil production capacity lies idle. No one can predict the price to which oil would fall if 10 mb/d were to be put on today's market, and I am not going to try. OPEC members will have to decide for themselves whether they would have been better off today with lower prices but closer to full production capacity. Clearly, the continued erosion of oil's market share poses a real threat to the medium-term interests of major producers. If oil prices had not jumped sharply in 1979–80 but had, instead, increased gradually at a rate of, let us say, 5 per cent annually in real terms, a barrel today would still cost close to $25, and OPEC production would be, I think, much closer to full capacity than its present 14–15 mb/d.

I am not going to assume success, however, in converting OPEC to free market principles. On the contrary, I think there is every reason to believe that OPEC, though currently strained, will manage to muddle through, even if oil prices drift marginally lower. If the oil market tightens in the early to mid-1990s, which I think it prudent to expect, OPEC may have another opportunity to choose between a policy of

administered price increases and a more patient and ultimately more stabilizing policy of allowing the market to
determine prices.

Removing Trade Barriers

In the meantime, it is in the interest of oil-consuming
countries to concentrate on removing barriers to energy trade
among themselves and on achieving, thereby, a diversified and
balanced energy mix. The principal forum for pursuit of this
objective is the International Energy Agency (IEA), which
maintains a constant effort to monitor barriers to energy trade
and to seek their removal. Whether IEA members will be as
vulnerable to oil supply disruptions in the 1990s as they were
in the 1970s depends in large measure on what they do in the
next ten years. If the IEA countries establish flexible, resilient
and transparent energy markets, based on an open trading
system, they will greatly reduce the potential for economic
harm arising from supply disruptions and associated sharp
price increases.

In discussing the removal of barriers to energy trade, I would
like to take an American point of view and concentrate, first, on
what is happening to make our own energy markets more
flexible and resilient and, secondly, on what we regard as the
principal barriers to increased energy trade with other OECD
countries. Three bilateral relationships are of particular
importance to us: those with Canada, Japan and Western
Europe. I would like to discuss each of these and then turn to a
specific issue that faces us all: the issue of refined product
imports.

Domestic Deregulation. Let me begin at home. The domestic
energy market in the USA is a very large one. We use about 38
mboe/d – 16 mb/d of oil, more than 9 mboe/d of natural gas,
almost 9 mboe/d of coal and about 5 mboe/d of nuclear and
renewable energy sources. The US Administration would like
to see these markets freed of artificial restrictions. President
Reagan removed all controls on oil prices in 1981. As a result of
gradual decontrol over the last several years, more than one-
half of the natural gas in the USA is now sold at market prices.

We would like to remove the remaining natural gas price controls as soon as possible, but even if the required legislative action is not taken, natural gas prices will eventually be decontrolled in any case, as older gas reserves are depleted. From an economic point of view, coal and uranium are virtually unregulated in the USA, and electric utilities are being freed of many of the economic restrictions imposed on them in the past by the Federal Government.

This movement towards deregulation has encouraged much more market-oriented behaviour throughout the energy sector. Oil, natural gas and coal are increasingly priced on a 'spot' or, at least, market-sensitive basis. The market for oil futures has grown rapidly, and a natural gas futures market is about to open. The futures market allows participants to hedge their risks and, at the same time, contributes to market transparency by serving as an additional indicator of market conditions. Competition has heightened, and we are now confident that our energy system, on the whole, can respond freely to changes in supply and demand. Even in a supply disruption, we would avoid price controls and allocation and depend on market mechanisms to restrain demand and distribute oil.

We would not, however, depend exclusively on market responses in an energy crisis. Assuring energy security, in our view, can justify government measures. The USA maintains a Strategic Petroleum Reserve (SPR) of almost 500 million barrels. We would use it early in a supply disruption to cushion our economy from the effects of a sharp increase in prices. Although use of the SPR would unquestionably represent a government rather than a market response, release of SPR oil would be by market mechanisms: the oil would be sold at auction to the highest bidder.

Trade with Canada. With the freeing of market forces inside the USA has come a change in our energy trade, especially with Canada. Canadian–US energy trade, which today amounts to about $10 billion per annum, provides a striking example of how market forces can bring mutual benefits. Canada today is by far our largest energy trading partner. It is our second largest foreign supplier of oil and oil products (900,000 b/d) and our number one foreign supplier of natural gas (26.9 bcm per annum) and electricity (39 billion kWh per annum). We, in turn, are Canada's largest supplier of coal (20 million tons per annum) and we export small amounts of crude and oil products to Canada.

US–Canadian trade is now prospering, but this was not the case at the beginning of the 1980s. Government intervention on both sides of the border was then stifling our bilateral trade in natural gas and petroleum. Canadian gas exports to the USA were based on a Canadian Government-administered, uniform border price, which ceased to be competitive as a gas delivery surplus developed in the USA. As a result, Canadian gas sales had plummeted from 90 per cent of licensed volumes in 1977 to only 43 per cent of licensed levels in 1983. Following extensive bilateral discussions between the two governments over a two-year period, the Canadian Government implemented a new gas export pricing policy in the summer of 1984 which allows US buyers and their Canadian suppliers to negotiate directly the price at the border. The new market-oriented policy has led to a 25 per cent drop in border prices (to an average of $3.26/mBtu), bringing great savings to US consumers. At the same time, Canadian gas exports to the USA this year are expected to increase by at least 30 per cent, which means that the value of Canadian gas exports will increase, despite the price drop.

Similarly, we are taking steps to remove barriers to US–Canadian energy trade in general. At the Quebec Summit on 17–18 March, President Reagan and Canadian Prime Minister Mulroney agreed to give market forces a major boost:

> ... by reducing restrictions, particularly those on petroleum imports and exports, and by maintaining open access to each other's energy markets, including oil, natural gas, electricity and coal.

Prime Minister Mulroney fulfilled his commitment with respect to oil when he decontrolled exports to the USA on 1 June. President Reagan reciprocated two weeks later by removing restrictions on the export of crude oil from the lower forty-eight states to Canada. Electricity trade, which is subject on both sides to extensive regulation, is expanding within limits imposed by the high costs of long-distance transmission. In the

USA we hope to see Canada's uranium industry freed of current requirements to upgrade the ore to uranium hexafluoride before export. We also hope to see fulfilled the Canadian Government's pledge to remove restrictions on energy investment, including the so-called retroactive back-in, so that US investment is encouraged, with beneficial consequences for trade between the two countries.

Trade with Japan. Our bilateral energy trading relationship with Japan, unfortunately, is not so thriving as our relationship with Canada. There are problems on both sides. On the US side, a major issue is the restriction, which amounts almost to a prohibition, on oil exports. There are six different laws in the USA that, in one way or another, restrict oil exports. Because of Canada's proximity to the USA and the historical relationship between the two countries (including the longstanding export of oil from Canada to the USA), we have been able to allow exports of crude oil from the lower forty-eight states to Canada.

Although the USA is a large net importer of oil, the Reagan Administration would, in principle, like to remove the ban on export of Alaskan oil because there are substantial economic advantages – in particular, lower transportation costs – in doing so. Under free market conditions, some Alaskan oil would be likely to go to Japan, Korea and other Pacific rim destinations. We have not yet reached the point of allowing such exports, largely because of domestic interests that fear such a step would weaken US energy security and harm the maritime fleet. The Administration would like to allow, under existing legislation, the export of small quantities of oil from the Cook Inlet area of Alaska. Although the limited amount of oil involved (less than 30,000 b/d) poses no significant risk to US energy security or maritime interests, the proposal is controversial and has aroused some Congressional opposition. It is still being discussed within the Administration.

On the Japanese side, we see the major problem arising from price controls in the energy sector. Japan allows refiners to charge higher than market prices for gasoline in order to subsidize fuel oil and kerosine. This price control system would appear to make it more difficult for natural gas and coal, which are the principal competitors to fuel oil in the electrical sector, to penetrate the Japanese market. We wonder whether the Japanese claim that it is uneconomical to convert more power plants to coal, and Japanese projections of limited growth in natural gas demand, are due in part to artificially low fuel oil prices. Without price controls, the prospects for coal and natural gas demand in Japan might look brighter, and our bilateral energy trade, which already amounts to more than $1.5 billion per annum, might expand signficantly by the 1990s.

Trade with Western Europe. With Western Europe, our trade in oil and oil products faces minimal barriers on both sides and has grown substantially. Our exports of oil products to Western Europe have reached 205,000 b/d, and we import 620,000 b/d of crude and oil products from Western Europe. In sharp contrast, our coal trade with Western Europe has stagnated in recent years. There are several reasons: the strong dollar has made US coal expensive relative to that of our Australian, South African and Polish competitors; and the economic slow-down in Europe – combined with the growing availability of French nuclear power – has reduced demand for coal-generated electricity. European restrictions are also limiting the potential market. The UK and West Germany subsidize locally produced coal so that it reaches the end-user at prices equivalent to US coal, despite significantly higher production costs in Europe. Although some steps have been taken in recent years to reduce these subsidies, the market for imports is still significantly smaller than it would be under free market conditions. We would like to see a real effort made in the next few years to put the West European coal market on a free market basis.

An Open Market Strategy for Refined Product Imports

So far, I have discussed our bilateral relationships with our major OECD energy trading partners. I would like now to discuss the matter of refined product imports. This issue concerns the OECD countries in general and will affect their relationship with oil-exporting countries for many years to come. It also challenges our capacity to act collectively to maintain open markets for the common good.

The problem of oil product imports arises because of the vast over-capacity in the refining industry that has developed since 1980 and the shift of some refining activity from consuming to producing countries. Much has been written and said about how the global refining industry reached the point where it has 8–10 mb/d of idle refining capacity and another 1 mb/d coming on line in the next year or so. My own view is that it really does not matter how this situation came about. The question is, how do we respond? Do we seek to protect our respective refining industries by erecting barriers to trade, or do we move towards a more open system and allow market forces to find an economic solution?

I am pleased to say that the principal industrialized countries, through the instrument of the IEA, have taken the first step toward a market-based solution – one that will avoid the 'invidious eye' that, in Adam Smith's view, creates 'discord and animosity'. At a ministerial meeting on 9 July 1985 IEA member states agreed to a communiqué that calls for a 'common approach whereby they would maintain or create conditions such that imported refined products could go to the markets of the different IEA countries and regions on the basis of supply and demand as determined by market forces without distortions.'

How are we to interpret this statement? It does not call explicitly for free trade or open markets, but it does, in our view, define open market conditions. This definition is contained in the phrase 'on the basis of supply and demand as determined by market forces without distortions.' We have no objection if Japan and Western Europe maintain licensing and stockholding requirements – even though we do not – so long as those requirements are otherwise compatible with GATT and do not affect the volumes and prices of oil product imports that would otherwise prevail; nor will we object to the current tariff levels, especially if the revenues are used for energy security purposes.

We believe that implementation of the IEA 'common approach' is the only reasonable basis for resolving the issue of refined product imports. If all IEA members – including

Japan, Spain and Greece – import oil products on the basis of supply and demand, the products coming from new refineries will be sufficiently dispersed to allow us all to make the necessary adjustments. Keeping those markets closed would only strengthen protectionist pressures elsewhere and lead to a wave of new restrictions that would leave all of us in the OECD area worse off.

Such a protectionist wave would also damage the interests of oil-producing countries, especially those that have invested in downstream operations. In our view, the interests of both producers and consumers lie in the direction of open markets. We in the OECD are doing our part, and the IEA plans to monitor carefully the implementation of the ministerial agreement. At the same time, we expect oil producers to avoid subsidies to their refineries and to ensure that uneconomic operations are not artificially maintained. Some producing countries appear to be maintaining energy resource prices below market levels in order to benefit export-oriented refiners and petrochemical producers. This practice has given rise in the USA to calls for legislation to take account of so-called natural resource subsidies in countervailing duty procedures. It would be preferable for producers to eliminate such subsidies, where they exist, before legal or legislative actions are taken in the USA and, perhaps, elsewhere.

The Developing World's Future Role in Energy Trade

Finally, I would like to turn to the world outside OPEC and the OECD. What is its future role in energy trade? Here I am thinking primarily of the non-OPEC developing countries. Despite the strong growth in oil production in non-OPEC developing countries during the past decade, there is still potential for increased oil and natural gas production and exports. Egypt, Mexico, Oman, Angola, Malaysia and other non-members of OPEC have expanded their oil production. In today's market, the question is whether they can capture the slow growth in demand – perhaps 1 per cent per annum – that can be expected between now and the year 2000 and, perhaps, also compete for OPEC's declining market share. A similar problem faces gas producers: are they willing to compete aggressively? Algeria has yet to develop into the major gas supplier its potential would indicate. A more market-oriented approach to gas sales might enable Algeria and other gas suppliers to slow Soviet penetration of the West European market.

Of particular importance to future oil and gas production in developing countries is their attitude towards foreign investment, which can be viewed either as a threat or as an opportunity. I would suggest that the threat is minimal and the opportunity is great. Brazil, which has been expanding production very rapidly, has been doing so essentially without foreign equity participation. Despite Petrobrás' (the Brazilian state petroleum company) remarkable and highly laudable effort, it would take a long time, at the current rate of activity, to explore all of Brazil thoroughly. Is it not wiser to speed up the process and to spread the risk? Brazil by 1990 will be almost energy independent if current plans are fulfilled. Could it not become an oil exporter, as well, by encouraging foreign investment in its hydrocarbon sector?

If developing countries do take a more market-oriented point of view and if they accept foreign investment, the developed countries will have to redouble their efforts against protectionism. The 'invidious eye' will be all too ready to see national interests threatened and to ask for protective quotas or tariffs. A coal mine in Colombia – one with a potential capacity in the year 2000 of less than 5 per cent of US coal production – has already led to serious coal tariff proposals in the USA. So far, we have been successful in fending off these proposals. In the past year, we have also seen proposals for an oil tariff, for oil product quotas, for restrictions on natural gas imports and for relief for our domestic uranium industry. It is the Administration's policy to resist proposals of this sort and to try to keep our energy markets open to fair competition.

Our job will be much easier if we can point to a broad consensus in favour of open markets, free trade and equitable treatment for foreign investors. It is unrealistic to expect our markets to remain open if others are closed or if others subsidize their products or restrict foreign investment. We would like to see the kind of commitment we have undertaken with Canada – to reduce restrictions and maintain open access to energy markets and energy investment – spread to other countries, both developed and developing, and become a world standard for energy commerce. If we succeed, energy trade will become 'a bond of union and friendship' that contributes to the prosperity and security of all our countries.

PART III

PRELUDE TO THE 1986 OIL PRICE CRISIS

14 DEBATE AT THE OXFORD ENERGY SEMINAR, 13 SEPTEMBER 1985*

Sheikh Ahmed Zaki Yamani

The situation today is very critical, very serious – and it needs some discussion. I am not going to talk as an oil producer. I am one, but I think the problem is a global one. It represents a serious difficulty in the future – in the far future – and a difficulty we have today that might increase. I was talking to my friend, Dr Chalabi, the other day, asking his advice on the subject I should discuss with you. He suggested a forecast about the energy situation, the oil situation. And then yesterday I was talking again with my colleague Husseini to see what the forecast is for the future. When we used to sit down to make a forecast, we would talk about the short term, the medium term and the long term; and usually the short term would be clear enough with a high degree of accuracy, the medium term would be less accurate and the long term would be rather vague – it was anybody's guess. I realized, thinking about it yesterday, that it is now the other way around. The long term is rather clear to me, the medium term is less clear and the short term is very vague, and I cannot see it very well. In the long term I have no doubt in my mind that there will be a shortage in the supply of oil. How serious it is, how great it is, remains to be seen and depends entirely on what we do within the short term. In the medium term there will be a period of some equilibrium, a situation of balance between supply and demand. And the short term is, as I said, vague and unknown to me.

I looked with Mr Husseini at the figures related to the long term. We looked at the present reserves, we examined a lot of scenarios, assuming for instance that we will have an increase

---

* This is the text of the contributions of the principal speakers on the Final Panel of the Seventh Oxford Energy Seminar, 13 September 1985.

in the consumption of oil on a yearly basis of 1 per cent. And when we arrived at the year 2000, we looked at the level of consumption and reserves, and we found that there will be a shortage in the supply of oil. Of course, by the year 2000, there will be so many oil exporters disappearing as such from the picture, most of the oil exported will be coming from the Gulf (and mainly from a few countries), and maybe we will return to the situation where one member country of the future OPEC, or whatever we will call it, will be reluctant to produce so much at that time. But we constructed a lot of scenarios and they were all hypothetical, and I thought I should not really waste your time with hypothetical studies, since what happens in the short term will have a very serious impact on that long term; and the medium term is, as I told you, in between, when we get over the present situation. Oil producers will then be in a more comfortable position and will be able to produce almost within their financial requirements. But what is the present situation? The way I see it, of course there is a surplus in the market – what they call a glut in the market – and there is a pressure to bring the price as low as it is convenient to the consumers. And here the consumers differ. We will probably hear from our good friend, Vicomte Davignon, what the various views of the consumers are on this. Here we have the non-OPEC producers relying on OPEC to protect the price of oil, and they feel free to increase production and play with the price of oil – their price – according to the market situation.

Inside OPEC, most of the OPEC member countries depend on Saudi Arabia to carry the burden and protect the price of oil. Now the situation has changed. Saudi Arabia is no longer willing or able to take that heavy burden and duty, and therefore it cannot be taken for granted. And therefore I do not think that OPEC as a whole will be able to protect the price of oil. So we have one of two scenarios or alternatives. Either it is left for everybody to produce as much as he can, and sell at any price dictated by the market and we will see real chaos, we will see a sharp drop in the price of oil – maybe to within the range of $15 per barrel, maybe less – it is very difficult to foresee. And, of course, we will have an international financial crisis, the banking community in the United States will suffer so much, we will have some political crisis in so many countries, oil producers within OPEC and outside OPEC. That is alternative number one, which I see for the moment as more imminent than before – probably at least for a certain period of time. Alternative number two is to see some sort of co-ordination between the non-OPEC producers and the OPEC producers, and also among the member countries within OPEC. And that co-operation will see non-OPEC producers reducing their level of production a little bit and staying at that level for some time until some OPEC producers are able to breathe. And then they can share in the increased consumption for the future.

Now I do not want to sound very pessimistic but I think this is the situation. I know that we will have some additional production coming from Iraq. It will probably start reaching the market by the end of this month or next month,[1] and gradually increase. I don't think that the Iraqis will really restrain themselves or agree to take any additional responsi-bilities within OPEC in order to strengthen the price level and protect it. And since I told you that Saudi Arabia will not carry on with the previous policy, any drop in the price level will definitely force certain member countries with additional capacities, like for instance Nigeria, to produce more in order to maintain a minimum level of revenues. At the price of, let us say, $27–28 for Nigerian Bonny, if it is sold at that price – I think it is a big 'if' – they derive a certain level of revenue. When that price goes down to $20 or $16, they have to produce at full capacity in order to get an even lower level of revenue. So, the lower price of oil is in itself a pressure on oil producers to produce more, which will create another pressure to lower the price of oil. Of course, we will see another scenario coming after that, and we will see some of the oilfields – existing new oilfields – no longer commercially viable. We will see develop-ments in new oilfields completely stopping, especially in the North Sea, and probably an end to exploration activities. And I do not know how we are going to solve the financial and monetary crisis.

I do not foresee an immediate possibility for a get-together of the oil producers, and therefore I do not rule out the possibility of a collapse in the price of oil, although probably not until after

[1] Speech delivered 13 September 1985.

this winter since, considering the present circumstances in the market with a very low level of stocks, I think we will easily carry on as we are, probably until the end of the first quarter of next year.

Now, to add some additional confusion to the situation, we have a political element in the area related to the Iraqi– Iranian war. We do not know whether the Iraqis will succeed in one of their attacks on Kharg Island in ruining the installations and depriving the Iranians of their oil exports. If this happens, we also know for sure that the Iranians will not let the navigation in the Gulf go smoothly, and there will be a serious interruption in the supply of oil which will create a world-wide panic. And probably we will see the price of oil shooting up – temporarily of course, for a few months – to – God knows – probably a level of $40 or so. Again, that is mainly a result of the low level of stock now in the market. That is one of the possibilities. Unfortunately it is an imminent possibility that we see in front of us. I want to tell you that I am worried, and I think the situation should worry everybody – in this room or in the official government departments in the consuming nations and the producing nations. I hope that I have whet your appetite for some serious discussions.

Thank you very much.

Vicomte Etienne Davignon

Well, the first thing that we must be grateful for is that very sobering picture of what we are up against. I should like to begin with your first point. I think it has always been the security of forecasters to be able to forecast faraway, because they would no longer be there when the things happened, and there is no doubt that applying that principle has helped my political career enormously. And so I am a little worried that we are now discussing the real thing, so that one can find out very quickly how mistaken one can be.

I would like to make the first point, which I think is very strongly in the minds of European consuming countries – and what I will now say is related to OECD European countries because the situation of the United States is quite different and I am quite sure somebody will pick that up. I think that we in Europe have found one thing very clear. This is that in our present situation – and of course we are speaking globally exactly as Sheikh Yamani has spoken – there is no longer an energy problem separated from a problem of global economic policy, budget, finance, debt and what have you. There is now one problem: the question is which are the elements of that problem that can be influenced by action. That is the question which comes to governments or to main companies: what is the element for which is there is a margin of influence? And none can be fundamentally changed so everybody is working on the margins. We have found that what literally devastates our economies in Europe is brusque changes. We cannot digest brusque movements, and this I think is very deep in our thinking, and in the way we react to what presently exists. There is a second element, which is of course of interest, and which shows how global these things are. It is that if you look at the statistics, you will find that on average in Europe the real price of oil calculated in our currencies has only begun to come down in 1985, way after what happened in the dollar area, because the revaluation of the dollar has cancelled out the movements of crude prices in terms of our balance of payments and our real price, and it is only in 1985, if you take an average in European units of account, that you see that price come down.

The third element is that it has now become clear to European governments that with the full evolution of energy policy, the variation of price, unless enormous and considered to be lasting, has very little impact on demand. I think that will remain so, so the price element will not have an impact on the economy, the demand and so on. So the question is twofold: what is the reality? And what is the perception? It has always struck me as an observer and as a participant in these questions that there is no other area that I know of where the perception takes over so much *vis-à-vis* the reality. As you just mentioned, if there was a very significant political difficulty in relation to transport: it would have the effect of panic, and this panic would have economic consequences that were in no way economically justified. It will happen, it has happened before – the post-Shah period in Iran is the most illustrative of that – and I think it is no longer contested and everybody knows that, but it will happen in any case. So the perception is very important. And if you look at the perception *vis-à-vis* the reality, looking at the figures before coming here, it struck me that in months which are traditionally not so good for the oil producers, the prices firmed. In the month of July, since production was lower and since, because of the level of stock that you mentioned the real level of the usable commercial stock was small, consumers had to continue buying as they did not have to do one year ago or two years ago. So if you looked at the reality from the consumer side, you could say the cartel is working and the cartel can still have a firming effect on prices, which appears in spot prices in Rotterdam, but the perception is quite different. (Having had the not very satisfying joy in my life of running a cartel in steel but not in oil, I always found that, when you run a cartel, if things are going badly it is not good and if an increase of demand appears that is about the worst thing that can happen to you because then everybody wants to have 100 per cent of the increase, so it is not great fun running a cartel but it can be quite interesting.) The perception is that, since there is a division among the members of the cartel over the distribution of production, as demand revives there will be an increased desire to meet this demand and so the opposite will happen – the prices will go down. So the perception is clearly that the prices will go down, although the reality has shown, and should in any case teach a lesson to the European consumers, that the flexibility that really exists on their side is not very great, as the price trend has shown over the past months.

What we would clearly prefer (and I think I can speak on that quite frankly since for the first time in quite a long while I have no public functions so my usual undiplomatic remarks can become even more undiplomatic) is a period of stability. I do not think that anybody in the various governments believes that their problem of balance of payments or their problem of economic growth would be helped in any way by great movements, great insecurity and great instability. Why is that not said? That is not said, in my view, for two basic reasons. The first comes through the point that you were making. It is that if we said that we wanted stability and that we wanted some sort of period in which stability could be maintained with the help of the consumer countries, this would probably lead to no response – not to no response because of a lack of interest, but to no response because maybe the conditions are not right.

And the second reason is that people basically dislike taking responsibility, and to do something different and new requires somebody (or a group of people) who is ready to stick his neck out, and unfortunately this time I don't see people who are ready to stick their necks out and it is very easy to explain why one does not stick one's neck out. There is always this marvellous possibility to invoke the market economy. The market economy is basically the law of supply and demand – you cannot go against the market etc. etc. Never having been an operator in the oil market but having read quite a lot about it, I find that the historical literature of the energy industry does not indicate very clearly that the law of supply and demand has ever been prominent in this area; but that does not stop you having great principles, and invoking principles is always a useful way of not dealing with the problem – or in any case a dignified way of not dealing with the problem. So, to sum up, my feelings are first, that while the situation may be different in the United States, there is still a profound preoccupation with energy problems inside the European consumer countries. Secondly, there is a feeling of vulnerability that remains in the short term. Thirdly, in all scenarios the preferred scenario is one of stability. Fourthly, unfortunately, in relation to that scenario of stability I see little prospect of an imaginative approach being taken for the various reasons that I have mentioned so I would conclude with some sadness that the possibilities of unsatisfactory movements are greater than the possibilities of stability at this time.

Mr Mario Ramón Beteta

The world oil market is in fundamental disequilibrium. Unused productive capacity – both upstream and downstream – has increased substantially in the 1980s. Demand for oil has contracted in a dramatic way. Such a state of affairs is not new: disequilibrium has characterized many phases of our industry's history. Today, our main concerns relate to the magnitude and pace of the adjustment process, and to the distribution of the costs and benefits that it implies. We are dealing with a commodity of critical importance to the economic welfare of producing countries and of great strategic relevance for the world as a whole.

In the short and medium terms, the behaviour of demand will not ease the process of adjustment. Energy conservation and inter-fuel substitution continue to reduce the demand for oil. The transition from the 1983–4 cyclical recovery in world economic activity to steady long-term growth will probably be characterized by a slower rate of growth than previously envisaged. Economic crisis in developing and industrializing countries has curtailed oil consumption in precisely those regions that were considered the main sources of growth in world demand. In the very short term, demand patterns have been seriously affected by speculative activity and inventory management. In the longer term, the extent to which consumption will react to lower nominal and real prices of oil is not clear. The elasticity of demand is not necessarily symmetrical with respect to upward and downward price movements. That is why producers remain sceptical of the potential longer-term benefits that downward price adjustments may entail.

These world oil demand conditions underline the importance of supply behaviour. In the short and medium terms, the basic problems with which we will have to deal have to do with supply management, if we are to maintain order and stability in the oil market. The output and pricing policies of OPEC, and of the main non-OPEC exporting countries, will have to take full account of the dangers implied by a deepening structural disequilibrium. All exporting countries must contribute their part in preserving stability. The implied burdens must be shared equitably. This constitutes a highly complex and sensitive political challenge to a number of sovereign nations. It will require enlightened statesmanship, imagination and discipline in order to cope rationally with current oil market conditions and prospects.

Price stability is in the long-term interest of producing and consuming countries. For both it is important that prices do not change abruptly in any direction. They must evolve in some reasonably predictable way. Adjusting to rapid changes in the price of oil poses difficult problems to the oil industry itself and to the world economy as a whole. Investment decisions are severely affected by price uncertainty. This is particularly true in the oil industry, where investment projects need long periods to mature. This explains why price instability today affects the future supply of oil and, consequently, the future price of oil. Drastic price cuts today may well mean steeper increases in the not too distant future.

If oil prices were to drop beyond certain levels – and these are difficult to define precisely – the stability of the world's financial system could be seriously affected. Bankers are well aware of the impact of price reductions on the financial health of the oil industry in which they are heavily involved. They are also concerned with the effect of an abrupt price fall on highly indebted oil exporters. As the flow of foreign exchange derived from oil fluctuates, servicing external debt can be severely hampered.

Governments in consuming countries have an important role to play with regard to price stability, without interfering directly with market forces. By their actions and through policy statements, governments contribute to the development of a market atmosphere that conditions the perceptions and attitudes of market actors. Confrontational positions do not benefit anyone. What is needed is a greater recognition that the working of the world oil system must be based on the reality of interdependence. Those in positions of responsibility must search for common ground, identifying and making explicit common interests and common risks faced by producing and consuming countries alike.

Allow me to concentrate on some questions of structure and strategy of non-OPEC oil supplies. We must have a better understanding of the role that this set of producers plays in the market and what can be expected from them in our search for stability. My remarks stem from the conviction that OPEC and non-OPEC exporters must commit themselves to the pursuit of a meaningful dialogue. My country has been active in establishing contact with other producers, members and non-members of OPEC. These have proved to be particularly fruitful. It is precisely in difficult moments like the present that we must exert our greatest efforts to keep channels of communication open and effective. Permanent dialogue can dispel misunderstandings and give us a fuller grasp of the implications of alternative courses of action.

Let us approach the world oil market through an Oxford looking-glass. Although not the one from Alice, it is in the tradition of Lewis Carroll, exhibiting a common interest in asymmetrical structures. In the simple model of the oil market that has been used in research carried out by the Oxford Institute for Energy Studies, the world is divided in two parts: one where shifts in demand and other shocks are largely accommodated by quantity adjustments, and the second one where changes in demand elicit only price adjustments. One part of the world – OPEC – operates as if supplies were totally price elastic, and the second – non-OPEC areas – as if supply were totally inelastic. Of course, there is a certain overlap in practice: some OPEC members have become very price responsive through a multitude of informal pricing mechanisms and there are some non-OPEC countries, like my own, that have not been following an output-maximizing strategy.

In this model the two groups are linked to each other in a straightforward manner: any imbalance in supply and demand in non-OPEC areas generates a change in price which is initially accommodated by OPEC members through a change in their export volumes. This reaction eventually corrects the original imbalance or disturbance in non-OPEC areas. It is in this way that the stability of the global system is preserved. However, there are situations in which OPEC is not willing or able to absorb all of the shift in the demand for its crude. It is then that OPEC prices are adjusted, formally or informally.

The relative size of the two parts in which the world is structured in this model, their change over time and the limits to which their respective shares may evolve are key variables.

Even if the OPEC region is seen as a residual supplier of oil and demand stays relatively flat, it is difficult to foresee a situation in which its market share continues to erode in a significant way. Output of non-OPEC countries as a whole is nearing its peak. In Latin America, the only significant increases that we shall probably see during the rest of this decade are in Colombia and Brazil, as long as Mexico maintains its self-imposed export limits. In Africa, only Egypt and Angola seem capable of further modest increases before output reaches its maximum level. In Asia, an expansion of production appears feasible only in Malaysia, although this country has restrained output growth in co-operation with OPEC. In the Middle East, Oman and Syria have more significant short- and medium-term potential.

The impact on the market of output from non-OPEC oil producers from developing areas is less direct. The market strategies of these very diverse countries vary significantly. If we exclude Mexico, their aggregate importance as exporters is limited, as a large proportion of their output is for domestic consumption. However, they have been substituting oil imports, thus reducing the size of other producers' markets. Countries that have become net exporters tend to adopt over-competitive prices. In many cases they do not have many options owing to prevailing domestic economic conditions, weak physical infrastructure and the limited marketing experience of their national oil companies. Greater contact with more established oil exporters might be useful.

Of greater importance and complexity is the role played by the non-OPEC developed oil exporters. The institutional framework in which their production and pricing policies are determined has become a key source of instability in the world market, especially when export volumes, incomes and the market shares of OPEC producers have reached their present level. Output expansion under conditions of profound market contraction is a dangerous policy, particularly when a few countries hold ample unused capacity and low-cost resources. One may follow a policy to pursue one's own interests, without regard to those of others, up to the point where by doing so one endangers the oil regime from which one benefits. I suspect that the time has come for those producers to review their strategies thoroughly and possibly to show more restraint regarding output growth.

In order to preserve stability it seems necessary that those countries that adjust prices, but are rigid with respect to quantities, should show greater flexibility with respect to output. Conversely, OPEC might benefit from more flexibility in setting its official prices. This could effectively contain some of the extreme forms of irregular pricing behaviour by individual OPEC members.

Price transparency is essential for market order in a system of administered prices. When official prices are rendered almost meaningless – and they are meaningless when discounting and irregular trading practices become general – we create the conditions that further weaken price sovereignty. Refiners become interested not only in lower prices but in mechanisms that render the downward adjustment process more predictable. This is the world of deemed netback arrangements and spot-related automatic pricing mechanisms. Producers not only lose control over prices: they may be allowing for an acceleration in the fall of prices.

Greater flexibility by those that follow output-maximizing policies and by OPEC in the administration of prices could open the way for the reconstruction of term relationships and contractual arrangements. These are the key to stability. The alternative is a cycle of intermittent crises of increasing frequency and intensity.

Mr Arve Johnsen

Having listened to the panel up to this moment, I have four observations to make, and whether or not they are related to our contribution to stability remains to be seen. Those four observations are as follows:

The first one is related to the Seminars we have held here since 1979 (and it so happens that I had been in on every one). It struck me this morning as I was listening that the situation was completely different in September 1979 from the one we are now facing in September 1985. The main theme in 1979 was as follows: how high could the oil prices go and how could we do something in each country about conservation and a reduction of the consumption of oil?

At this Seminar in 1985, I have a feeling that the question is now quite the opposite, namely: how far down can the oil prices go? And I would like to make this particular observation because my third observation has to do with the forces that have been working between 1979 and 1985 – because a lot has happened between those two years. However, before I proceed to that, my second observation is related to what has been said by the speakers so far this morning and, to quote Sheikh Yamani, there are two alternatives: either the one that would lead to chaos – and we could actually call it confrontation to some extent – or the other one that would take the form of co-ordination internally in OPEC and between OPEC and non-OPEC countries. May I offer a new word in English which is a combination of these two and which would read – I don't think you will find it in the Oxford dictionary – it would be the combination of co-ordination and confrontation reading as 'co-frontation'. You may consider this just for a minute. By combining it this way I am hinting at the situation where many of us would like co-ordination but in which there are also forces at work, which we do not always command, that might to some extent prefer to see some kind of a confrontation; and here I think we have a difficult conflict of interest between the various powers. Let me also briefly point to the fact that in addition to that Vicomte Davignon drew our attention to the alternatives of stability versus instability and ended up with a vote for instability considering everything in the short term, and then it came in nicely from Mr Beteta in terms of equilibrium versus disequilibrium with the preference for the latter rather than the former, which is to say the same as was said by the two previous speakers in different words.

So far we seem to have a fair measure of consensus, and I am always sceptical of consensus because we had a number of consensuses during the 1970s and the early 1980s and they haven't always come out the way they were supposed to.

My third observation is related to what I would call the market behaviour between 1979 and 1985 and also to what I would call the power struggle there because, whether we like it or not, we are talking about a power struggle in the oil market just like in any other market. Now then, what has happened in the market between 1979 and 1985? I offer just two points of view there: one is related to the demand side and the other one to the supply side. Regarding the demand side, there is no doubt that energy saving has taken place to an extent that we could not foresee in 1979. It is in insulation, it is in the new types of car – and we have not seen the end of that – it is in the new types of aircraft. Amongst other things, a lot of work has been done in order to develop new materials; composites, light material. Why? In order to reduce the energy bill, whether you are a car owner or you use aeroplanes or you use energy in your own home. And as far as I can observe this is going to be a permanent, long-term, new aspect on the demand side.

From my point of view, regarding what has happened on the supply side during these years, high prices in the initial part of this period for oil and oil-derived products led to high profits, high investment and increased new production. Now, with these two forces at work on the demand side as well as the supply, we see some of the results as per 1985, but my fourth observation is related to another activity, particularly among the producers of energy, which may have an even more lasting effect than what has happened so far. I would like to connect it with the initial statement by Sheikh Yamani that in the short term he wasn't quite certain, in the medium term he saw balance, and in the long term he saw shortage, and he was looking towards the year 2000. I came to think of Lord Keynes who said that in the long term we are all dead – and as Vicomte Davignon said it is easy to predict about the long term because no one will hold you responsible for that. I will offer at the end of my statement here an opposite view that, in the long term, there may not necessarily be a case of shortage and you may ask me how on earth it is possible to have such a point of view, and that brings me to my fourth observation and the two key concepts related to my fourth observation which are: (a) technological change and (b) substitution. I should like to elaborate a little bit on these and see whether or not they will lead to more stability. As a side comment I would 100 per cent support what has been said on this matter, namely that we should all try to work for a measure of stability, with as little abrupt and sudden change as possible. Now then, as for technological change, I would like to take only one example. I am of the opinion that natural gas may turn out to be as essential during the twenty-first century as oil has been during the twentieth century, and I would remind you that there are large resources of natural gas left unused. Today, a lot of research and development is being put into the following process: how to produce natural gas, from remote areas and in cases where you don't have very large reserves, by a new process combining liquefied nitrogen with liquefaction of gas. By doing that, you could reduce the energy loss by at least half of what it is using the traditional set-up and it is my guess, maybe even my assessment, that in five years' time, we will have this new technology whereby natural gas in remote areas and smaller quantities will become competitive in the market and add to the already existing reserves. On the refining side, similar research and development work is going into how to convert natural gas to gasoline not via methanol but rather directly. I would not be suprised if, in another six years' time, we could meet here and conclude that this research and development has had a basic breakthrough. It is my personal opinion that in six years' time it will have done so, not only on the production side, but also on the consumption side, and that brings me to my last point concerning substitution.

It is my opinion that we have a tendency when we discuss the oil market to become a little narrow-minded in so far as the base for substitution is somewhat broader than we sometimes think. In other words, and now I am speaking as a producer, when I come to the conclusion in 1985 that if I don't do anything about this substitution and about new technology over the next few years, then there will be a shortage in the year 2000, then I will do everything possible to see to it that there is no such shortage, because if there is a shortage there will be no further equilibrium, no further stability, and we might have an abrupt change again. So my conclusion is that I would like to work along these lines of technological change and substitution towards the year 2000, in order to see to it that there is no such instability.

Professor Franco Reviglio

I welcome the opportunity to reflect on the question of the relationship and the dialogue betweeen producing and consuming countries, in their work together for stability. In 1984, the world economy showed signs of recovery from its worst recession since the Great Depression more than fifty years ago. The various geographical areas have benefited from the world recovery through the mechanism of trade, although to different degrees. In 1985, however, the economic recovery is showing signs of weakness. The risk that it may be interrupted, or at least that it may pass by entire geopolitical, geographical areas is great. In this respect, a conditioning influence seems to be played by monetary and financial factors. Very probably the international economic problems are aggravated by the failure to find an agreement on a new world monetary order.

Industrialized countries on the whole, and especially the richer countries, have the greatest responsibilities in this field. To every 1 per cent of GDP growth in the industrialized countries there corresponds an increase of 2 per cent in the exports of developing countries. Every percentage point increase in the interest rate of the dollar causes higher currency expenditure or pushes up the foreign debts of the developing countries by about $4 billion. These data give an idea of the interdependence of the various geopolitical areas and of the rising internationalization of the economic facts. The responses to these problems have often been inadequate with solutions based on regional or national interests and short-term benefits. Nationalistic and protectionist tendencies are still developing, bringing with them the danger of aggressive behaviour, which would interrupt the process of economic integration under way.

Events in the energy sector before and after the oil shocks of 1973 and 1979 have been very significant in this respect. Producing and consuming countries have based their policies almost exclusively on their own interests with practically no attention to their relationship of interdependence.

We all know how unsatisfactory the results were for everyone concerned. Co-operation was and still is the card to play. However, co-operation in this sense, of long-term joint planning to establish genuine integration of markets with production, is still only the aim we hear about at conference after conference. It is, however, something that is still far too rare in actual projects and undertakings.

Failures have also marked the few attempts made in recent years on the international political level to reconcile the individual interests with the more general need for development. The lack of results at the political level, although representing a major obstacle to common undertakings, should not be regarded by the business communities as an alibi for lessening their efforts in the field of co-operation.

If one looks at the present situation in the oil market sector, one finds a great deal that is paradoxical. Huge funds are used to finance take-overs and mergers or to repurchase shares outstanding. At the same time, upstream investment is declining in real terms year after year despite the huge increase in the cost of oil exploration. Money is invested in mature oil systems such as that of the USA, which have already been extensively explored, or in areas like the North Sea, Alaska, and the Canadian Arctic, where difficult environmental conditions raise costs tremendously and the possibilities of finding giant fields are lower. Far more promising areas in the Middle East, North Africa and even Latin America are ignored and around 50 per cent of OPEC production capacity remains unused.

With the present relative abundance of oil and the correspondingly weaker price trend, some observers take a rather simple and short-term view of the energy situation and tend to play down the question of dialogue between consuming and producing countries. However, a long-term approach cannot leave out of account the facts that oil demand will pick up again, particularly if prices continue to weaken, and that a substantial part of the oil reserves located in the OECD countries will be depleted in the course of the 1990s. If you consider the energy intensity in GNP since 1973, you realize that it was in 1984 that the intensity stopped declining for the first time. I am not sure that Vicomte Davignon is right when he says that variation of the price of energy has little impact on demand. I think that this decline of substitution that we can see looking at this ten- or eleven-year period shows that, in some way, declining prices are responsible for declining substitution. Since its foundation ENI has actively pursued a policy of co-operation with the oil-producing countries. At the end of last year, our group had oil-prospecting rights in twenty-seven countries (not including Italy), covering a total area of about 5,000 square kilometres. 70 per cent of these rights were located in Third World countries and 45 per cent in Arab nations. In the same year, 1984, AGIP helped Third World countries to produce about 34 million tonnes of oil of which 21 million tonnes were produced in Arab countries. The group's investments abroad in the oil sector are expected to be around $5 billion in the next three years. 80 per cent of this sum will be invested in local Third World projects including about 47 per cent to be invested in Arab countries.

ENI has also done work at the theoretical level to demonstrate the need for concerted policies on the part of diverse groups of countries and the advantages to be gained by integrating important sectors. I am referring to the interdependence model presented in Rome at the ENI/OAPEC seminar of April 1981 as subsequently developed by a joint ENI/OAPEC team. I am also referring to the joint ENI/OAPEC study of the refining industry in the Arab world, a study that has pointed out the risk of over-capacity in the years to come as well as the need for adequate forms of integration between the downstream activities of the developed countries and those of the Arab nations. And integration is probably still the way to be followed so as to restore reasonable conditions of stability to the market, and to avoid the risk of another energy shock.

In the 1970s, the oil producers took over the crude oil and the upstream businesses, but not the downstream one. Therefore, they have to sell their oil, or the oil products manufactured in the new export refineries, to the oil companies, which control the market. This is a weak posture because it breaks the market into segments that have different supply and demand balances, making the whole oil industry unstable and difficult to run. Involvement of the oil producers in the downstream activities of the consuming nations and the involvement of the consumers in the upstream activities of the producing countries may be a remedy, provided it is pursued in a balanced and equitable fashion, taking into account the interests and problems of both parties. The state oil companies of the producing and consuming nations can play an important role in implementing such a policy, and ENI is certainly open to work along these lines. I also want to stress that a fundamental disequilibrium, as Mr Beteta has said there is in the oil market today, can be avoided only by increasing development and economic growth: otherwise the risk is that we may find very transitional equilibria in the short term at lower and lower equilibrium points.

Mr Jack Crutchfield

I should like to take this opportunity to point out the substantial amount of common ground in the views that have been expressed already. In fact, I would even suggest that the long-range view expressed at the outset by Sheikh Yamani is not necessarily inconsistent with that that Mr Johnsen is suggesting. Those two possibilities, it seems to me, can in fact exist at the same time in the future, if you accept that the real meaning of stability, which is a much used word here, is not stagnation when we are talking about the oil industry. Let me, if I may, take just a few minutes, in spite of an earlier warning to stay away from this aspect of the subject, to suggest that our understanding of what is going on now and what is likely to happen in the future will benefit from our not losing sight of the economic market factors that are in play. At least perhaps I can get up with dignity if I pursue that course. I propose, if I may, and admittedly in a drastically over-simplified way, four points for consideration.

First of all, in spite of the fact that governments, for a long time, in all parts of the world, have very successfully controlled our industry within their national boundaries, I would suggest that the international aspect of our business always has been and remains today basically a free market, subject to the fairly simple and classic laws of supply and demand – and I say that with all due respect to some of my fellow panellists who have participated importantly and vitally in the management of the reactions to those forces and the moderation of those forces from time to time.

Secondly, our industry is characterized importantly by a very high investment intensity, very large economies of scale and very substantial risks. Now then, the natural results of those economic characteristics in this industry are always very high fixed costs, very low variable costs and a very slow ability to react to the market signals, even when those signals are correctly perceived.

My third point is really simply that if you wrote a solution to the equations that you can write from points one and two, the natural result of those first two points is an expectation that an industry with those characteristics will operate in a very cyclical manner and with very long-term cycles, and that it will constantly move between an excess of producing capacity and a shortage of producing capacity. And as it makes those moves – and this is key to the point I am developing – the forces at work continually push it in the opposite direction: when you're at the top of the cycle they are pulling you down and when you're at the bottom of the cycle they're ready to pull you up. I think in the long term some of the points that Mr Johnsen suggested are the kind of things that are a natural reaction to the perception of an onset of shortage. And they try to correct it.

My fourth point is a more near-term one and I think it has important consequences for what we are saying today, and that is the very substantial separation during the 1970s of the economic interests in the upstream and the downstream portions of our business. This did not change the fundamental economics of either part of the business, but it seems to me it does give rise to the possibility of independent cycles occurring in the two different parts of our businesss. It is entirely possible that we could have too much oilfield producing capacity and too little capacity to transport, manufacture or market those barrels or vice versa. Now where does all this lead me in terms of viewing today's situation? I think what we are experiencing today is the natural back side of a mountain, if you will: we are on the downward slope of a long-term cycle in our industry. It is probably an unusually sharp cycle because of the coincidence of a downturn or surplus of capacity in the upstream part of the business, at the same time a surplus of capacity in the downstream part of our business, and, at least at the outset, a downturn in the demand for our products. That cycle comes from outside our industry: there is no reason why it should not, from time to time, compound our problems, just as from time to time it might mitigate them and make them more simple. I think one very revealing aspect of this part of the cycle that we are in right now is suggested by the behaviour of markets for crude oil. I see today's situation very much as a transitional one. We have moved almost completely from the period in the 1970s when I think it was fairly easy to characterize the market as a sellers' market, that is a market in which security of supply commanded a premium. That resulted in very long-term contracts at prices set by the seller, and the buyer's interest was very much in access and in security of supply. And undoubtedly the cycle is now taking us to a market of the opposite sort, in which there is a premium available in the market for security of output and as we approach that period I think the instruments – the contracts if you will – to provide that are in the process of being invented right now. Now, in between, we are probably moving very unsatisfactorily to a very heavy dependence on the spot market, which I would suggest is not in the interest of either the buyers or the sellers because we are in an industry that has to rely on the longer term. Predictability and the ability to construct reliable forecasts are in the interest of all of the parties. Now all of this really leads me to a fairly optimistic view of the future, because, if you will accept even part of what I have suggested, the surest thing about going down the slope of the back end of a cycle is that there is a bottom and that the part of the curve that we are on now is going to be followed, surely as can be, by an upturn in which we will all be celebrating our health. Whether that will be in six years or some longer period of time, in my personal view, does not count. I think these economic factors are indeed very important and that is not to suggest a lack of appreciation for or understanding of the political element. I should not use the word understanding – I don't understand the economics or the politics – but the political part is very critical to what is going on – I'm not trying to minimize that – but I hope at the same time we won't lose sight of some of the fundamental economics that are really just about what we have been saying here.

Dr Ali Attiga

Today I feel at a bit of a disadvantage because, although I am among old friends, I am the only one of those present on the panel who has no experience of either selling or buying oil. But because I am among friends, I think I will offer or advance perhaps some questions, and also some observations about what I have heard.

Working as I do in an intergovernmental agency where we try to look at the common denominator if there is one, I find it difficult to get excited about one scenario as against the other, because I tend to see more than two sides to a coin. My first question perhaps is about the first scenario offered by His Excellency Sheikh Yamani, whom I very much thank on behalf of the Management Committee for honouring us in this Seminar for the third time. He has been a great supporter of this Seminar on our Council of Ministers: in fact, he was the man who carried the day when this decision came on committing OAPEC to the Seminar and also to the Institute. I also want to thank him for being so clear and so explicit, even though we may think his view is a bit pessimistic about the possible scenarios – the first scenario that is, namely that which he said may be more imminent – that everybody would go for his own and sell at whatever price he could get. My question is that if there is that much more production coming in order to keep the revenue the same, if that is possible, what guarantee would there be that the market would take that much more production – at any price?

My second one is that even if the market would take it so that we had a sudden increase in demand in response to a decrease of prices, what guarantee would there be that that increase in demand would ultimately firm up the prices? We could have a case where demand increased by 2 per cent but where, because of the excess capacity and because of the anxiety to get more revenue, production increased by a greater percentage, and we would have a situation close to that of the 1960s when the demand for OPEC oil was increasing at the rate of 10 per cent but prices were deteriorating. And indeed, if producers go as far as becoming disorganized and not able to talk to each other on their common interest, they may not be able to get back together again when they want to, when demand starts firming up. So there is a risk that if each producer sells at any price he can get for whatever volume he wants to produce, he may not find the buyers for that greater volume, and prices may deteriorate even if demand increases; and that will simply give the oil importers the chance to impose a tax on oil and take a greater share of the price of a barrel of oil as they did in the 1960s. That is a fear that I see associated with the scenario that one would produce a higher quantity even at a lower price in order to balance the revenue, and I very much fear that if that happens the producers' loss may be so great that it would take them a long time to recover.

My second observation concerns Vicomte Davignon's plea for stability – and we have all been pleading that course ever since I started participating in such discussions. But as always the question is: who will contribute to that stability or who is contributing to the instability? In the 1970s, and the early 1980s, it was a common thing to accuse OPEC of being responsible for the instability, even though everybody would say in the same discussion that OPEC was the residual producer and therefore it was simply responding to changes in the quantity needed to balance the market. Except for the short period of the war in 1973 and the political decisions with regard to the embargo, which was very mild and very temporary, OPEC has always been prepared to supply whatever has been demanded. The instability has been on the demand side. The demand side has been erratic: you may say it's market forces, but I want to make the point that it is *managed* market forces. Today we see a market for OPEC oil that is being deliberately managed by the state in each of the consuming countries. We see decisions to limit the imports from OPEC by a certain quantity irrespective of price, and to divert resources to look for oil in more expensive places, to invest resources in substitutes which, as we now see, are no more economical than finding more oil and producing the present oil. So the source of instability in my view is really the demand from the industrial countries. It has been determined that OPEC oil should be pushed out, and that is where the confrontational aspect comes. I think Mr Arve Johnsen said he favours the combination of co-operation and confrontation. I want to say that I think that has been the rule, but the co-operation has been on one side from the OPEC producers and the confrontation has been emanating more from the industrial countries. OPEC producers have co-operated with the consumers on a bilateral basis and that is unfortunate. If they had been able to co-operate on a more collective basis, I think we would have seen better results. But the consuming countries outlined their confrontational approach from 1974 on, namely to reduce their dependence, not just on oil, but more particularly than that, to reduce their dependence on OPEC oil and especially on oil from our area in the Arab countries. So I would say when we plead for stability we really ought to examine what the industrial countries are doing to contribute to the instability, not only on the oil demand side, but also on financial matters – on the rates of exchange, on monetary policies. The inflation which followed the increase in the price of oil in the 1970s was really a deliberate inflationary policy. Money supply was increased in the United States and in other industrial countries to demonetize the oil price. It is those who have the power over the world economy who can contribute to stability or instability, and oil producers have very limited power, and diminishing power, over the production of only one commodity in the world economy, which at its best today amounts to no more than 18–20 per cent of total world trade. Sources of economic instability are many, and more of them are in the hands of the industrial countries.

Another point I want to comment on – and I was very pleased to hear Professor Reviglio commenting on it so explicitly – is the scenario for development. I think the potential for increased demand for oil should come and can come from the developing countries, from the Third World, whose oil consumption is very low and in many sectors has not even started. But to develop that potential we need a greater rate of economic development in these countries and here is where the industrial countries together with the oil-exporting countries can engage in a great deal of co-operation.

The resources that have been saved since 1974, through conservation of oil, through more efficient use of energy, through substitution and hence through a reduction of the oil bill that is paid by industrial countries, together add up to an enormous amount. If some of those resources, with some co-operation from the oil producers, are diverted towards accelerating development in the less developed countries, then we will see a greater demand for goods and services all over. I think that that scenario has not received enough attention, and I think it really is the hope for the future. We tend to forget that two-thirds of the world's population is still very energy hungry – and indeed hungry for everything – and that we must take them into account, and here again I think that more of the burden should fall on the shoulders of those who possess about 90 per cent of the world's trade and who possess the key to the basic economic policies in the international field.

My second observation concerns oil and the need to look at oil as a bridge to the future. It is a bridge for our generation in oil-producing countries to reach a state of sustainable economic growth without oil – that has to come. It is a bridge for the industrial countries to enable them to get their substitution in order in time before oil resources are ultimately exhausted; and therefore our look at the use of oil resources should be a long-term outlook and here I completely agree with His Excellency Sheikh Yamani's warning about the shortage in the long run. I also agree with Mr Johnsen in saying that we should try to manage and pre-plan so that we don't get these abrupt changes due to shortages, but nor should we have these abrupt changes due to surplus. And here, when we met six years ago in 1979, the consumers were pleading with the producers for two things: security of supply and stability of price. I think now producers, especially OPEC producers, ought to ask their oil consumers for security of demand and stability of price. And that ought to be a contribution from the industrial countries which would do a great deal to enhance stability and to allow for long-term planning which would avoid serious shortages in the long run.

Finally, I would like to say that we need more co-operation among oil producers, both within OPEC and between OPEC and non-OPEC countries, but especially within OPEC. Unless we get more co-operation among oil producers, it will be very difficult to attain meaningful co-operation between them and oil consumers, and here I think oil producers would have an opportunity to enhance their co-operation if they put more reliance on their intergovernmental institutions, in the same way that oil consumers use their intergovernmental institutions to chart a common policy, to make common declaration, and to provide for a common position. That would be helpful whether in dialogue, whether in scenarios of co-operation with consumers, or in confrontational scenarios.

So far I am afraid intergovernmental institutions in the oil-exporting countries have not been given a sufficient role and bilateral relations and bilateral policies have been the rule. I know that any sovereign state would never give up that privilege: all I say is that even if implementation is bilateral, common ground can still be explored on a common basis, and that is what is happening in the consuming countries. Developing countries in general – not only oil producers, but developing countries in general – despite the number of intergovernmental institutions they have formed, have generally left them aside and tried to conduct their business with the industrial countries on a direct bilateral basis, and that I think has been one of the major causes for the lack of co-operation among developing countries, whether oil producers or non-oil producers. So, as a servant of an intergovernmental institution, I would say in this forum that we need to put greater emphasis on what can be done through such institutions *vis-à-vis* the co-operation that we can have both with the industrial consuming countries and also with the developing countries, and I will conclude by saying that we should never forget that the potential for energy consumption in the next twenty or fifty years lies in the economies of the developing countries.

Dr Fadhil Al Chalabi

I believe that in analysing the likely situation in the short term His Excellency the Minister showed a very clear vision of what may happen given the present situation in the market and the pressures to which OPEC countries have been subjected for the last few years.

As the world demand for oil has fallen, OPEC as a group has been playing the downward swing producer and Saudi Arabia has also been playing this role within OPEC. Clearly enough, when the swing was in its downturn, this role was possible for a while and OPEC found itself in a comfortable situation defending the price by holding back its production until it reached a certain limit, beyond which the downward swing of production could not go any further. OPEC had to reduce its production ceiling from 17.5 mb/d to 16.0 mb/d and its production to less than 16.0 mb/d and Saudi Arabia reached to lowest production level since the 1960s.

This is a limit to the extent of the possible swing, beyond which it is very likely that a situation of chaos would prevail. The world energy situation today depends on one price set by one group, which is the price set by OPEC. This price has become so fragile and so difficult to defend that the whole energy situation in the world might be disrupted. Non-OPEC producers have been systematically undercutting the OPEC price to maximize their sales and to reach their maximum capacity. They benefit from the OPEC price in investments that would not otherwise be feasible. But they always undercut the OPEC price by a sufficient margin to allow them to move as much oil as possible. If we put Mexico apart, since it has been co-operating with OPEC for the last few years, we see that all other producers have been systematically expanding their production capacity at the expense of OPEC, taking for granted that the OPEC price will continue to be the cushion for their own investments and taking for granted that OPEC would go on defending the price, which they undercut in order to capture a higher share in a shrinking market.

It is in fact not only the non-OPEC oil producers who depend on this fragile price equilibrium: it is also the producers of other sources of energy. Without the OPEC price, coal would not have gained as much as it has during the last few years, and investments in nuclear energy wouldn't have been pushed as far as they have. But we are now facing a situation which could be considered a turning-point in the history of the world energy order. I cannot see how this imbalance can be sustained. I cannot see that OPEC will continue to be the only price defender by systematically holding back its production and undermining its development programmes and the financial and political equilibria inside its member countries. I cannot imagine that within OPEC one country could act as the downward swing producer accepting the whole reduction of output. This is a situation by nature precarious and unstable, that would engender or generate a downward spiral in the price that would hurt everybody. It would hurt OPEC countries for sure because even in the present situation OPEC countries would be better off maintaining the price than facing a downward spiral. Non-OPEC countries might continue to produce but any price collapse would definitely undermine their investment and future capacity. Non-oil energy producers would be affected by the collapse of the price, either because they would have to defend their energy production by protectionist means or because oil would again displace coal as was the pattern historically.

The other point that is related to the possibility of a price collapse is the impact this eventual development of the energy situation would have on the consuming countries and the extent to which the consumers could play a role to prevent chaos. I believe that in adopting a systematic policy during the last ten years of reducing their dependence on OPEC oil, and especially on Arab oil, the consuming countries have been resorting to means of increasing pressure on OPEC, not necessarily through the market but rather through protectionist measures and deliberate policy actions.

They have also been playing a role in increasing the pressure on OPEC through the management of stocks, and stocks have been fluctuating in such a manner as to affect the short-term market equilibrium. I believe that consumers would not benefit from any price collapse in the long run because, apart from the short-term destructive effects on the financial system, the banking system and possibly trade as described by His Excellency the Minister, a collapse of the price would affect their future energy and economic equilibria, because, unless they resorted to very heavy protectionist measures, a collapse in the price would create the conditions for greater dependence on imported oil in the future than has been the case up to now.

To conclude, Mr Chairman, I believe that, unless there are some trilateral co-ordination policies between the OPEC and non-OPEC producers and the consumers, the oil situation and the world energy situation in general will become so precarious that we will be threatened with imminent chaos.

I cannot see from what has happened in the past how this trilateral co-ordination could take place. Everybody talks about stability but their actions have quite the reverse effect. Non-OPEC countries always talk about co-operation with OPEC, but when it comes to actual policy initiatives they do the opposite. They continue to increase their production at the expense of OPEC, thus cornering OPEC more. Mr Beteta has just said that non-OPEC countries have a very grave responsibility in striving for stability and that this can only be done by means of some restraints on their production, but this is not taking place. We see that the producers from the North Sea and sellers from the Soviet Union and other producing countries are playing a very destructive and negative role in destabilizing the market and weakening the price structure. Representatives of the consuming countries also talk about stability – and they need it – but stability for them would entail that OPEC should continue to carry alone the burden of a pricing structure from which they benefit.

Mr Chairman, I believe there is some structural rigidity and some political short-sightedness in the non-OPEC producing countries as well as in the consuming countries in preventing rather than creating the conditions for dialogue and co-operation. Recently in the IEA, Austria, Sweden and a few consuming countries have been tabling a proposal to open a dialogue with OPEC, and this proposal has been turned down very strongly by the major industrialized countries – mainly the USA, the UK, even a country like Japan which depends so heavily on imported oil. Unless something is done, I believe that what has been predicted by His Excellency the Minister will happen and that everybody will suffer from it.

Mr Robert Mabro

Well, I think we have had a very excellent definition of the problems that are facing the world at large and, as many of the speakers have emphasized, there is a very strong interrelationship between what happens to oil, what happens to energy, what happens to development, what happens to the financial sector and even what happens to political stability in certain regions of the world.

I think the panel has expressed very well what we have been feeling and perceiving throughout the Seminar. We have perceived that there is a serious problem, and I would divide the Seminar into two groups: a larger group, where the problem is perceived, and a group that is trying to deny its existence by maintaining that the market, left to its own devices, and market forces will solve everything by themselves.

I am taking a position for the first time. I am saying it is a dangerous delusion that markets left to operate on their own are going to bring us stability, growth and correct allocation of resources. You should know as oilmen that all the oil markets operating in the world today are fiscal creations. The North Sea market is a fiscal creation. Most of the US market is a fiscal creation. People buy and sell oil not in order to get the best oil they need for the refineries or to get the best commercial deal: they buy and sell oil to minimize their tax bills – and so they should if the tax law allows that. So they should: they are private companies, wanting to make profits.

When markets are the result of distortions, they cannot be called upon to bring about an undistorted equilibrium. So we have perceived the problem. There is no point throwing smoke-screens. There is no point saying if you are a non-OPEC country that there is nothing you can do, because the non-OPEC countries will be hurt as much as the OPEC countries.

There is no point hiding behind facile excuses. I think we have reached the point where the problem has been posed and we could spend some time trying to raise questions about what can be done, however modestly, to face the situation and to improve its outcome.

PART IV

STABILIZATION AND LONG-TERM STRATEGIES

15 THE ECONOMIC DEVELOPMENT OF THE OIL-EXPORTING COUNTRIES (1981)*

Ali Attiga

Perhaps much too much has been said and written about the economic misfortune of the oil-importing countries on the one hand and the assumed socio-economic bonanza of the oil-exporting countries on the other hand. Whenever the causes of economic recession, inflation, unemployment, trade deficits or exchange rate fluctuations are discussed, whether in the news media or in the professional literature, the cost of imported oil is usually identified as the major single cause behind these well-known and time-honoured economic problems. At the same time, the oil-exporting countries are usually shown as the recipients of great transfers of wealth from abroad. If any of the advanced oil-importing countries experiences a balance-of-payments surplus, it is usually welcomed as a sign of good economic performance and a normal trade advantage. Even after the major increase in the price of oil, some of these countries occasionally showed substantial trade surpluses, but it was often argued that such surpluses were the result of economic recession and could not be regarded as real wealth.

The 'Strange Cake'

On the other hand, whenever the oil-exporting countries show any trade or balance-of-payments surpluses, it is generally argued that such surpluses represent great wealth and a heavy burden on the international monetary system. Such surpluses are often seen as a strange sign of changing economic fortune and should therefore be quickly reduced or eliminated and turned into deficits whenever and wherever possible. Perhaps

* Lecture delivered at the Third Oxford Energy Seminar, September 1981, and published as a Special Supplement to *Petroleum Intelligence Weekly,* October 19, 1981.

this attitude illustrates an Arab proverb which says that 'a cake in the hand of an orphan is a strange thing.' In order to do away with this 'strange cake', economists, bankers and, of course, politicians quickly identified recycling of so-called oil surplus funds as the major challenge facing the money and capital markets of the advanced oil-importing counties.

The fact that these countries as a group receive the oil they purchase and generally keep the payments they make for the oil, either in the form of receipts for goods and services or as deposits in rapidly depreciating assets, is often overlooked in the discussion of the so-called recycling problem.

The Exporters' Problems

In discussing some aspects of the problems of economic development of the oil-exporting countries, I wish to reverse the equation by arguing that the very difficult socio-economic problems of these countries and the high security and political risks which are facing them are often conveniently ignored or greatly minimized. Yet I am afraid that when the history of the oil era is finally written, it may not be an exaggeration to expect that the oil-exporting countries may be shown to have gained the least or lost the most from the discovery and development of their oil resources. Let me briefly explain what I mean.

Prior to the major oil price increase in 1973–4, the oil-exporting countries lost the most in terms of their finite natural resource endowment. At the same time, the oil-importing advanced countries gained the most from their imports of cheap oil and the preservation of their coal resources, which they are now finding of great strategic importance and high economic value. Undoubtedly, that period greatly contributed to the present maldistribution of conventional energy resources between the advanced countries and the OPEC member states.

Thus it may not be widely known that in terms of total conventional energy resources, the OPEC countries have only about 11 or 12 per cent while their contribution to total commercial energy consumption is about 25 per cent. For the OAPEC area the figures are 8 and 16 per cent respectively. In terms of financial returns for the export of oil during the 1950s and 1960s, the producing countries were often not able to collect the necessary funds for the normal requirements of their public expenditure and private consumption. Great development opportunities were generally lost and many necessary investments delayed for lack of sufficient funds. In fact, many oil-exporting countries had to resort to foreign borrowing and to deficit financing in order to cope with the heavy burden of imported and domestic inflation, as well as with the rising cost of development. During that period, all of the oil-exporting countries generally tried to increase their oil production as the only means to raise their export revenues.

The Internal Impact

If the external factors affecting the oil exporters prior to 1974 were highly unfavourable to their economic development, the internal impact of oil on their socio-economic development was even more difficult to understand or cope with.

It is not an exaggeration to say that the initial impact of oil exploration and discovery on underdeveloped, subsistence economies tends to act like an aggressive, beautiful and wealthy lady. In the same way that the sudden presence of such a lady in any gathering of lonely men would result in immediate and exaggerated expectations, the news of oil exploration and discovery in a poor underdeveloped economy would bring about a sudden rise in expectations and a rapid rush of people from the interior to the urban centres. This is usually the beginning of the adverse impact of oil on economic development.

The second and almost simultaneous phase of adverse developments associated with the early stages of oil discovery is rapid inflation and monetary expansion in the few urban centres, where the oil companies with their highly paid personnel and service agencies are usually concentrated. The oil-induced domestic inflaiton, combined with the increasing migration of people from rural and traditional sectors of economic activities, greatly increases the demand for consumer goods and services which, in turn, aggravates the inflation and migration problems.

Rural–Urban Migration

In order to cope with this difficult and politically disturbing situation, governments of oil-exporting countries generally try to rely on imports, using the foreign exchange gained from the domestic expenditure of the foreign oil companies and whatever revenues they have received from the oil sector. Usually this trend accelerates with the increase in foreign exchange revenues in response to increasing demand for greater quantities and more varieties of goods and services. In such a situation the effect plays its full role. The ultimate result is usually empty countryside and crowded cities. Since at this stage of the impact of oil on economic development governments do not receive sufficient revenues from the export of their finite oil resources, they generally lack the means with which to finance large rural development projects needed for stopping or reversing the rural–urban migration.

Illusion of Real Growth

At this stage of our story, the impact of oil on economic development in the exporting countries no longer resembles the beautiful lady described above. Rather, it becomes more like a wild horse running in all directions and breaking all the farm fences which were constructed for normal domesticated animals. In this sense a rapid increase in oil income tends to accelerate internal socio-economic conflicts in all directions. It also gives rise to rapid economic growth which is easily mistaken for real economic development. Perhaps this illusion is the most serious obstacle facing economic planners in the oil-exporting countries.

Since the substantial increase in the financial liquidity of the oil-exporting countries following the oil price adjustments, the impact of oil became more like a wild horse than was the case in the past. This is because the oil economies were already conditioned to living on their capital assets. They have accommodated their habits and institutions to modern standards of consumption and have become used to looking at their oil revenues as real income, which is far from the truth.

Exporters become Consumers

Politically they have already been fragmented into relatively small entities with little or no scope for economic integration. Indeed, the impact of oil has tended to destroy the traditional economic integration of their production with consumption, both individually and between them and their neighbours. With oil revenues paying the bill, the wild horse quickly moved them to new economic territories, where their main function became consumers of the latest and the most expensive products of the advanced oil-importing countries. Their consumer and service sectors, which gained the most from the oil revenues, became almost fully integrated with the productive sectors of their import markets. Regrettably, this is the situation in which the oil-exporting countries find themselves today.

Revenues mask Realities

Saying this does not mean that these countries have not experienced rapid economic growth and, in certain cases, even socio-economic development under the impact of oil. On the contrary, many of them show several manifestations of economic development. All of them invested substantial sums of capital in building and expanding their physical infrastructure. Their educational and health services are expanded and improved beyond recognition when compared with the recent past. For a significant portion of their population the standard of living has risen to a very high level, and nearly all groups of people have gained something from the oil wealth. All this is undeniable.

But what is more difficult to understand is that these positive gains of oil-induced growth tend to increase rather than decrease the dependence of their economic and political activities on the quantity and price of crude oil exports. They tend to give the illusion of finding a short cut to the long and difficult process of economic development. By providing the needed foreign exchange, the export of crude oil makes it easy for governments and individuals to avoid facing the political and economic realities of their regions and the possibilities they offer for economic co-operation and ultimate integration. The availability of oil revenues makes it easy to buy ready-made products and services from wherever they like, at whatever price they are able and willing to pay.

Economic Choices are Few

This may give the impression that the oil-exporting countries have a wide range of economic choices at their disposal. Unfortunately, the opposite is the case. As exporters of one commodity and importers of thousands of consumer and capital goods and services, they have only a few options. Their export and import markets are under the control of a few industrial advanced countries. Their domestic currencies and foreign assets are, in fact, dependent on the monetary and fiscal policies of even fewer countries. Their access to modern technology and know-how is highly restricted by a combination of their own internal limitations and the terms and conditions usually imposed by the technology-exporting institutions and governments. Their strong feelings for internal security and external defence needs, whether real or exaggerated, readily induce them to spend an increasing portion of their oil revenues on the purchase of suitable and unsuitable modern arms and other military hardware. Because these countries can pay for their civil and military imports in cash, they provide attractive markets for the exporting countries. All these features of the oil-exporting economies reinforce their dependence on foreign markets and tend to diminish their indigenous drive for self-reliance and regional co-operation.

Productivity Destroyed

Let us return to the impact of oil on internal economic development. Perhaps the most serious adverse impact of oil-induced inflation and excessive rural or nomadic–urban migration is the destruction of the traditional productive activities of the people, without replacing them with new forms of productive employment. On the contrary, what usually happens is that people who were partly productive in their subsistence economies join the unemployed or, more correctly, disguisedly unemployed personnel of the public and semi-public sectors.

Those who join the private sector, where such opportunities exist, generally become either traders, speculators, small shopkeepers or just common labourers in the construction sector. In any case, the whole population becomes more one of urban consumers than of producers or entrepreneurs. For all of them, oil money provides the easiest and most attractive source from which to increase their income. Of course, those with economic muscle and political power manage to get much more of it than others. But in all cases, a sharp dichotomy develops between real productive efforts and monetary rewards.

Oil Exports gain Control

At this stage the whole economy, public and private, becomes almost wholly dependent on the export of oil. Governments, in addition to their normal functions, become central economic powers around which all public and private activities concentrate. There are only a few oil-exporting countries with very large rural areas, such as Indonesia and Nigeria, where this situation may not fully apply, but it is only a matter of degree. In essence even these two countries are heavily dependent on oil. As the demands of the public and private sectors for more consumption and higher levels of expenditure increase the pressure on the governments, their natural response is to try to raise more revenues from oil exports, either through increases in price or quantity or both if market conditions permit.

However, when governments follow such a simple and free-spending policy, they will quickly find themselves tied to a very high plateau of public expenditure and commitments which can be supported only by a high level of oil production even in the face of market gluts. At this stage, oil exporters will be faced with a pure buyers' market. When oil gets control of the economies and governments of the oil-exporting countries in the manner described above, it again becomes like dealing with a wild horse: you can ride such a horse only to the extent you can tame it and control its speed and direction.

Untaxed Profits Assumed

In several of the OAPEC member states there are active and affluent private sectors. They are usually active in trade, services and real estate speculation. Their notions of reasonable profits are far too high for any sustainable economic activities. They do not accept the concept of modern taxation and cannot see the need of applying it to their business profits or personal incomes. Their notion of the government's role in the private sector is that of spending oil revenues through large purchases of goods and services, financing the business needs of the economy, and subsidizing all sorts of economic activities, including consumption. All of this, of course, reinforces the heavy dependence of the economy on the export of oil. But the central question is whether the continuation of such dependence can ever lead to sound economic development. Can it lead to alternative sources of income and employment, when oil resources are exhausted through exports and domestic consumption? If the answer is negative, then what can the oil-exporting countries do to reduce their high dependence on the export of crude oil?

The Devastating Dilemma

There is no single answer to the needs of all oil-exporting countries regardless of their non-oil resource endowment, state of socio-economic development and type of political institutions. But in my opinion all the major oil-exporting countries are faced with a common dilemma. If they choose to accelerate the spreading of oil revenues to all segments of their population, they will face the devastating danger of destroying the individual and social incentives for productive activities and may eliminate the need for gainful employment. All citizens can easily become recipients of guaranteed government pay, the duration and size of which will depend on the fortunes of the oil export markets. This course of action will, of course, also guarantee the rapid depletion of oil resources long before the attainment of sound economic development.

    If, on the other hand, the government of an oil-exporting country decides to channel the oil revenues into the economic life of the people gradually and only in return for productive economic performance, it will face the risk of a frustrated population whose needs are many and whose wants are insatiable, but whose skills and economic performance are widely varied and in most cases need to be discovered and professionally developed. The real problem in following this kind of policy is that it takes a long time and requires sound development policy, skilful economic management and, above all, flexible and stable political institutions. Unfortunately, all these requirements are difficult to attain, especially in developing countries, and certainly they cannot be purchased from abroad. They can only be developed internally through hard work by a dedicated and able leadership willing to learn from the lessons of trial and error. All this takes a long time and lots of luck.

Another common difficulty facing many oil-exporting countries is the maldistribution of income between different groups of people and within specific groups. If there are no adequate fiscal measures to cope with this problem through taxation and other means, it will inevitably work against political stability, social justice and national unity. Such a trend may lead the individual and different groups in society to look in different directions outside their countries for coping with their sense of insecurity, frustrations and ambitions.

How to Mitigate Adverse Effects

If these are some of the major problems and risks facing many if not all the major oil-exporting countries, then what can be suggested to mitigate the adverse effects of oil on sound economic development? I can suggest three broad lines of policy action.

(a) In order to lessen the adverse impact of crude oil exports on the economy, it would seem sensible for many countries to produce less of it and encourage the export of oil products and other manufactured goods and services whenever possible. Encouraging trade among developing countries may be more helpful in the long run than continuing heavy dependence on the markets of the advanced countries. This approach would prolong the life of oil resources and make their digestion in the usual development process more feasible. It will also save more oil for the needs of the non-oil developing countries who must depend on oil for a very long time.

(b) All available means, including cheap energy, should be used to encourage domestic production of goods and services in order to reduce the excessive dependence on imports. This line of action will also require the adoption of adequate fiscal policy designed to promote economic development, diminish excessive luxury consumption and real estate speculation, and improve the distribution of income in accordance with real economic contribution to the productive process.

(c) Regional co-operation and economic integration should be promoted through joint projects and common institutions. Perhaps this line of policy is essential for lasting success in the implementation of the first two suggestions.

This is the area where regional organizations such as OAPEC have a vital role to play. For the last eight years OAPEC has been doing all it can to play its role to the extent that political realities and available resources and information have allowed.

16 THE NEED FOR AN OPEC CENTRAL TRADING AGENCY (1983)*

Robert Mabro

OPEC has recently been giving much attention to the discussion of long-term strategies. The work already done on this subject is certainly valuable, and the debate between those who prefer to increase OPEC's 'market share' and those who emphasize 'maximization of revenues' could be fruitful, if it revealed the relative merits and weaknesses of the respective positions.

But this concern with long-term strategy, however important, may be distracting OPEC from more immediate and urgent tasks. The situation facing OPEC today can be described in stark and simple terms:

— The world petroleum market continues to be slack. Of course a supply accident caused by warlike acts in the Gulf region can always occur. Such an accident would most probably provoke a price explosion, but is unlikely to remove the underlying weakness of a market that has already been badly battered by the two price explosions of the 1970s.

— Non-OPEC exporters, except Mexico, are not really co-operating with OPEC in its attempt to stabilize world oil prices. Though most of them are perfectly aware of the significant losses that producers would suffer if OPEC failed, they are happy to delegate the difficult task of price administration to OPEC. They seem to believe that OPEC is both willing and able to perform indefinitely this task irrespective of costs and sacrifices. Taking advantage of OPEC's protection, the UK and Norway are able to enjoy the fruits of higher production (some 20 per cent increase in

* Paper published in *Petroleum Intelligence Weekly*, December 5, 1983.

UK output in the past year), and the Soviet Union can play with impunity competitive price games which have a significant impact on the market given the large volume (1.0–1.5 mb/d) of Soviet exports.

— OPEC continues to play the role of a residual supplier to the world. Such a role is fairly easy to perform when volumes of production are comfortable, but becomes costly and troublesome when OPEC's output falls below 19 or 20 mb/d. The output swings have tended to be absorbed to a very large extent by two or three countries – notably Saudi Arabia and Nigeria. It has always been recognized that Nigeria suffers unduly from being the Atlantic Basin 'swing supplier'. Today, even Saudi Arabia finds that fluctuation of its export volume around a low average is an unacceptable burden.

How does OPEC cope with these problems? The short-term market-stabilizing strategy agreed in London last March certainly was the best arrangement that would have been produced in the circumstances. Nobody doubts that it fulfilled for a while the objective of stabilizing prices around the $29 marker. But this does not mean that the arrangements are flawless, nor that they can be relied upon to continue performing effectively in their present form.

The London Agreement fixed the main structure of price differentials, allocated production quotas to all OPEC members, defined an overall output ceiling of 17.5 mb/d, attributed to Saudi Arabia the role of residual supplier, and lowered the marker price from $34 to $29.

It is my judgement, however, that market stabilization from April to this December was achieved through a much simpler device: the manifestation by OPEC member countries of a remarkably high degree of price discipline.

Main defects of the London system are, first, that price differentials are fixed too rigidly and without variations for too long a period. These relative prices are now out of line with market realities for the simple reason that market conditions change all the time.

Secondly, the overall output ceiling does not seem to mean very much. It is an irrelevant number which OPEC cannot reach when demand falls short of the ceiling, and which OPEC is too happy to exceed when demand is higher than 17.5 mb/d. To say that the ceiling is not operative is to cast doubt on the ultimate significance of quotas, although their merit as guidelines for agreed market shares by OPEC members is not in doubt.

Thirdly, the swing supplier role of Saudi Arabia is not clearly defined. Nobody seems to know exactly whether Saudi Arabia is supposed to vary its output only within the 17.5 mb/d ceiling or whether it can go beyond this overall limit, at least temporarily, to meet an upsurge in demand.

Besides these technical difficulties, there are more significant defects of the London Agreement and of the post-London developments. These are: (a) the lack of a credible and effective OPEC strategy *vis-à-vis* non-OPEC exporters, and (b) the failure of current policies to relieve OPEC from its burdensome role of residual oil supplier to the world.

It would seem therefore that the priority task for OPEC is to concentrate on current problems. Our proposed strategy outline would involve:

— A clear perception of OPEC's perennial objectives.
— Policies aimed at stabilizing the market through a new approach to trading and marketing.
— Use of these same policy instruments to induce co-operation of non-OPEC exporters.

Whether labelled long or short term, the substantive point is that the strategy, however defined, should attempt to solve today's problems. If successful, the strategy may have to continue to be implemented over many years because today's problem may well be the threat of a long period of market weakness and demand stagnation punctuated by unwholesome price explosions.

Let us consider the three elements of proposed strategy: price administration, a return to long-term contracts and the establishment of a central OPEC trading agency.

210   *Robert Mabro*

Price Administration

The only perennial objective that OPEC has to identify for itself is the need to retain (with or without the involvement of other oil exporters) a strong hold over the administration of oil prices. This is what OPEC has always been about since its establishment in 1960. There is no point defining long-term objectives in terms of market shares or maximum revenues because these aims are neither meaningful nor possible to achieve unless producers are able to administer prices. This is the prerequisite. To lose control is to risk the loss of a considerable part of the rental element in the current price of oil. In different market circumstances, loss of control could mean high rates of depletion and wasteful use of oil resources.

Ability to administer prices allows producers to set them at levels appropriate for a variety of objectives: protection of market shares by erecting a low barrier against substitutes when competition from non-OPEC oil or from other fuels becomes too threatening. Or it could be maximization of revenues when short-term circumstances are favourable, provided that producers remain prepared to return to a more defensive price position when the lean period succeeds the fat years.

A Return to Long-term Contracts

The second point is how to retain control over price administration when markets are slack, and when competition of non-OPEC exporters spreads to weaker or more vulnerable members of the organization. My view is that the only solution is an attempt within OPEC to reduce the impact of the export fluctuations that induce members to break the rules of price discipline.

Price discipline breaks down in ways that by now have become sadly familiar. Price discounts are given either directly or in disguised forms. Some members, imitating non-OPEC exporters, 'play the market' as best as they can for the incremental barrel to the detriment of their long-term interests.

In short, oil-exporting countries are selling too much oil through short-term contracts and spot transactions, a tendency which may lose them the grip they still have over a very slack market.

Any worthwhile strategy must reverse this tendency. OPEC starting on its own could take advantage of its position as residual supplier to force companies to return to long-term contracts, even if it has not yet secured co-operation from other exporters. This would turn weakness into potential strength. We should not forget that the residual supplier has enormous power over that final amount of oil that buyers treat as the residual. By definition, buyers have nowhere else to go for the 15–17 mb/d that non-OPEC producers working close to capacity cannot deliver.

The proposed trading agreement would set a certain volume, say 16 or 17 mb/d in today's conditions, to represent OPEC's base-load output. This would be divided up into members' quotas – similar but not necessarily identical to current ones. The base-load output should not be set so high as to be more than actual demand for OPEC oil, nor so low as to leave a large proportion of this demand outside it. The number may be revised every quarter in the light of the most recent demand forecasts.

In short, the base-load output, except for minor demand fluctuations, should represent the bulk of so-called 'OPEC residual supplies'. OPEC countries will then offer their traditional customers long-term contracts at official prices for the base-load output. Companies may be allowed a 5 per cent tolerance but no more. There would be a collective OPEC sanction on any company or buyer withdrawing from a long-term contract without assigning his commitment to another acceptable entity. The sanction could be access barred from all OPEC base-load output for three or four years.

This contract would be easily enforceable if restricted to the amount of oil that can be correctly construed as the OPEC residual supply. The temptation to extend the arrangement to a larger volume is self-defeating.

This system will reduce to some extent the variations of demand for OPEC oil, shifting some of these fluctuations to non-OPEC producers. There will still be some seasonal movements, and these should take place above the base-load level if this is set correctly. OPEC will want to meet this extra demand.

This is not an assumption but a direct reading of current behaviour which clearly shows that demand is always satisfied in aggregate even when it exceeds the 17.5 mb/d ceiling.

An OPEC Trading Agency

In order to meet incremental demand above base-load, OPEC would establish a trading agency. This agency would offer oil from all member countries in ratios that would reflect an agreement on relative quotas for incremental output. These 'incremental' ratios need not be identical to base-load quotas, but subject to negotiation.

Prices of incremental crude, except for the marker which remains the fixed reference price, would be open to monthly bids. The interaction of bids and relative availabilities under the relative quota system would determine price differentials at the margin. An automatic quarterly revision of the price structure in long-term contracts would ensue.

As there would be no set limit to incremental supplies, just a proportion of crudes from different countries, the bidding process would not lead to price explosions, but would continually adjust price differentials in relation to changing market circumstances. OPEC would remain fully sovereign in determination of the marker price, which could be revised from time to time by the governing Conference.

Creation of such a trading agreement, with peak-load long-term contracts and direct OPEC sales of incremental oil, would provide OPEC with a very powerful policy instrument *vis-à-vis* non-OPEC exporters. The first advantage of this system, already mentioned, is the reduction in output fluctuations. Non-OPEC exporters would have to absorb part of the demand fluctuations.

Another advantage is that it would provide OPEC with the means to intervene directly in the market. To control incremental supplies is to control market prices. All non-OPEC exporters are market oriented. If OPEC, God forbid, were to engage in a price war against non-OPEC producers it could lower the price on incremental supplies without having to lose a penny on base-load sales, which would continue at official prices under long-term contracts.

This is a formidable deterrent. If put in place, OPEC would be able to avoid actual price wars to induce co-operation on sensible producers' policies. The ability to control both the residual and the margin in a slack market is real market power. Few oil experts would be brave enough to challenge it.

This scheme involves two types of difficulties: practical and political. It requires a willingness by OPEC member countries to co-operate in trading. New institutional arrangements will have to be carefully and intelligently designed. Finally, discussions and a new agreement on quotas (for both base-load and incremental outputs) are needed once again. But these discussions will have to take place in any case, whether the present system continues or is replaced by a different strategy.

An open-minded assessment of the advantages and drawbacks of this scheme would reveal, I am sure, that oil-exporting countries still possess the means to administer the price of oil in an effective manner.

17 OPTIONS FOR OPEC LONG-TERM PRICING STRATEGIES (1981-5)*

Fadhil Al Chalabi

Introduction

The great structural changes in the international oil industry during the 1970s, especially as far as oil prices are concerned, are widely believed to be the result of collective actions and policies of OPEC's member countries. The latter are generally considered to be the main instrument for achieving the required changes in the world oil relationships, so that without the collective approach to recover the producers' rights of sovereignty over their national resources from the multinational oil companies, member countries, taken individually, would not have been in a position to bring to an end the era of oil companies' domination.[1]

However, there are some who believe that OPEC's major actions on prices were no more than a series of reactions to external events which took place, mainly in certain member countries, and which had the effect of reshaping the oil market before OPEC as a group could decide to undertake any real change, or to confirm the change that had taken place or, at best, to carry it further. According to this belief, OPEC's actions and policies did not reflect a strategic thinking towards setting long-term common objectives for member countries within a defined system for the process of change and to be implemented in stages.

It is true that the major turning-points in the successive stages of structural transformation in the industry throughout

---

* Originally delivered as a lecture to the Third Oxford Energy Seminar, September 1981. Revised and expanded early 1985.

[1] See the author's book *OPEC and the International Oil Industry: A Changing Structure*, Oxford University Press, 1980.

the 1970s were associated with events or developments in certain member countries which caused the creation of new market conditions that outran the then prevailing price structure. Before any collective decision was taken by OPEC, oil prices in the free market took over the OPEC official prices and warranted the correction of those latter prices in the light of new conditions.

That was, for example, the case with the first major change in the industry's structure when the Tehran Agreement with the oil companies was concluded early in 1971. When prior to it OPEC met in Caracas in December 1970 and decided to negotiate collectively with the oil companies for a new set of relationships, including the levels of prices and taxes, it did so in a market structure that was already changing, mainly because of the action taken by Libya in 1970 in cutting back its oil production in order to force a new relationship between the Government and the oil companies. The resulting shortage of 'short-haul' oil was further aggravated by a political event, namely the blow-up of the Saudi Tapline which further deprived the Mediterranean of about half a million barrels per day. Consequently, official prices of oil lagged considerably behind the market, a fact that enabled OPEC negotiators in Tehran to change the price structure and, more generally, the relationship with the oil companies. It is interesting to recall that the pattern of change, especially concerning the fiscal structure (the increase of the tax ratio from 50 to 55 per cent) was already accepted by the companies in Libya, as well as in the Gulf, well before the conclusion of the Tehran Agreement. In this respect, i.e. the fiscal relationship between the oil companies and oil-producing countries, the Tehran Agreement did nothing but to confirm and improve a new pattern in the oil industry which was already established prior to it.[2]

It should also be remembered that the price 'shock' of 1973 was partly due to the political events in the Middle East, namely the Arab–Israeli armed conflict and the oil embargo decided upon by the Arab oil-exporting countries indepen-

---

[2] It should be recalled, however, that the major change in the system of setting both the oil prices and their levels in the Tehran Agreement was solely the result of the collective negotiations between the OPEC oil-producing countries of the Gulf and the oil companies. See Al Chalabi *op. cit.*

dently of OPEC. It has to be recalled here that the Arab member countries of OPEC decided to impose the oil embargo only one day after the 1973 OPEC Conference Meeting in Kuwait which decided to take over the pricing of its oil from the multinational oil companies and to increase the price level by 70 per cent.[3] The great price flare-up which took place in the market as a result of the oil embargo was such that when OPEC met in Tehran in December 1973 to decide a further 130 per cent price increase, prices in the free market were already more than three times the OPEC official price levels decided in Kuwait only two months earlier.[4]

Similarly, the oil market developments of 1979 and 1980 constitute a typical case of OPEC price-making decisions as a reaction to market changes rather than the reflection of a strategic thinking towards achieving long-term objectives of reshaping or influencing the market itself. It was the revolution in Iran which created a temporary oil shortage that disrupted completely the market, independently of OPEC action, so that any price decision taken by OPEC was soon outpaced by the market. We merely have to recall how OPEC's decision in December 1978, in Abu Dhabi, in favour of an average price increase of only 10 per cent for the whole of 1979 was shattered only two months later under the pressure of the market. Further, all oil developments in 1979 and 1980 show that almost all OPEC's subsequent price decisions during that period were nothing more than reactions to the market which had taken over from the OPEC price setting.

The effect of the national policies was no less great, and at times crucial in reshaping the structure of the ownership and management in the OPEC area as a whole. Suffice to recall that without the nationalization of oil in Iraq in the summer of 1972, the companies would not have been in a hurry to accept the principle of equity participation by Gulf countries in the oil concessions, and later to implement it in such a manner as to lead to the total take-over of the industry by the government in agreement with the oil companies. These structural changes in relationships between governments and companies transformed the price system and the oil market structure in favour of OPEC.

[3] *Ibid.*   [4] *Ibid.*

Past Endeavours for OPEC Strategies

To attribute OPEC's actions in achieving the great structural transformation in the oil industry to exogeneous factors alone, as is sometimes argued, would amount to an over-simplification of the transformation process.

While it is true that some of those changes were triggered initially by developments inside member countries, it was, nevertheless, collective action on the part of OPEC that was instrumental in bringing them to fruition and generalizing what had started as a mere local event into a common pattern, which was to shape the whole structure of the oil industry. In many of the other cases of structural change in the 1970s, the initiative was taken by OPEC itself, and not by member countries who applied the new decisions later on. On the other hand, the examples mentioned earlier show the inherent nature of OPEC as a vehicle of change resulting from the inter-action of multiple forces. In fact, the collective action of OPEC in undertaking the change cannot be dissociated from the national policy actions taken individually by member countries, nor can the latter be looked upon in isolation from the collective action. It is the combination of the national policies with the collective policies that was responsible for reversing the status quo, and consequently OPEC should not be considered merely as a forum for collective decision-making, but rather as a process where all forces of change were interacting and complementing each other on both the national and the international levels. The structural transformations were actually the result of this interaction of inter-governmental policies, so that any successful action taken individually by a member country, could, by itself, trigger a process of change which would affect the collective decisions of OPEC in the same manner as collective decisions affected the national policies of member countries.

It is no less an over-simplification to assume that, during its lifetime, OPEC was not able to formulate any strategy for the change. Since the late 1960s, OPEC had been making endeavours to look into long-term policy objectives within a framework of 'global strategies', although those objectives changed in nature and emphasis as the structure of the international oil industry, and hence OPEC's priorities, changed. As early as 1968, OPEC issued its Declaratory Policy Statement (resolution no. 90) by which it specified certain policy objectives to be attained by member countries, at a time when OPEC's main preoccupation was to assert its members' inalienable right of sovereignty over natural resources, a right of which they had been deprived by the system of oil concessions.

Looked at in retrospect, that document was surprisingly pioneering in that it underlined those forces of change in the governments' relationship with the international oil companies that were to be reflected, some years later, in the structure of the international oil industry. The policy objectives incorporated in the Declaratory Statement heralded, in one way or another, the change in the relationship with the companies through collective action. The document stipulated, for example, that prices of oil had to be determined by the governments concerned and not by the companies; that the exploitation of national petroleum resources had to be made, as far as possible, directly by the state; that the relationship with the oil companies, including the implementation of the principle of participation (and ultimately the complete take-over) had to be continually revised in the light of the 'changing circumstances'; that the control of oil operations, including the implementation of the principle of conservation of oil reservoirs, had to be exercised by those governments, etc. Undoubtedly, such policy objectives played a tremendous role in reversing completely the governments' relationship with the companies and caused the eventual downfall of the system of oil concessions. In this sense, therefore, that document could indeed be considered a 'strategy', albeit modest, adopted and implemented by OPEC countries in a manner such as to lead to the subsequent changes in the price system and the structure of the oil industry.

However, OPEC's objectives of the late 1960s were soon surpassed by the dramatic events of the 1970s which created a new situation, warranting a new 'strategy'. Having shaken up the old system of pricing raw materials in world markets, the OPEC revolutionary experiment appeared, especially to the industrialized countries, to be a signal of change towards a new era of international economic relations in which developing countries, exporters of raw materials, could change the old economic and political status quo, especially the price-determination system of primary commodities, in their favour. For OPEC, on the other hand, this great change resulted in the organization emerging as a new force that could have a say in shaping the new international economic order. In other words, OPEC's objectives were no longer confined to the protection of its members' basic interests *vis-à-vis* the oil companies, but now embraced also endeavours to regulate the international relations in matters of energy and development.

It was in this context that the Special Session of the United Nations was held in 1974 to deal with the problems of energy and development, with a view to establishing a new and more equitable international economic order through international negotiations or 'dialogue'. It was also in this spirit that a Summit Conference of OPEC Countries was held in Algiers in the spring of 1975 in which Sovereigns and Heads of State met to adopt a 'Solemn Declaration', a collective policy instrument, which was meant to serve not only as a 'global strategy' for the North–South dialogue, but also as a guideline for long-term OPEC policies, including the future pricing of oil and the prerequisites for international development for OPEC and non-OPEC developing countries. The fiasco in which the dialogue, or the CIEC (Conference for International Economic Co-operation) as it was officially called, ended, after about two years of protracted negotiations, indicated the resistance of the developed countries to any real change in the existing economic order. In contrast to OPEC's position, they wanted to solve their energy problems without considering the global problems of raw materials and development.

Meanwhile, the concerns of the industrialized countries about the cost of oil supplies were soon outpaced by the new developments which took place in the mid-1970s, some of which had the effect of changing further the structure of the international oil industry. The OPEC policies of declining oil prices, in real terms, pursued between 1973 and 1978 helped the industrialized countries to absorb the effects of the initial shock, as the real cost incurred by them in acquiring OPEC oil was decreasing continually, especially in the non-dollar industrialized zones. At the same time, further major changes in the structure of oil supplies were increasingly felt in the world market as the dominant role of the international major oil companies in pricing and marketing oil in those markets began to wane in favour of the national oil companies which had emerged as the new power in those markets.

The developments in the management and ownership of the oil industry in OPEC member countries had created a new situation in the market, whereby the major oil companies were gradually losing access to cheaper crude oil in the major producing areas. Their dominant role as the real mediators between the oil-producing and oil-consuming countries was fading, especially in setting the supply and cost of oil entering international trade.

It was within the context of these structural changes in the international oil 'scene' that OPEC envisaged the adoption of a long-term strategy, which would enable it to formulate its position *vis-à-vis* the major issues of energy and development. The idea was first conceived at a Consultative Meeting of OPEC Ministers held in Taif, Saudi Arabia in the spring of 1978. In the summer of that year, the OPEC Ministerial Conference formally established the committee at ministerial level under the chairmanship of Sheikh Ahmed Zaki Yamani, Saudi Arabian Minister of Petroleum and Mineral Resources, composed of the five founder members of OPEC, Iran, Iraq, Kuwait, Saudi Arabia and Venezuela, with the addition of Algeria. At the same time, another committee was formed, at a technical level, under the same chairmanship. After about two years, this Expert Committee drew up a report in which it tried to reach an overall concept of long-term objectives for the protection of member countries' own interests as well as those of the world economy, both in the Third World and in the highly industrialized, developed nations. The report was discussed by the Ministerial Committee on Long-Term Strategy and finally submitted to an Extraordinary Meeting of the Conference, which was held in Taif in May 1980.

Later in September of that year, a Tri-Ministerial Conference was held in Vienna, comprising the Ministers of Foreign Affairs, Oil, and Finance of the OPEC countries to discuss the global strategy in preparation for a Summit Conference which was scheduled to be held in Baghdad in November 1981. A policy statement as well as a plan of action were expected to be endorsed at that meeting. They would have defined the major long-term policy objectives for OPEC, not only with regard to pricing, but also in relation to problems of international development and the relationship with the other developing countries, as well as the conditions for global negotiations with the industrialized countries. The Summit was, however, postponed owing to the armed conflict between two member countries, Iran and Iraq.

In the next section, we shall only be concerned with issues relating to oil prices in OPEC's long-term strategy.

A New OPEC Long-term Price Strategy: Objectives and Limitations

The objectives of any long-term global strategy for OPEC should naturally stem from the basic needs of its member countries: broadly speaking, OPEC countries are developing countries in the process of economic development and rapid social transformation. Depending almost totally on the export of one commodity, oil, those countries tend inevitably to gear all their present and future development to the value and volume of oil exports to world markets. In other words, as long as those countries are in a state of economic and social underdevelopment, and until such time as they can achieve an adequate structural diversification of their economies towards lesser dependence on oil revenues, the volume and value of their oil exports will continue to determine the level and the shape of their existence.

At the same time, being a depletable resource, oil amounts to a national capital that should be conserved as much as possible for future generations. The rates of oil depletion should, therefore, be compatible with the present and future energy and development requirements of those countries. On the other hand, serving as a 'residue' to fill the gap between the world demand for energy and the energy supplies from outside OPEC, export oil availabilities from the OPEC countries play a tremendous role in shaping the world energy outlook. A world energy balance can be achieved only when sufficient

OPEC oil is being made available in the world market to cope with world demand. Moreover, the magnitude and frequency of the changes in the cost of those oil availabilities contribute to determining the pace and health of the world economy.

A global strategy for OPEC countries should, therefore, try to strike a balance between, on the one hand, all those 'inputs' for long-term common objectives of all member countries, namely, the achievement of their present and future economic and social development within the framework of a balanced world energy outlook and, on the other, a healthy world economy whereby energy problems are dealt with globally as part of an overall context of international development which would be conceived within a negotiated pattern of a new international economic order.

However, for a heterogeneous group of countries like those of OPEC, which differ widely in their economic and social structures, and hence in their national interests and priorities, the great complexity of the issues involved in reaching a common global strategy will inevitably lead to a great diversity of technical views as well as political positions. OPEC countries differ enormously from one another in their levels of economic and social development, population, per capita income, financial requirements for development, absorptive capacity for spending on development, hydrocarbon production capacities, potential for developing those capacities in the future, political systems, etc. The so-called financially 'surplus' oil-producing countries enjoy large oil production capacities, and hence a greater share in the world total energy market, which exceeds by far their requirements for development. The financially 'deficit' countries, on the other hand, possess a much higher capacity for development and greater long-term potential for diversified economic structures, but enjoy a small share in a world energy market which is unlikely to grow in the future. Against these two categories of financially 'surplus' or 'deficit' countries, there is the third category of OPEC countries whose members have a high potential for a greater share in the world energy market as well as more diversified economic structures.

This basic structural difference among the various groups of OPEC countries may lead to different positions concerning the issue of the long-term price strategy. The very strong financial position of the 'surplus' countries may make them look, for example, not to the immediate increase in the per barrel income (higher prices in real terms) but rather to the likely impact of higher prices on determining their share in the world energy market as well as the worth and security of their financial reserves and foreign investments.[5]

The 'deficit' group, on the other hand, tend to push for as much of an immediate increase in their per barrel income as possible in order to alleviate the financial pressures of short-term economic development requirements. Because of their high absorptive capacity for development, and hence their greater potential for structural diversification of their economies in the long run, those countries look forward, in theory at least, to reducing the dependence of their future development on oil revenues. The growth prospects of the non-oil sectors of their economies are much greater than those of the 'surplus' countries, which, because of the lesser potential for economic diversification, find themselves in a state of continuing and heavy dependence on oil revenues.

With little potential for internal investments, mainly because of the lack of other natural resources such as water and land, but also owing to the scarcity of manpower, the 'surplus' countries will look to their foreign financial investments as one means of income diversification, aimed towards lesser dependence on oil revenues. This is how in a country like Kuwait, for example, the income derived from private and public foreign investments in the form of returns on capital, interests and profits, is currently accounting for more than half the country's foreign currency requirements for importation.[6] In other words, the financial surplus which results from producing oil at levels higher than development requirements could constitute, through sound foreign investments, a source of economic growth and diversified income generation. The continued flow of revenues from oil exports is therefore crucial in securing future development in such OPEC countries where the absorptive capacity for national development is structurally limited. Conversely, because of the high absorptive capacity for

---

[5] Presently, there is no surplus country within OPEC.
[6] See Central Bank of Kuwait Annual Report, 1981.

investment in the second group of OPEC countries, the national priority for expenditure is to invest as much as possible inside the countries themselves.

On the other hand, the present large production capacities of the 'surplus' countries reflect also huge oil potential that could be developed further in the future. With a rate of production of 1.5 mb/d, Kuwait's present recoverable oil reserves would be enough to sustain more than 124 years of production. That country's oil potential could be further increased through investing in exploration and enhanced recovery such amounts of capital as could be sustained by the financial 'surplus'. This situation is almost the opposite of that in a 'deficit' country, like Algeria, where a rate of production of 1 mb/d can be sustained for only twenty-two years, and where the prospects for increasing the low oil potential are limited and would, at any rate, incur high capital outlays that could not easily be met, given the financial pressures and the priorities for spending on other development programmes.[7]

Paradoxically enough, the surplus countries which because of their surplus are the least needy of any short-term expansion in their production capacities are, at the same time, better placed than others to invest in such an expansion, not only because of their greater hydrocarbon potential, but also because of their adequate financial capabilities, which allow them to embark on huge investments in exploration and enhanced recovery without jeopardizing their development plans in the other sectors of their national economies. This is why, for example, it is in the long-term interest of those countries to have a pricing policy which aims at striking a balance between maximizing their short-term income and keeping as much dynamic world demand for their oil in the future as possible.

These varied national interests among OPEC member countries would naturally be reflected in varied positions and national economic and political priorities, when the definition of objectives for long-term pricing policies is at issue and when the choice of appropriate means for attaining these objectives

---

[7] With the reduction of production of Kuwait and Algeria to 1.05 and 0.66 mb/d in 1983, the respective reserves/production ratios have increased to 175 and thirty-eight years.

and of the time span required to implement these means is
discussed.

Major Issues for an OPEC Long-term Pricing Strategy

With such diversity in the structures and national priorities of
OPEC countries, optimizing the oil price has, in the long run,
naturally to take into consideration a host of factors related to
those various interests, as well as the interests of the international community. Only through looking into the combined
national interests of the members, which constitute the
minimum common denominator for all, can a long-term price
strategy for OPEC be found and serve as a basis for their collective action. It is in this way that the community of national
interests of all member countries can be preserved.

It is, however, necessary to analyse the basic price-related
issues before any options for long-term pricing strategies can be
discussed.

(*a*) *Oil Prices and the Oil Terms of Trade*. There is no doubt that
the financial requirement for economic and social development
is the most direct factor influencing OPEC in its oil pricing
policies. This factor is important both in the long and in the
short term. To optimize the price of oil in order to ensure an
adequate revenue per barrel will continue to be one of the main
issues in the debate on the oil price strategy.

But financial requirements for development differ between
OPEC member countries: they are significantly different
between Nigeria with its 82 million inhabitants and a per
capita revenue of $500 and the UAE with 855,000 inhabitants
and a per capita income of $14,000. Financial needs differ
between countries such as Algeria, Iraq and Iran with their
considerable potential for structural diversification of their
economies and some of the Gulf countries where this potential
is much smaller. How can we reconcile divergent national
interests when long-term pricing strategy has to be defined for
the whole of OPEC in terms of development needs?

In our view a common denominator in oil pricing policies
which could reflect all the national interests of OPEC member
countries may be found in the concept of improving the oil

terms of trade, or at least, in preventing them from deteriorating, i.e. the preservation of the purchasing power of a barrel of oil by protecting the price in real terms from any erosion due to inflation or currency fluctuations.

This principle has always been favoured by OPEC and was incorporated in several resolutions passed in the 1960s well before the 'oil revolution' of 1973. This principle was accepted by the oil companies and is embodied in the Tehran Agreement of 1971 and the agreements known as Geneva I and Geneva II. Further, the Solemn Declaration of the Algiers Summit emphasized, with considerable stress, the need to protect the purchasing power of the OPEC barrel against inflation and currency fluctuation.

Certain conceptual and technical problems may, however, arise from the application of this concept and lead to some differences in views and positions. Among those problems is the measurement of world inflation in order to assess the movement of oil prices in real terms. The price movement of the industrialized countries is generally taken as a measure of world inflation. This can be either the OECD export price index or the internal GNP price deflator, or both with certain weights. Certain OPEC countries argue, however, that using those indices does not reflect in reality the degree of the erosion of the purchasing power of the oil. According to them, it is only the landed cost into the OPEC countries of the goods and services imported from the industrialized countries. The movement of this latter cost indicates a much higher rate of world inflation as OPEC countries' foreign trade statistics indicate that the average price increases of OPEC imports are greater than those indicated in the OECD price export indices. For this purpose some OPEC experts suggest to construct an OPEC import price index based on the movement of the landed cost of OPEC imports as a measure of world inflation.

Taking the OECD export price index as a criterion to measure world inflation, the OPEC average price of about $34 in September 1981 would represent an increase in real terms of about 30 per cent in comparison with the OPEC price of $10.84 per barrel in January 1974. But if, on the other hand, the OPEC import price index were taken as a measure for the erosion in the purchasing power, the $34 of September 1981 would be equal in 1973 dollars to 10 per cent less than the price of January 1974. A third result could be obtained if a combination of the two indices were taken as the measure for world inflation, in which case the said price of $34 per barrel would be marginally higher in real terms than the price of $10.84 in 1973 dollars. Figure 17.1 shows the difference in the real price movement using each of the three methods for the measurement of world inflation.

Another technical problem could arise from the selection of the base year for the calculation of the cumulative inflation. Against January 1974, which we have just taken as a base period for the measurement of the cumulative change in the real price of oil, another approach for selecting the base period for the measurement of the impact of inflation on the price of oil could be the date at which any decision on prices was taken, because any such decision is supposed to consider, amongst the various parameters for the price setting, the erosion in the purchasing power that was accumulated prior to it. For some

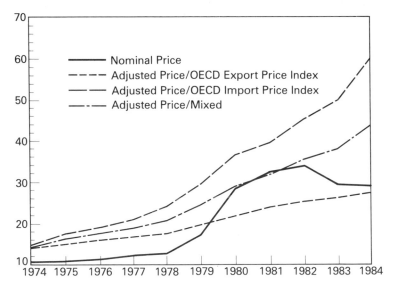

Figure 17.1 Nominal and Adjusted Prices of Arabian Light. 1974–84. Dollars per Barrel.

others, the base period should be sought on a longer period, dating back as far as the 1950s and so on.

Although measuring the movement of the dollar *vis-à-vis* the major international currencies poses fewer technical difficulties than world inflation, a difference in views may, nevertheless, arise in the applicability of the measure in periods of an appreciating US dollar. When the agreements of Geneva I and Geneva II were concluded with the international oil companies,[8] the adjustment of the price to preserve the real value of the barrel had to be made symmetrically as the situation dictated. In other words, an upward price adjustment was made when the dollar depreciated *vis-à-vis* the other currencies in the same manner as a downward adjustment of the price was triggered whenever the dollar appreciated *vis-à-vis* the other currencies (but only to a certain cushion below which no further downward adjustment in the price could be made). With the collapse of the Tehran Agreement and related agreements with the international oil companies, including the two Geneva Agreements, this formula was abandoned without being replaced by any other adjustment mechanism. OPEC did not make any upward adjustment of the price when the dollar was persistently depreciating between 1975 and 1979. Nor did OPEC lower its price in mid-1980 when the dollar began to rise in value against other currencies.

(*b*) *Oil Prices and the Cost of Alternative Sources of Energy*. Another major issue in relation to OPEC long-term pricing policies is the linkage that could eventually be sought between the price of oil and the cost of alternative sources of energy. It is often argued that the intrinsic value of oil as a depletable resource should always be measured in terms of the cost of its replacement. Accordingly, the difference between the price of oil and the cost of its substitutes is an 'economic rent' which must ultimately be taken by the producers through equating the price of oil with the marginal cost of producing a barrel of oil equivalent from substitutes. Hence, among the widely acclaimed concepts governing the OPEC long-term oil pricing policies during the 1970s is that which advocates that prices of oil should be moving upwards in a predetermined path until

[8] For a description of those agreements, see Al Chalabi, *op. cit*.

they reach parity with the cost of producing a similar amount of energy from a substitute for a barrel of oil.

The problem, however, is the definition of the substitute itself. When refined, a barrel of crude oil yields a spectrum of products destined for different uses, certain of which could be met by available resources of energy: for instance, fuel oil could be replaced by coal, gas or nuclear energy (especially in generating electricity). Some other uses, however, cannot be met, except by synthetic oil obtained by the liquefaction or gasification of coal through a complex manufacturing process. The latter are usually referred to as the 'premium uses', such as transportation, the chemical and petrochemical industries, etc. Selecting the product or the use as a base for substitution has, therefore, far-reaching effects on the measurement of the energy price/cost parity, and hence the determination of oil prices. If the substitutability of coal is taken as a yardstick for the parity comparisons, the average price of oil ($34 per barrel, September 1981) was much higher than the cost of its replacement.[9] At a technical cost of $6–13 per barrel of oil equivalent, US coal could generate the same amount of electricity as could be produced by a barrel of fuel oil at a cost of $27. In North West Europe, the technical cost of coal to generate the same amount of electrical utilities is estimated to be in the order of $10–24 per barrel of oil equivalent. If an estimated average cost of $18 per barrel of oil equivalent is taken from those ranges as a base for the comparison of energy cost/price parity, the current average price of OPEC oil is about twice as high as the cost of coal in terms of oil equivalent. The OPEC price is also much higher than the cost of generating the same amount of electricity from nuclear energy which, according to the most recent estimates, would amount to $7–20 per barrel of oil equivalent (in France, the UK and the USA).

By contrast, and in spite of the successive increases in OPEC prices, especially those effected in 1979 and 1980, the average price of oil in 1981 was still much less than the cost of producing a synthetic barrel of crude oil from coal. According to some estimates, the marginal cost of syncrude would amount to $60–

---

[9] The current (1985) average official OPEC price is $28 per barrel.

70 per barrel. For some OPEC experts, the real measure for the price parity for oil is the cost of producing synthetic fuel from coal gasification or liquefaction, since it is only such a barrel that could fully substitute for a barrel of oil lifted naturally from the oil reservoir.

For some others, however, the substitutability of certain oil products by coal or nuclear would justify taking the cost of those alternatives into consideration, besides that of synthetic oil, in order to arrive at a weighted cost average for the substitutes of all the various products obtained from one barrel of crude oil. When taken as a measure for the oil price parity, this approach of weighted cost of substitutes would result in a price which is about 25 per cent higher than the OPEC price of $34 per barrel in September 1981.

However, measuring the price parity with the marginal cost of producing synthetic fuel from coal liquefaction or gasification poses some serious technical and economic problems. Being still in the state of research and development, enormous technical problems might have to be surmounted before any commercial quantities from this source of energy could be produced. This is why, for example, estimates for the cost of producing synthetic crude change dramatically over time. Between 1977 and 1981, the estimated cost of producing a barrel of syncrude moved from more than $40 to about $70 per barrel of oil equivalent. Hence it is often argued that as long as synthetic crude cannot be produced on a commercial scale, no definite cost structure for this source of energy can be defined and, as a consequence, no definite cost/price relationship for oil can be established.

Furthermore, problems of the per barrel cost cannot be taken as a yardstick in isolation from those related to the scale of economies and the production capacities that could be installed in quantities sufficient to make substitution physically feasible. Moreover, certain environmental and infrastructural problems would require to be solved, as the scale of production increased. Lastly, problems related to the technological change, as well as to the cost of fuel used for the processing of coal, would have a bearing on the final cost structure and supply curve of this rather remote source of energy. It is estimated, for example, that by the year 2000 this source of energy would contribute only 4 per cent of total world energy requirements.

All these conceptual and technical problems arising from the definition of the substitutes for oil, and their cost, would continually add to the practical difficulties of linking the price of oil to the cost of its substitutes. Owing to the continuous advances in technology and ever changing environmental requirements, with their attendant costs, the nature of the relationship between the price of oil and the cost of its alternatives for some time to come will be elusive, thus causing the oil price movement to work continually in tandem with the changing cost of producing syncrude.

On the other hand, setting the oil price in a mechanical and inflexible upward motion towards an elusive and changing target would naturally deprive OPEC of the flexibility necessary for fixing the price in the light of changing conditions. It could be in the interest of OPEC, for example, not to apply any formula of automatic linkage of the price to the marginal cost of producing syncrude if world demand fell sharply short of the necessary level to meet minimum short-term expenditure requirements. Furthermore, a mechanical price linkage would inevitably accelerate the process of substitution of oil by other sources of energy, including those of a remote kind like the synthetic fuels (the necessary investments for which would be encouraged by such a linkage).

It is true that the continually rising price resulting from the linkage would help OPEC countries to achieve rapidly their oil conservation targets and secure continuous increases in real oil revenues; but it could also lead to a reduction in world demand for OPEC oil at a much faster rate than was desired by OPEC in the light of member countries' long-term requirements for economic and social development.[10]

---

[10]   The decline in world demand for OPEC oil, which started in 1980, is partially due to an accelerated process of substituting fuel oil by other sources of energy, especially coal and nuclear energy. Between 1973 and 1984, the consumption of fuel oil in the USA, Western Europe and Japan was cut by half (from 560 to 280 million tons per annum – *BP Statistical Review of World Energy*). In fact, this dramatic decline in the use of fuel oil is the main cause for the fall in world oil consumption as gasoline and middle distillates were virtually stable during this period.

Oil Prices and the Conservation of Oil Reserves in Producing Countries

Long-term oil pricing policies play a crucial role in determining the rates of depletion of existing reserves, as well as the addition of new reserves, whether through oil discoveries or through increasing the recoverable reserves by enhanced recovery methods. Low oil prices dictated by the oil companies' policies led in the past to very fast depletion of OPEC oil resources, so that, in spite of major oil discoveries in the 1950s and 1960s, the life-span of OPEC oil, especially that of the Middle East, was dramatically reduced.[11] It is also to be recalled how, after striking extremely low-cost giant oilfields in the Middle East, the multinational oil companies gradually lost interest in investing in exploration or enhanced recovery so that the rates of adding new reserves dwindled appreciably. This is why, in the 1950s and 1960s, the cumulative production from existing reserves was only about 11 and 27 per cent respectively of the total reserves added during the period, a situation which was completely reversed in the 1970s when cumulative production reached levels about twice as high as those of the added reserves.[12]

Prior to 1973, OPEC was, therefore, left with high rates of resource depletion and very low rates of reserves addition. It was only through higher prices in the 1970s that those high rates of depletion were arrested leading to an observable reversal in the life-span of the reserves. After declining to its lowest level in the mid-1970s (thirty-five years at the then prevailing production rates) the life-span of the OPEC oil reserves has increased to the extent that current reserves (1984) would be enough to sustain more than eighty years of

[11] Between 1955 and 1975, proven recoverable oil reserves in the Middle East were multiplied by four times, from 97.2 billion barrels to 395.5 billion. The life-span of those reserves declined, however, dramatically. In terms of reserves/output ratio, OPEC Middle East oil reserves in 1955 were enough to sustain about 140 years of life on the basis of the production rates at that time. In 1975 that ratio had declined to forty-five years.

[12] However, this situation has once again been reversed since 1980 when cumulative production became less than added reserves, as a result of the reduced rates of production of OPEC.

production at present annual rates. Figure 17.2 shows the evolution of the reserves/output ratio over the years.

Whether as a source of energy to meet the domestic energy requirements for industrialization and social welfare or as a source of finance for development programmes or, finally, as a base for hydrocarbon-related industrialization, reserves in the OPEC area will be needed as much in the future as they are now. To over-deplete oil resources could, therefore, be detrimental to the energy and financial requirements for future development. On the other hand, the fact that OPEC's present development is totally dependent on the proceeds of oil sales in the world market pushes its members to increase production (at a certain price level) to meet the continually rising cost of imported technology, equipment, materials, food, etc. In other words, over-conserving these resources for the future, at the expense of present requirements for economic and social development, could be no less detrimental to member countries' development and social welfare. There should, therefore, be a balance between present and future energy and development requirements. The question is, however, how such a balance can be struck and what role price policies should play.

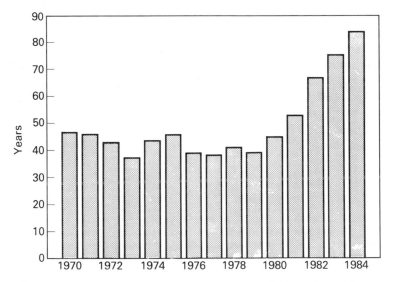

Figure 17.2 OPEC Oil Reserves/Production Ratio. 1970–84.

It is sometimes argued by some OPEC experts that the rates of depletion of OPEC resources should be tied to the rates of development, so that no OPEC member country will produce more than it can spend on development. The reasoning behind this approach is that production over and above those requirements could amount to sheer waste of a national capital that cannot be replaced. Accordingly, leaving in the ground such additional quantities of oil as are not required for development would optimize the utilization of oil resources, especially since the financial surpluses resulting from over-production are becoming increasingly vulnerable to the vagaries of world inflation and currency fluctuations. It is estimated, for example, that, in 1980, OPEC countries taken as a group were producing some 13 mb/d more than was really needed to meet the financial requirements for their development, especially their imports.[13] According to this approach, therefore, prices should be set at such higher levels in real terms as would cause rates of production to fall to levels commensurate with development requirements. It is also often argued that, in defining those requirements, a rational approach to expenditure on development must be adopted with a view to avoiding unnecessary spending that would amount to sheer waste of national resources, or making unnecessary investments that only serve prestige purposes.

A counter-argument to this 'ultra-conservationist' approach could be found in the fact that cutting production rates to such low levels would, as a result of the oil shortage in the market, necessarily lead to market disruptions and uncontrollable price flare-ups that could be detrimental to OPEC itself. Apart from the negative effects on the world economy which would certainly be created by that approach, the resulting price levels would be completely out of context in any long-term pricing

---

[13] It was estimated that the total import requirements of the OPEC area in 1980 amounted to about $132 billion. At the then prevailing oil prices this would have necessitated earnings in foreign exchange equivalent to the export of 11.3 mb/d, whereas the total OPEC exports in that year amounted to 24.6 mb/d. OPEC's external balances have been completely reversed in 1982 and specially in 1983 and 1984 when the group became a net borrower with increasing financial deficits. OPEC's deficit in 1983 amounted to $18 billion and is estimated to be in the order of $11 billion in 1984. This happened as a result of the steep decline in total OPEC production combined with the $5 per barrel cut in the price decided in March 1983.

strategy. Prices would in this case be determined by a convulsive market rather than by 'optimization' through long-term planning. Moreover, higher price levels, whether determined in a 'market' characterized by a shortage, or in accordance with a planned approach towards reduced production, would again result in financial surpluses, i.e. total revenues which exceed development requirements.

A more powerful criticism of the 'ultra-conservationist' argument is that due account must be given, not only to the existing recoverable reserves but also to the possibility of developing potentially new reserves. Existing recoverable reserves are not the whole of the story. The potential is higher and not yet well known. The alarming trend of the 1970s of fast depletion rates overtaking those of added new reserves should not be taken as the only indication of the capacity of future oil supplies within OPEC countries. The stagnation in adding new reserves during that period was largely caused by the very meagre investment efforts made in the OPEC countries in general, but in the Middle Eastern Arab producing countries in particular. Although the latter area accounts for the bulk of crude oil entering the world oil trade, its share in world capital expenditure for oil and gas exploration and production in 1977 was only 6.5 per cent. About 90 per cent of that expenditure went to the OECD countries, with the USA accounting for 50 per cent of the world total.

This very small share of upstream investment in OPEC can be well illustrated by comparing the number of wells drilled in 100 square kilometres of prospective areas in 1976. Whereas 780 wells were drilled in the USA, only twenty wells were drilled in the entire OPEC area. Against a world drilling activity increasing by more than 80 per cent, there was a net reduction in that activity in the OPEC Middle East, where the number of wells drilled actually dropped by about 10 per cent. This happened in an area where investment risks for expansion are the lowest in the world, if such risks are measured by the comparative success ratios of drilled wells. In 1979, that ratio reached about 90 per cent in the OPEC area against a world average of less than 66 per cent. Furthermore, in the USA, where more than half of the world's drilling activities occur, only fifteen barrels of oil could be obtained per foot of drilling, whereas in the Middle East OPEC countries, the return per foot of drilling activity could be counted in terms of a few thousand barrels.

On the other hand, net improvements in the methods of recovering oil from existing reservoirs could substantially add to total recoverable reserves and compensate for depletion in the Middle East, where the average recovery factor from the oil in place is 25 per cent. If, for example, this factor is increased to 35 per cent, which is technically feasible and economically viable with current oil prices, such improvements could alone add new reserves of about 145 billion barrels. In other words, an increase of ten percentage points in the efficiency of recovery techniques used in the Middle East would prolong the life-span of its reserves by more than twenty-five years at 1981 production rates.

Moreover, the present known gas reserves in the OPEC area amount to less than one-third of what could be discovered and developed in the future. This is without counting the flared associated gas, which at current (1984) production rates is equivalent to about 1 mb/d of oil.

As far as conservation is concerned, therefore, prices should not be allowed to fall to such levels as to accelerate the depletion of reserves as was, for example, the case during the companies' days, or to levels which would reduce the incentives for the producers to invest in expanding their production capacities. High potentials for adding new hydrocarbon reserves in OPEC countries can be exploited only at a price level that makes the exorbitantly expensive investments attractive enough. At the same time, however, oil prices should not be allowed to shoot up so much as to create a situation of over-conservation in the sense of keeping more oil in the ground than is really required in terms of present and future economic development, or to drive away world demand for any future expansion of the production capabilities.

Oil Prices and the World Energy Balances

OPEC oil serves as a 'residue' to fill the gap between the world total energy requirements and total energy (oil and non-oil) supplies from outside OPEC. The greater the gap, therefore, the higher the demand for OPEC oil. The smaller the gap, the lower the demand for OPEC oil. Consuming countries try first to satisfy their total demand for energy by resorting to their own supplies of energy, including petroleum produced in their own countries, before they enter international markets for the purchase of oil offered for sale by oil-producing countries. The difference between their demand for energy and their supply constitutes a gap or deficit that should be filled by the importation of energy, mainly from the OPEC countries. Consequently, the existence of oil availabilities offered by OPEC in sufficient quantities to the world market to fill that deficit of energy is of crucial importance for ensuring the equilibrium between world energy supply and demand. In other words, oil supplies from the OPEC countries are necessary to prevent any scarcity of energy resources in the world market.

The world energy equilibrium would, therefore, depend on the relationship between the magnitude of the world energy deficit and the OPEC production capacity. In the case of an abundant excess capacity for supply of OPEC oil, the world energy balance could always be maintained through an upward or downward 'swing' of OPEC output in response to variations in the energy gap (although, of course, there is a limit to OPEC's ability to play this role). By contrast, in the case of a limited capacity of supply from OPEC, greater demand would mean increasing pressure in the market, which would be reflected in higher prices and, in certain cases, uncontrollable market disruptions.

The magnitude of the energy deficit of the consuming countries would, naturally, depend on the growth rates of their total demand for energy, on the one hand, and that of their energy availabilities on the other. In the era of cheap energy, demand for energy in the consuming countries increased at a high rate, whereas their energy production, especially of coal and oil, decreased. The result was an energy deficit that was growing considerably in the consuming countries, especially Western Europe, in favour of OPEC oil. Consequently world demand for OPEC oil grew so sharply that during the 1950s and 1960s, the production of OPEC oil quadrupled every ten years. In contrast, in the era of expensive oil since the 'oil revolution' of the 1970s, the energy deficit of the consuming countries not only stopped growing but, on the contrary, it was reduced.

Most of the forecasts made in the years 1977–9 of world energy supply and demand showed that the world may risk an energy scarcity in 1990 and beyond. For example, according to the estimates made in the late 1970s, the world energy demand could be between 143 and 155 mboe/d (or an average of 150 mboe/d), almost half of which (48 per cent) must be supplied by oil resources. After deducting the oil production outside OPEC, these forecasts estimated world demand for OPEC oil to be 36–49 mb/d by 1990. Such a level of required production from OPEC would by far exceed OPEC's production capacity, which, on the basis of the present recovery factors from existing oil reserves, would amount to 33–36 mb/d.

However, that 'pessimistic' outlook of an eventual world energy disequilibrium in the future was suddenly reversed following the oil events of 1979–80. As we will see later, it is not only that the new forecasts did not indicate any oil shortage for the years 1990 and beyond but, on the contrary, they indicated an excess capacity of OPEC oil in relation to world demand.

According to forecasts made in 1980–81, world demand for energy (outside the Socialist bloc) would be 116–140 mboe/d for these years, an average of 121 mboe/d or 20 per cent less than the forecasts mentioned earlier. The reductions in the forecasts for the world energy requirements are more dramatic for oil. According to those estimates, the world oil demand for the year 1990 would be 52–59 mb/d, an average of 55 mb/d or 24 per cent less than the estimates made in the late 1970s. The fall in the world demand for oil would be more spectacular when it comes to OPEC oil. Those same estimates give the world demand for OPEC oil as being 24–31 mb/d, an average of 29 mb/d or a reduction of 33 per cent compared with the old estimates. The later forecasts (made in 1983) gave a much lower demand for oil in general, and OPEC oil in particular, in 1990, namely 23–27.5 mb/d or an average of 24.5 mb/d. Table 17.1 gives a comparison of the forecasts made during the various periods of the required production from OPEC to meet world demand in 1990.

However, future world energy balances cannot be isolated from the movement of oil prices, in real terms, which is likely to

Table 17.1:   Forecasts of Non-Communist World Demand for Energy, Oil and OPEC Oil for the Year 1990. Million Barrels of Oil Equivalent per Day.

		Range	*Average*
Forecasts made up to 1978[a]	World Energy Demand	143–155	150
	World Oil Demand	64–79	72
	Required OPEC Production	36–49	43
Forecasts made in 1980–81[b]	World Energy Demand	116–140	121
	World Oil Demand	52–59	55
	Required OPEC Production	24–31	29
Forecasts made in 1983[c]	World Energy Demand	109–125	113
	World Oil Demand	47.5–53	49.5
	Required OPEC Production	23–27.5	24.5

Sources: [a] US Congressional Research Service, Texaco, Exxon, OECD, Pirinc, WAES, CIA, Mitsubishi. [b] IEA, Chase Manhattan, Conoco, BP, Texaco, Exxon, Shell, Gulf, Socal, World Bank, Bank of Paris. [c] IEA, Chase Manhattan, Conoco, BP, Texaco, Department of Energy, Chevron, Cambridge University, Standard Oil Company of Indiana.

take place. It is that movement which will determine whether the world will pass through the cycle of an energy shortage, or surplus (over-capacities in OPEC oil production). Low prices, in real terms, would tend to encourage an increase in demand for oil,[14] as consumers found little incentive to reduce consumption of energy or undertake efforts for energy diversification. It is only higher prices, in real terms, that would create the incentive for the consumers to conserve more energy and to shift partially to other available sources of energy, such as coal and nuclear, as well as for investment in other sources of energy. Other things being equal, cheap oil means high growth rates of world demand for OPEC oil that cannot be met by

[14] What is meant here is the lower price paid by end-consumers in the consuming countries as lower prices in the world market for crude oil may not be passed through to end-consumers because of the fiscal policies of the governments of the consuming nations. Recent experience has shown that the fall in world oil prices is not always translated into lower prices paid by end-consumers as, in many cases, it is the treasuries of these governments which benefit from the difference and not the consumers themselves.

existing capacities, whereas expensive oil is bound to reduce world oil demand, not only to levels capable of maintaining an adequate balance between world energy supply and demand, but even, perhaps, to the extent of creating substantial surplus energy capacity.

Looking at past energy trends may help us to understand the relationship between the prices of oil and the world energy balance. Had the very high growth rates of consumption of oil during the era of cheap energy continued, the required level of oil production from the OPEC area would by now have exceeded 50 mb/d. With existing OPEC capacities, such a situation would have created a catastrophic imbalance in the world energy market. It was only after the first major price increase in 1973 that these rising past trends were reversed, resulting in the growth of world demand for OPEC oil being totally arrested — as it did not substantially surpass, in any year in the 1970s, its peak of 1973. However, after the sharp drop in world demand for OPEC oil, a relative revival took place when, as a result of the conservative pricing policies being pursued at that time, OPEC oil prices, in real terms, went into decline. With the oil price increases in 1979 and 1980, another sharp drop in world demand for OPEC oil occurred: so that between 1979 and 1984 oil consumption in the OECD area fell from 41.6 mb/d to 34.6 mb/d, a fall of 18 per cent.

The reversal in oil consumption trends in the industrialized countries can be attributed in the main to the movement of the price in real terms. Higher real prices have led to more serious efforts on the part of those countries substantially to increase the efficiency of the energy use, resulting in an enormous reduction of the energy component per single unit of economic growth.

In fact, following the major price changes, a structural change in the relationship between energy consumption and economic growth has taken place, whereby economic activity in the industrialized countries can now be sustained with much lower energy consumption than before. Although part of the decline in energy (especially oil) consumption in the industrialized countries can be attributed to the economic recession in the world economy during the 1970s, the major part of that decline, however, has been due to the change in the energy structure, so that a revival in economic activity need not necessarily be reflected by higher levels of oil consumption.

A comparison of the movements of certain indicators of growth rates of energy in the periods before and after the 'oil revolution' may help in showing the structural change that we mentioned. Between 1967 and 1972 the accumulated growth in the OECD amounted to about 26 per cent requiring an accumulated growth of energy consumption in the order of 31 per cent and oil consumption in the order of 44 per cent. During the seven years that followed the oil 'shock' of 1973, the accumulated growth of the economic activities of those countries was reduced to about 18 per cent, requiring an accumulated growth of energy of only 2.6 per cent, whereas the oil consumption during that period fell by about 5 per cent (i.e. negative growth).

The same reversal of the relationship between energy consumption and economic activity could be measured by the change in the amount of energy needed to achieve a certain value unit of the GDP. Whereas in 1972, 4.4 boe of energy were needed for each $1,000 worth of GDP in the European OECD countries, only 3.7 boe were required in 1980. This structural change was much more pronounced as far as oil was concerned owing to the fact that consumers made serious efforts to meet demand by substituting mainly coal for oil. This is why coal consumption in the OECD countries kept increasing whilst oil consumption kept decreasing so that, during the period 1979–84, coal consumption in those countries rose by 13 per cent compared with a decrease in oil consumption of the order of 18 per cent.

To put it another way, the Western economies were, prior to 1973, growing at high rates, generating an even higher growth rate of energy consumption, the increment of which was taken entirely by oil, as the growth rate of oil consumption was much higher than the energy average. After 1973, a complete reversal of trends occurred, as the Western economies started growing at a slower pace, which required much lower growth in energy consumption, the increment of which was taken mostly by sources other than oil. The result was that there was virtually no growth in oil consumption. On the contrary, there was a decline in absolute levels, indicating a negative growth.

One of the explanations of this phenomenon is the change that had occurred in the pattern of energy elasticities in the consuming countries. When oil was cheap, its price elasticity of demand was extremely low, so that oil price variations did not produce an important impact on the behaviour of consumers. By contrast, when the world entered into the era of expensive energy, these patterns changed dramatically, so that the price elasticity of demand increased enormously. This means that any price increase would entail a significant reduction in consumption as a result of the price variations. This is why there has been such a noticeable reaction of consumers to the post-1973 price movements and, more especially, to those of 1979–80. Higher prices in real terms led to greater savings of energy, especially oil, during the initial period of the price rise, a situation which started to ease as a result of the decline in the OPEC oil price, in real terms, during the period 1975–8. The same trend could be witnessed in the elasticity of substitution, as higher oil prices have increased the pace of substitution in favour of available sources of energy, notably coal.

While the main cause for those drastic changes in the energy situation can naturally be found in the reactions of consumers *vis-à-vis* the price increases, the factors related to government policy actions have also played an important role. Energy problems in the developed countries have acquired a strategic nature, so that policy objectives in matters of energy can be achieved by consuming countries through government intervention, without there necessarily being a direct reference to existing price levels in the international market. By this means, governments of the industrialized countries have taken drastic measures, through fiscal policies as well as quantitative controls, in order to impose the required change in energy consumption, especially of oil.

The process of change towards a better world energy balance has been especially facilitated by the recent major price increases, whereby the average price of OPEC oil has increased in early 1981 by more than 170 per cent over that in 1978. This is why the new forecasts of future world demand for OPEC oil have been indicating much lower production requirements from OPEC than its present production capacities permit, i.e. an excess capacity of production is now envisaged, instead of the oil shortage forecast for the mid-1990s in 1978–9. These developments have created the conditions for a world energy equilibrium as the figures concerning required production of oil to fill the world energy deficit are well below the existing production capacity in OPEC. In other words, a surplus production capacity is envisaged today whereas at the end of the 1970s forecasts were indicating an oil shortage. The more recent forecasts went as far as predicting that the situation of surplus will last until the end of the century at which time demand for OPEC production will not exceed 28 mb/d, or an average of some 15 mb/d less than the forecasts made in 1978. The predicted level of world demand for OPEC oil includes production which will be needed to meet domestic OPEC energy requirements estimated to be in the range of 8 mb/d by that time.

Oil Prices and OPEC's Share in the World Energy Markets

OPEC price explosions not only helped in establishing a new structural relationship between economic growth and energy consumption in the industries directed towards a lower energy component of growth, but also triggered a process of change in the world energy mix, whereby oil will have to play a relatively smaller role in meeting future world energy requirements. Moreover, OPEC pricing policies have created conditions for change in the world oil mix itself, leading towards a lesser share of OPEC oil in the world oil supplies. In other words, oil became the energy 'swing' in the world energy balance and OPEC oil became the 'swing' in the world oil supply. A process of historical transition in the world energy structure is currently under way towards a new situation whereby the world, and especially the industrialized countries, will have to reduce their dependence on oil imports from OPEC countries.

This trend reverses the post-war energy transition into heavy dependence on OPEC oil, during the era of cheap energy when the multinational oil companies maintained an artificially low level for oil prices. Past low pricing policies resulted in a steadily increasing share of oil in the world energy balance at the expense of traditional sources of energy, mainly coal, which kept losing ground, so that its share in the world energy production dropped from 60 per cent in 1945 to 30 per cent in 1975. Low oil prices had likewise the effect of preventing technological development towards the utilization of other sources of energy, including natural gas and nuclear energy. The result was that the share of oil in the total world energy supply increased dramatically from 23 per cent to 46 per cent during the same period. Naturally, it was OPEC oil which took the brunt of that expansion, so that OPEC's share in world energy production increased from 5 per cent to 23 per cent with all the consequential adverse effects that were discussed earlier, namely the fast depletion of OPEC oil reserves and the creation of a great potential for world energy imbalance.

However, as soon as energy became 'expensive', oil started to lose ground in favour of other sources of energy. After having reached a maximum of 54 per cent in 1973, the share of oil in the total world energy supplies, outside the Socialist bloc, was reduced to 50 per cent in 1980 and to 46 per cent in 1983. It is estimated that this trend of a falling share of oil in the world energy consumption will continue so that it may reach 45 per cent in 1990 and 41 per cent in the year 2000.

By contrast, it is expected that the consumption of coal and nuclear energy will increase. From a maximum of 18 per cent reached in 1979, the share of coal in the world energy total consumption, outside the Socialist bloc, is estimated to reach 26 per cent in the year 2000 and the share of nuclear energy would increase from 3 per cent to 10 per cent during that same period. In this structural shift in the world energy consumption, in which oil loses its predominant role in favour of other sources of energy, it is OPEC oil which is taking the total brunt of the loss of oil share. This is actually taking place in favour of oil produced outside OPEC.

One of the structural effects of OPEC's pricing policies was that the oil price increase stepped up investments in the expansion of oil production capacity in a number of oil-producing countries, outside OPEC, such as the UK and Norway in the industrialized world, and Mexico, Egypt, Malaysia, Oman, Angola, etc. in the developing world. The increase in oil supplies from these countries started to play a significant role in the world energy balance at the expense of

OPEC oil. Production from these countries kept increasing and displacing OPEC oil in world oil markets so that total non-OPEC oil supplies in the world in 1984 represented a net addition of about 7.5 mb/d compared with 1976.

Since the first major price increase in 1973–4, an exponential increase of oil exploratory efforts has been taking place in the oil-producing countries outside OPEC. This can be made evident by comparing the number of wells drilled in the world before and after the 'oil revolution' of 1973–4. Between 1960 and 1973, this figure was reduced from 55,600 wells to 35,400, or an average annual decrease of 3 per cent. By contrast, the total number of wells drilled in the world in 1980 reached 84,000, or an average annual increase of 12 per cent compared with 1983. The bulk of these efforts is being made in the developed countries, especially the USA, which alone accounts for 50 per cent of the world total. This increase in world exploratory efforts was made at the expense of OPEC countries where the number of wells drilled, especially in the Middle East, was reduced. It is obvious that these investments in exploration would not have been economically viable without the price increase made by OPEC as such investments continued to decrease during the era of cheap energy. In fact, the price 'revolution' of OPEC had the effect of radically changing the structure of comparative costs of production in the OPEC countries compared with those outside OPEC. It also changed the concept of the economic oilfields. In this context, it is enough to invoke the example of the North Sea, where the average cost of production of a barrel can, in certain instances, exceed $22 per barrel (including the amortization of investment capital). This cost may be even higher if we consider the expensive investment necessary for an increase in production capacity in that area. Such costs would never have been economically justified if the oil price had not increased to levels surpassing those costs. It is true that when investment started in the North Sea at the beginning of the 1970s, the average cost of production in that area was estimated to be in the order of $3 per barrel, i.e. higher than the then prevailing price in the world market, a fact which indicates that other factors, besides comparative costs, are taken into consideration when developing oilfields, namely the security of oil supply.

Nevertheless, the bulk of these investments were made when all indicators were pointing towards a price rise. Moreover, the investments which were made for the expansion of production capacity in the North Sea would not have been undertaken without an important price increase.

After reaching a peak of 67 per cent of world total oil supplies, outside the CPEs, in 1973, OPEC's share in those supplies continued to decline. In fact, for the first time since 1962, its share in those supplies became, in 1981, lower than that from outside OPEC and continued to shrink so that, by 1984, it had fallen to 43 per cent.[15]

This dramatic fall in OPEC's share in world oil supplies stems from the fact that the newcomers in the world market, especially those in the North Sea, Mexico, Egypt, Oman and others, were able to displace OPEC oil in the world oil market through undercutting OPEC's price as the only means to maximize their market share at the expense of OPEC oil. This displacement was made possible by OPEC's pricing policies themselves, as OPEC defended its price by allowing its production to fall; customers took first the cheaper oil before turning to OPEC to lift the more expensive oil, a policy which finally led OPEC to become the world oil swing producer.

This falling trend of OPEC's share in the world energy supply has created immense problems for OPEC and its future role in the world oil trade.

In the very long term, the world transition towards a lesser share for OPEC oil in the world energy balance is inevitable. World energy requirements are bound ultimately to outpace the development of finite fossil resources, since OPEC's capacities are simply not large enough to meet both the increase in world demand for its oil and its own domestic energy requirements.

However, problems of the world energy transition are not the same for the oil-producing countries as for the industrialized world. For the developed countries, the problem lies mainly in the relationship between the cost of imported energy and economic growth. During the era of cheap oil, great wealth and

[15] OPEC's share of world oil supplies, outside the CPEs, is estimated to be under 30 per cent in 1985.

technological transformation were generated in those countries through their heavy dependence on imported oil at a cost of next to nothing. Now that oil has become expensive, such dependence must be substantially reduced, and a new energy era created, where oil no longer plays a dominant role in the overall energy balance. For this reason, oil conservation in the consuming countries should go beyond merely avoiding waste, to realizing profound structural modifications in production systems, which would secure growth with much less energy and a greater accumulation of technology. Among the policy objectives in the industrialized countries was that fuel substitution, especially by coal and nuclear energy, should be made in major steps, overcoming infrastructural and environmental problems. Furthermore, accessible oil from non-OPEC sources, preferably those in the industrialized countries themselves, should be encouraged, and more remote sources, such as solar energy and synthetic oil from coal, should also provide a real possibility for diversification in the longer term.

While agreeing with the consumers on the long-term target of ultimately reducing the share of their oil in the world energy supplies, producers may take a different stand on the speed and timing of that reduction and the period during which the energy transition is achieved. The main concern of producers is to speed up the structural transition of their economies from the present stage of underdevelopment, where dependence on oil revenues is virtually total, to a higher level of economic and social transformation, where dependence on oil revenues will be drastically reduced and replaced by diversified income generation. Oil is the producers' only effective instrument for this structural transformation and should, therefore, be looked at, not only in terms of existing capacities but also taking into account the potential for increasing those capacities by adding new oil and gas reserves. For this reason, the development needs of the producing countries may require that the world energy transition, and hence the determination of their share in the overall world energy balance, be achieved within a time horizon compatible with the needs of the structural transition of their economies. Future developments in most of the OPEC member countries will continue to depend on the proceeds of oil exports to world markets until sufficient structural changes in their economies are achieved, and diversified sources of income created, thus reducing the predominant role of oil revenues in their development.

No matter how oil-producing countries differ in economic and social structures, it is fair to estimate that the time horizon needed for achieving such structural changes in their economies will generally be longer than that envisaged by the industrialized countries for the energy transition. If the latter is made at a much faster rate than the former, development prospects in the oil-producing countries may be compromised before an adequate level of economic structural change has been realized. Consequently, there should be a balance between the pace of economic and social development in the oil-producing countries and the pace of transition in Western countries towards a lesser dependence on imported oil from OPEC. The faster the rate of development, the greater are the incentives for the oil-producing countries to co-operate with the consuming countries in smoothly accelerating the energy transition. Otherwise, a wider time horizon for the transition towards a drastic reduction of the world's energy dependence on OPEC oil may be necessary, to allow for a similar reduction in the producing countries' dependence on oil revenues being achieved.

Oil prices could play a crucial role in shaping this time horizon and, consequently, in determining the share of OPEC in total world energy requirements. Although the energy objectives in the industrialized countries are no longer left to be achieved by market forces alone, but are also influenced by direct and indirect government intervention, it is nevertheless true that the level of the oil price in the international market will determine the pace and timing of the world energy transition into a new energy mix. Substantially higher prices in real terms in the future will no doubt accelerate the pace of the world energy transition and hence speedily reduce OPEC's share in total energy requirements. Lower real prices would contribute to decelerating the speed of energy transition, and hence widen its horizon.

Consequently, OPEC price policies should be the instrument by which oil-producing countries can influence the determination of their share in the world energy market in a manner to be compatible with their long-term economic and social development requirements.

Generally speaking, therefore, prices should not be so high as to accelerate the process of energy transition towards a much lesser share for OPEC oil in the world total energy balance before OPEC countries have achieved an economic 'take-off' towards lesser dependence on oil revenues. Neither should oil prices be so low as to keep OPEC's energy share at a level that could not be sustained by existing capacities, nor to lead to an over-depletion of oil revenues.[16]

It could, however, be argued that since the industrialized countries have embarked on investment policies to speed up the transition, OPEC pricing policies to shape the pace of transition could be counteracted by government policy measures, including fiscal policies and taxation on products inside their markets so as to create an internal price structure that would favour the energy transition irrespective of the price levels in the world markets.

In fact, such policies have been already discussed by the industrial countries since the creation of the International Energy Agency (IEA) following the OPEC oil 'price revolution'. It was that Agency that introduced the notion that a minimum real price for crude oil from OPEC countries must be maintained even if the OPEC price in the world market dwindled to lower levels. In other words, should OPEC prices in the world market fall below a certain minimum level, all countries should impose on imported oil such tariffs and taxes as are necessary to maintain that minimum inside the industrial countries (the famous $7 per barrel in real terms announced by Henry Kissinger in 1974).

On the other hand, while OPEC's policies, in general, were aimed at reducing the pressure of world demand for its oil, such a reduction should not be so much as to affect OPEC's share in the total world oil supplies in a way as to adversely affect its member countries' economic and social development. The price should, therefore, not be so high as to encourage the

---

[16] The above argument about the importance of OPEC's share in the world energy market draws heavily on the author's intervention in the OAPEC/Italy/South Europe Seminar in Rome on 7 April 1981 entitled 'Problems of World Energy Transition: A Producer's Point of View' published in *OPEC Review*, Vol. V, No. 2, Summer 1981.

continuous investment in expensive oil in a way as to create new sources of oil supplies which would compete with OPEC oil. By the same token, the price should not be so low as to create pressure on OPEC supplies and to increase OPEC's share in the world oil market beyond its financial and development requirements.

One of the arguments used against the utilization of pricing policies as an instrument to increase OPEC's share in the world oil market is that it is extremely difficult to find a common pricing policy of OPEC that can satisfy the conflicting economic interests of member countries. It is often argued that OPEC member countries differ enormously in terms of their share in the world market as well as the time horizon necessary for achieving the required structural transformation of their economies so that, for some countries, what matters most is to have as high an income per barrel through higher prices as possible irrespective of OPEC's share in the world market whereas for some others, with huge oil reserves, maintaining a high share in the market is a crucial long-term policy objective, especially given that for those countries generally the achievement of the required structural change would take a very long time owing to their limited non-oil resources. The structural heterogeneity among member countries, especially concerning the development levels achieved by each one of them and the potential for structural diversification of their economies, would prevent the adoption of a unified policy position *vis-à-vis* the long-term pricing policy as a means to synchronize OPEC's share in the world energy and oil markets with the required structural change of the individual member country's economy.

Oil Prices and the World Economy

OPEC's conservative pricing policy between 1974 and 1978, with the consequent deterioration in OPEC's price in real terms,[17] was, to a large extent, caused by the concern shared by

[17] Between January 1974 and December 1978, OPEC did not increase the price of oil except twice (in September 1975 and December 1976) and at 10 per cent each time. During that period, however, the cumulative world inflation was in the order of 62 per cent. On the other hand, the dollar depreciated continually with a cumulative decrease

OPEC policy-makers about the negative effects of prices on the world economy, especially after the initial shock of 1973. Many OPEC countries, particularly Saudi Arabia, were opposing any price adjustment, even those necessary to offset the adverse effects of world inflation and the then depreciating dollar, on the basis that such adjustments might endanger the world economic recovery after the long economic recession. Those countries thought that maintaining low price levels in real terms would alleviate the pressures on the balance of payments of the oil-importing countries and would strengthen the anti-inflationary efforts undertaken by the industrial countries, thus helping to achieve a sustained world economic growth.

It is certain that substantial and sudden price increases would adversely affect the balance of payments of the oil-importing countries. However, in the case of the majority of the industrial countries the deficits in the external balances resulting from higher oil prices would be self-correcting, at least partially, after a certain lead time, which differs from one country to another depending, mainly, on the structure and pattern of trade of those countries with OPEC.

Experience shows that the increase in oil revenues as a result of the price adjustment strengthened the trend among the OPEC producing countries to spend more on imported goods and services from the industrial countries. In many cases, OPEC member countries spent more on importing such goods and services between 1974 and 1979 than their oil revenues. Even in those OPEC countries with low absorptive capacity for development, development expenditure resulted in a dramatic increase in imports. Generally speaking the growth rate of trade between OPEC and the industrial countries was higher than that of oil revenues. This was especially true during the period 1974–9 when OPEC oil revenues increased from $87 billion to $189 billion, or an average annual rate of growth in the order of 14 per cent. This rate is much inferior to that of the growth of imports by OPEC member countries which, during that same period, reached 22 per cent per annum on average. The total value of imports of goods increased from

of its value reaching 13 per cent. The result was that the price of oil in real terms deteriorated tremendously. In the dollars of October 1973, the price of oil in December 1978 of $12.70 was equivalent to $6.90. See Al Chalabi, *op. cit*., p. 95.

$32 billion to $107 billion during that period.[18] The growth of this trade has naturally led to a reduction (or even disappearance) of the current account surplus of OPEC member countries.[19]

In other words, the increase by OPEC member countries of their imports of manufactured goods, services, technology, foodstuffs, and, more especially, imports required for economic development, from the industrial countries would by itself create the self-correcting element in the balance of payments of the oil-importing developing countries. The extent to which the industrial countries' balance of payments are self-correcting would naturally depend on the distribution of trade among the countries which supply the goods and services. Countries with huge export potential to the OPEC member countries would have their balance of payments self-corrected much faster than other countries which have a lesser trade relationship with OPEC.[20] It goes without saying that the bulk of OPEC trade is effected with the industrial countries.[21]

In spite of the fact that this situation was changed following the substantial increases in oil revenues in 1980, the tendency to

[18] These figures do not include two main items of trade between OPEC and the OECD, namely the purchase of armaments (for which figures are not available) as well as services, such as freight, insurance, banking services, technical services and the cost of the transfer of technology, etc. In adding these two items to the total trade, the process of recycling of the oil money, especially towards the OECD countries, would be enhanced. Between 1974 and 1979 the total value of imported services by OPEC countries increased from $12 billion to $42 billion, or an average annual increase of 23 per cent. It is obvious that such services are, in the main, imported from the industrial countries.

[19] This surplus, that is to say the balance of current accounts of the OPEC countries, fell from $68 billion in 1974 to only $5 billion in 1978. Following the price increases of 1979–80 the surplus increased dramatically again. However, with the dramatic decline in oil exports after 1982, OPEC's external balance shifted from a situation of surplus to one of deficit.

[20] As an example, the value of French merchandise exports to OPEC countries increased from $1.1 billion to $10.7 billion during the period 1972–80, an average annual growth rate in the order of 30 per cent. These figures do not include the cost of the value of French services imported into the OPEC area; nor do they include the armament trade between France and the Arab countries.

[21] The pattern of total imports of OPEC member countries shows that the USA accounted for 17 per cent, Japan for 15 per cent, West Germany for 13.5 per cent, France 8.6 per cent, the UK 8 per cent, Italy 7.6 per cent, and the rest of the OECD countries for 14 per cent. This is to be compared with a share of only 3.7 per cent for the Socialist bloc. The remaining 12 per cent represents trade with the developing countries.

achieve balance in the trade between OPEC and the OECD
countries would continue, especially in view of the fact that
revenues are expected to fall as a result of the freeze in prices
and the reduction in oil export volumes.

This same tendency for the recycling of oil money is also
applicable in so far as the financial movements are concerned.
The OPEC financial surpluses which are not re-channelled to
the industrial countries in the form of increased trade are in
reality recycled again to those same countries through the main
international financial markets of the industrial countries.[22]

Whenever this type of recycling takes place, the recipient
countries benefit in balancing their external payments and can,
therefore, counteract the effect of the oil imports on the balance
of payments even if their current account balances are in
deficit. Here again, the structure of the financial movement
plays an important role in the correction of the imbalances of
the external payments. Certain countries, such as the USA,
where the bulk of the so-called petrodollars is absorbed by a
highly developed financial market, are less adversely affected
by the oil price movements than other developed oil-importing
countries which do not enjoy high concentration of financial
markets. For this reason the increase of oil imports into the
USA should not create a real problem for the external balance
of this country, taking into account the very strong concentration of financial surpluses of OPEC countries invested in the
USA in the form of treasury bonds, bank deposits, etc.[23]

By contrast the oil-importing countries from the Third
World do not generally enjoy the same advantages as the

---

[22] The following table shows the evolution of the financial investments of the OPEC
countries and their distribution by categories during the period 1974–9, in billion
dollars:

Type of Investment	1974	1975	1976	1977	1978	1979
Bank Deposit	30	11	14	13	5	42
Short-term Government Bonds	5	0	−2	−1	−1	4
Long-term Government Bonds	3	5	7	8	1	1
Other Capital Movement	8	12	14	13	12	16
Total	46	28	33	33	17	63

[23] It is estimated that the share of the USA in the total placement of oil-exporting
countries' investments was in the order of 30 per cent in 1981.

industrial countries in the area of recycling oil money through increased trade with OPEC or through the financial flow of capital. However, it is a mistake to consider the effect of oil prices on the developing countries as being uniform for all of them. Such effects differ enormously from one country or group of countries to another in accordance with the level and structure of the industrial development attained by each. For example, there are certain developing countries which enjoy a significant potential for exporting commodities and manufactured goods, such as Taiwan, South Korea or Brazil, which are better placed than the other developing countries to enjoy the effects of the recycling of oil money through trade. For these countries, the increase in trade with OPEC has partially, at least, offset the adverse effects of the oil price movement on their balance of payments. Because of their high level of industrial development, this limited number of developing countries absorb the bulk (more than three-quarters) of the total oil imports into the Third World.[24]

It is for the same reason that those same countries account for the major part of the Third World's external debts resulting from borrowing from the international banking system. Because of their high level of industrialization the growth rate of their investments is too high to be met by the national saving of capital. Consequently, it is these external debts, and not the oil imports, which are behind the increasing deficit in the balance of payments of those countries. It is true that the oil price increase has aggravated the problem of external payments of those countries but the effect of world inflation on those payments is much more serious than the effect of the oil price.

The situation is totally different when it comes to the majority of the nations of the Third World, whose level of industrialization is very low. For these nations, oil represents but a very small portion of their total imports, simply because their economic development is weak, which is reflected generally by a low level of oil consumption and, hence, oil imports. However, poor countries of the Third World enjoy

[24] The eight countries concerned are: Brazil, South Korea, Taiwan, India, Turkey, Thailand, Cuba and Yugoslavia.

OPEC financial aid in a manner that could, in many cases, offset the adverse effects of oil price increases. This is especially true for the least developed countries which received from OPEC countries during the 1970s enormous amounts of aid in the form of grants or concessionary aid so that in many cases the amount of aid received surpassed the increase in their modest oil bill. Moreover, for some developing countries, such as Egypt, India, etc., higher oil prices attracted foreign investment in their indigenous oil sector.

On the other hand, the effects of the oil price increases on world inflation have been unduly exaggerated. It is true that the oil price increases contributed to the acceleration of the world inflation rates but the contribution of oil in inflationary trends is very modest compared with the other factors of the economies of the industrial countries. Most of the studies published in those countries show that the effect of the increase in the oil price on inflation rates in the world is negligible. It is estimated, for example, that a 10 per cent increase in the price of oil could add, on average, 0.3 per cent to the inflation rates of the OECD countries. The effect varies, of course, in accordance with the degree of dependence on imported oil so that in such countries where dependence on imported oil is weak as a result of the existence of indigenous energy resources, the impact of oil prices on inflation is very weak. By contrast, in countries of high dependence on imported oil the effect of oil prices on internal inflation is much greater. Generally speaking, however, in the very high rates of inflation in the industrial countries, non-oil factors, such as the evolution of wages, play a much more important role in generating inflationary trends than oil prices. It is interesting to note, for example, that during the five-year period from early 1974 to end 1978, OPEC had virtually frozen its price. Nevertheless, inflation in the OECD countries during that period persisted at very high rates. Between January 1977 and December 1978, when oil prices were also frozen (after an increase of 10 per cent in December 1976), the accumulative rate of inflation in the OECD countries was about 18 per cent.

Finally, the oil price movements have far-reaching effects on the terms of trade as an effective means of transfer of wealth through the channels of international trade. They could also have some effects on the economic growth of the oil-importing countries. Exorbitant prices in real terms could adversely affect the propensity to invest and consequently the trends for the capital formation in the importing countries. It should be stated, however, that such an effect on the GNP growth of the oil-importing countries would depend on the economic structure and the ability to channel resources towards the most productive sectors of their economy, as well as their overall macroeconomic policies. Japan, for example, has a dynamic economy in spite of the fact that it is totally dependent on imported energy and that the cost of oil in the national economy accounts for a very high ratio. Nevertheless, that country succeeded in achieving the highest rate of growth in the whole OECD area. Japan was able promptly to redistribute its resources towards more profitable investments, such as the industries with very high technological content and which could lead to a very high national productivity as well as enhanced commercial competitiveness in the world markets. This latter fact may explain the surplus of the Japanese balance of payments during the 1970s in spite of the very high oil bill. The growth of investments in such sectors of the economy could generate additional revenue that would counterbalance the adverse effects of the increase in oil prices on the national economy.

It should, however, be admitted that the variations of oil prices would have a great impact on the world economic activities, including those of the OPEC countries.

A healthy world economy is a prerequisite for economic and social development of OPEC countries, as they depend totally on the import of technology as well as of capital and manufactured products from the industrialized countries. Moreover, the stability of the world's economic and monetary activities has a direct bearing on the worth and security of OPEC countries' reserves, especially those with financial surplus.

It is generally admitted now that the effect of oil prices on the industrialized countries, especially as far as inflation is concerned, is much less than has been suggested. It is also argued that the effects of higher prices on the balance of payments are offset by the various channels of recycling the oil money, including expanded trade with OPEC countries and increased financial flows from OPEC towards the major financial centres of the world, which are mostly located in the industrialized countries. Nevertheless, sudden and sizeable increases in oil prices could undoubtedly jeopardize the health of the world economy and, more especially, the developmental effort of the other countries of the Third World.

More importantly, the state of the world economy has an immediate impact on the world demand for OPEC oil, hence the level of OPEC exports into the world market. While it is true that the far-reaching structural changes that took place in the world economy following the price 'explosion' led to a lesser energy demand per GNP unit and that the growth in the world economy is no longer accompanied by a commensurate growth in demand for oil, it is still a fact that one of the major short-term factors that contributed to the dramatic fall in world demand for oil, especially in the OECD countries, was their low level of economic activity. It is, therefore, in the interest of all oil-producing countries that a steady growth in the world economy be always achieved and that, for this reason, oil prices should not fluctuate sharply and suddenly in such a way as to affect this growth.

This is why it is sometimes argued that small and gradual increases in oil prices in real terms, such as those which are commensurate with the growth rate of the economies of the industrialized countries, could be easily absorbed by the world, and would not impede any picking-up of the economic activity. It is not only that such increases would be in line with the pace of the industrial growth, so that no disruptive effects could be created beyond the absorptive capacity of the world economy, but such increases would, in fact, be justified by a higher demand for oil as a result of the sustained growth of the world economy.

However, some OPEC experts argue that what matters most for OPEC countries is to dedicate this finite resource to economic and social development inside OPEC countries at the fastest rates possible. This could be done only if the increase of oil prices, in real terms, were commensurate with the growth rates of the OPEC member countries themselves and not with those of the major industrialized countries, who, as experience has already shown, are suffering, not from oil prices as much as from a structural impediment to higher growth rates of their economies and who could, with a certain lead time, absorb the increases in oil prices.

Options for an OPEC Long-term Pricing Strategy

The foregoing analysis of OPEC long-term pricing strategies shows that the policy options open to OPEC countries are varied and conflicting. The validity of any price option would depend, of course, on the objective to be sought and the assumptions to be adopted. Those could be as varied as the national priorities of the member countries of OPEC and their respective economic and oil structures. Any workable option for a collective price strategy for OPEC must be based on a common denominator which reflects the minimum community of national interests of member countries, and on which an agreement could be reached. Such a minimum is not necessarily the optimum for all, as the differences in national priorities would lead some members to push for policies that could not secure unanimous agreement.

The problem is, of course, how to define this minimum. Broadly speaking, the main premiss for any minimum common denominator stems from the fact that no matter how the members of OPEC differ in their structures and national priorities, they all need to maintain the flow of oil revenues in real terms required for their development for as long a time as necessary to achieve the structural changes of their national economies towards lesser dependence on those revenues.

This would require a pricing policy that takes into account not only the present development requirements but also the continuous flow of oil revenues needed for a long time to come in order to meet the future development requirements. In other words, oil revenues should be protected against any deterioration in real terms and should, at the same time, be based on a price level that would keep a fairly dynamic world demand for OPEC oil within as wide a time horizon as possible. By the same token, the availability of oil to meet member countries' future energy requirements is as important for securing future development requirements as the financial flows. Therefore oil reserves should be preserved as much as possible. Oil conservation, however, must be looked at dynamically in the sense that the present OPEC proven and recoverable oil reserves should be increased and the right conditions for investing in new capacities should be created. A dynamic conservative approach means also that future generations' requirements should not be met at the expense of present development requirements. The oil which is depleted today in order to meet those latter requirements should be compensated tomorrow by new capacities which meet those of the future generations. Lastly, OPEC oil is crucial in achieving the world's energy balance and the healthiness of the world economy.

It should be emphasized here that any analysis of the options that OPEC may choose for its long-term pricing policies is based on the hypothesis that, in acting in the market, OPEC can administer the price of oil at a certain decided level, which it can protect only by letting the organization's production vary in accordance with the variations of the world demand for its oil. It is likewise admitted that in administering its price, OPEC can provoke reactions on the world demand for oil itself and can, for this reason, influence that demand, at least partially, in accordance with the strategic objectives to be defined for the long run.

It is generally thought, however, that the long-term pricing trends are essentially determined by the pricing interactions of both producers and consumers through supply and demand, instead of being the result of short-term and accidental factors operating in the free market. Nevertheless, this free market constitutes an indicator of the immediate state of supply and demand and can, hence, contribute in setting the price in the short run.

However, OPEC can only administer the price and, hence, enforce a price strategy when two conditions are met: first, the existence of a sufficient productive capacity of OPEC in relation to the world demand and, secondly, the predominance of OPEC exports in relation to the total volume of all world oil trade, i.e. an adequate share in the world oil markets.

The history of oil prices clearly shows that in the short and medium term, OPEC can manage the oil price, if only it has sufficient productive capacity to satisfy, at any moment, the world demand for oil. In other words, OPEC's ability to administer the price is strengthened when the market is in balance. OPEC can, in this case, fix a price level below which none of the members could sell its oil, whereas total production would be adjusted by member countries, upwards or downwards, in the light of the variations of world demand for oil. The surplus capacity of OPEC helps, therefore, to maintain and protect the price level.

In allowing its production to decrease in response to the world demand, OPEC can achieve a market equilibrium and can, therefore, control this market with a certain price level that it fixes itself. In turn, its capacity for price management is eroded when its productive capacity runs short of an increasing demand. In 1979, OPEC effectively lost its control of the price management in following an imbalanced market. That is why, for example, its decision in the summer of 1979 to establish a ceiling of $23.50 per barrel was shattered by a disrupted market two or three months later.

In the long run OPEC's capacity to manage the oil price is determined by its dominating share in the total volume of the world oil trade and the role it can assume as a leader of price fixation in the world market. In other words, in order for OPEC to administer its price on the basis of any option of its long-term strategy, it should continue to control the bulk of the world oil trade. The action taken by OPEC in changing the structure of the market and the oil pricing system would never have been possible without its predominant situation in determining the volumes of oil entering the world market. We should not forget the fact that during the turning-points in the history of oil pricing in the 1970s, OPEC's share in the world trade of crude oil was about 90 per cent of the total oil traded. That share was reduced to 60 per cent in 1984 as a result of the new structural changes in the world energy market, when the share of OPEC in the world energy consumption was reduced from 31.5 per cent to just above 24 per cent. If we assume that this falling trend of OPEC's share in the world market continues at the same rate observed during the last few years, the organization would suffer from a progressive loss of its power to influence the world market to the extent that it would erode gradually its leadership role. When OPEC controls the bulk of world oil trade, other exporters outside OPEC, such as the Soviet Union,

Norway, the UK, Mexico, etc., can but follow the evolution of price in the world market as decided by OPEC. Such a situation could be considerably modified, in case of a drastic decrease of OPEC's share in the world international markets.

With this in mind, the following options for an OPEC long-term pricing strategy could be envisaged:

(a) *Predictable Real Price Rises: Parity with Alternative Fuel Costs*. The first price option that won wide support in the late 1970s among OPEC experts is the concept of administering the price of oil on the basis of predictable, gradual increases of prices, in real terms and within a predetermined price path which leads ultimately to parity with the marginal cost of producing synthetic oil from coal liquefaction and gasification. It is often argued that, only with a long-term price strategy based on a minimum of 'predictability' of a rising trend, could both producers and consumers 'plan' and smooth out their structural adjustments: the consumers would be able to secure a smooth transition towards lesser dependence on OPEC oil and, in the same manner, producers could secure minimum real increases in their oil revenues which could help them to achieve the structural transition of their economies.

This would mean that, irrespective of any fall in world demand or a 'glut' in the market, a minimum, or a 'floor' price would have to be fixed by OPEC at a certain unified level and set in motion within a planned trajectory of periodic and automatic upward adjustments. These adjustments are to be determined in accordance with certain agreed parameters, which are mainly related to maintaining the price in real terms as a minimum and adding such real increases as deemed feasible to gradually and mildly reduce the gap between the price of oil and the cost of these alternatives.

This option for an oil price mechanism was first adopted by the Long-Term Strategy Committee of OPEC under the chairmanship of Sheikh Ahmed Zaki Yamani, and made part of the Committee's report to the Extraordinary Meeting of the OPEC Conference held in Taif in the spring of 1980. The ensuing price formula was accepted by the large majority of the OPEC Conference but was opposed to by some member countries. Consequently the discussion on the formula was left open-ended, especially with the postponement of the Summit Conference which was scheduled to be held in September 1980 and which was supposed to discuss, among other things, the Long-Term Strategy price approach.

In such a 'planned' approach of price administration, it is naturally assumed that in time of a depressed market, producers would undertake the necessary downward adjustments in their production levels to support the 'floor' price against the pressure of a fall in demand. If, on the other hand, a tight oil market results in higher prices than the 'floor', OPEC prices could be adjusted over and above the 'floor' to reflect such market conditions. The higher price level would either become a new 'floor', from which the mechanism of automatic upward adjustment would be applied, or be frozen, i.e. the application of the automatic formula would be suspended until the original 'floor' caught up with the new price. Taking either of these two courses of action in pricing oil in times of 'shortage' would depend on the nature of that shortage, and whether it was judged to be temporary, and hence a reflection of accidental and conjunctural conditions, or permanent, and hence a reflection of long-term imbalance between supply and demand. With the former assumption, the higher price should be forgone and the 'floor' be restored (freezing the higher price) whereas the latter assumption justifies raising the 'floor' to a higher level.

According to this strategic view of fixing oil prices in the long run, the definition of the floor price can essentially be found in the concept of a continued improvement in the terms of trade until a point where prices in real terms reach the parity level with the marginal cost of producing synthetic fuels.

As to the composition of the 'floor', three elements can be envisaged. First a price adjustment should be made periodically to offset the eroding effects of world inflation in order to maintain the price in real terms. To this end, OPEC may choose the OECD export price index as a measure of magnitude of world inflation and the deterioration in the terms of trade. A second adjustment element in the 'floor' price is meant to offset the movement of the dollar *vis-à-vis* the other currencies. For this purpose, the currency basket of the Geneva I Agreement plus the US dollar itself could be taken as

a criterion for measuring the worth of the US dollar in relation
to those currencies. The adjustment of the price on account of
the dollar movement would, according to this approach, work
both ways, i.e. when the dollar depreciated the price should
automatically increase to compensate for the fall in purchasing
power against the dollar, whereas, with the appreciation of the
dollar, prices would be corrected downwards in order not to
gain unduly in purchasing power. Finally, a quantum increase
in the price in real terms should be added over and above that
price so as gradually to narrow the gap between the price of oil
and the cost of producing a synthetic barrel of oil from coal. A
criterion for measuring this third component of the 'floor'
would be to equate the quantum real increase in the price of oil
to the growth rates of the GNP of the major industrialized
countries. As a support for choosing this parameter, it may be
argued that such rates would indicate the capacity of those
economies to absorb the price increases in real terms. In other
words, the real increase in the price of oil should not only seek
long-term parity with the marginal cost of alternative sources of
energy, but also, by being gradual and relatively small, help to
sustain the world economy. Those small increases would, on
the other hand, secure to the oil producers a minimum increase
of real income to cope with the increasing cost of their
economic and social development. Moreover, this approach
would facilitate long-term energy balances. Gradual real
increases in the price would improve the economic viability of
consumers' investments in alternative sources of energy which
would gradually reduce the demand for OPEC oil in a smooth
and slow transition period towards a new world energy mix.
Small and gradual price increases would not at the same time
prematurely accelerate the reduction of OPEC's share in the
world energy market and create a situation of permanent over-
supply. Moreover, such a price formula would meet the producers' long-term requirements for a moderately higher rate of
conservation of oil reserves needed for future generations.

However, while agreeing in principle on this price option for
a long-term pricing strategy, a minority view was expressed
within the Long-Term Strategy Committee concerning the
parameters for measuring the movement of price, in real terms,
as well as the real quantum increases. According to that view,

adopting parameters related to the economic performance of the industrialized countries, for measuring both world inflation and economic growth, would favour those latter countries at the expense of the producing countries. Instead of linking the price of OPEC oil to the OECD export price index and the quantum increase to the growth rates of the industrialized countries, the OPEC import price index could be envisaged as a measure for imported inflation into the OPEC countries, and the growth rates of the economies of those latter countries themselves as a parameter for the real increase. In defending this criterion which represents a maximum price adjustment, it is sometimes argued that the very small gradual increases in real terms resulting from the application of other parameters would help the developed countries to smooth out their energy transition and economic growth without securing to the OPEC countries themselves the transition towards higher development, since such small real increases would not be enough to offset the rising real cost of development in the OPEC countries. Furthermore, it would not substantially narrow the gap between the price of oil and the cost of alternative sources of energy, hence depriving the producers of the 'economic rent' necessary for their future development.

The results obtained from the application of either parameter, i.e. rates of economic growth and inflation in the industrialized countries versus those in the OPEC countries, would obviously differ enormously. Had, for example, those two parameters been applied since 1974, the adjusted price resulting from the application of either of these would be as shown in Table 17.2.

This minority view blocked an agreement on the Report of the Long-Term Strategy Committee and it was not further pursued by the OPEC Conference. Meanwhile, important developments took place in the world oil situation that made this option inapplicable, especially the important price increases that took place in 1980 and the subsequent drastic decline in world demand for OPEC oil.

(*b*) *Flexible Price Formulae: The Concept of an Equilibrium Price.* Instead of adopting a price strategy based on the inflexible predictability of a rising trend, as was originally suggested by

Table 17.2: Adjusted OPEC Prices. 1974–84. Dollars per Barrel.

Year	Aggregate Index A	Adjusted OPEC Price	Aggregate Index B	Adjusted OPEC Price
1974	126.89	13.75	146.71	15.90
1975	142.86	15.49	173.58	18.82
1976	149.30	16.18	211.78	22.96
1977	168.58	18.27	249.56	27.05
1978	198.86	21.56	294.27	31.90
1979	238.18	25.82	371.81	40.30
1980	273.21	29.62	453.14	49.12
1981	263.12	28.52	469.12	50.85
1982	248.27	26.91	515.56	55.89
1983	241.97	26.23	559.42	60.64
1984	241.50	26.18	691.80	74.99

Notes: 1. Base year: 1973 = 100, for both indices.
2. Aggregate Index A uses the OECD export price index and the economic growth rates of the industrialized countries, and includes the currency basket of the Geneva I Agreement plus the US dollar for measuring changes in currency fluctuations.
3. Aggregate Index B uses the OPEC import price index and the economic growth rates of the OPEC countries. Dollar movements are reflected implicitly in this index, which is denominated in dollars.

the Long-Term Strategy Committee, an alternative option of long-term pricing could be based on the concept of a dynamic 'equilibrium price' that could be determined by OPEC from time to time in the light of the world energy outlook and member countries' long-term requirements. According to this concept, OPEC would monitor the long-term movement of world demand for its oil and determine the level of its prices with a view to seeking a balance between its 'desired' production level, i.e. its 'desired' share in the world market, and the 'required' production from OPEC in order to meet world demand. The price determination would, therefore, depend on the reaction of the consumers to the price changes on the one hand and the investors in oil and non-oil energy sources on the other hand. When, for example, world demand for OPEC oil declines to levels which are considered by OPEC to be lower than its 'desired' production, prices would be set in order to stimulate world demand for OPEC oil. In other words, when OPEC oil becomes expensive in relation to the cost of non-OPEC oil or the cost of alternative sources of energy, then OPEC prices could be reduced as a means to deter further investment in new energy capacity which would compete with OPEC oil. This policy option implies that prices could be used as an instrument to maintain a certain level of world demand for OPEC oil which would correspond to OPEC's 'desired' production in the light of its financial requirements. By the same token, when world demand for OPEC oil increases to levels higher than OPEC's 'desired' production, then oil prices should, in real terms, be increased as a means to dampen demand to achieve a balance between supply and demand at the 'desired' production level.

The philosophy behind this concept is that instead of allowing its share in world energy requirements to be determined by consumers and producers outside OPEC, both in the upper and lower levels, OPEC should plan its share in the world market and should, for this purpose, use the price instrument to achieve its 'planned' production levels. It is this price which could enable OPEC to set the required pace and time horizon for the world transition towards a lesser dependence on its oil from both the supply and demand sides. On the supply side, i.e. oil supplies from outside OPEC, OPEC could set an equilibrium price which would secure for it a certain share in the market so that investments in oil supplies outside OPEC would be determined in the light of the 'desired' share of OPEC in the world market. From the demand side, the price could also be used as an instrument to achieve that share by stimulating or dampening demand as the case may be.

With certain lead times the price elasticity of world demand for OPEC oil could be carefully observed. Consequently, OPEC could price its oil in such a manner as to cause the pace of the reduction of its share in the world energy market to be commensurate with the time horizon for the structural transition of their economies from total dependence on the oil revenues to a diversified income generation through higher levels of economic and social development. Oil prices should, therefore, not be so low as to increase the pressure of world demand for OPEC capacity, and thus accelerate the rates of depletion of its resources; but, at the same time, they should not be so high as to drive OPEC oil out of the market before other income sources are generated within member countries' national economies.

Another aspect of the dynamism of this concept is that, in evaluating OPEC's capacity of production, it is not only the present recoverable oil reserves that should be taken as a basis for setting the price equilibrium between supply and demand, but also, as was explained earlier, the potential for increasing this capacity through more exploration and enhanced recovery. Long-term prices should, therefore, be set at levels which would secure supply/demand balance by creating the right conditions for increased oil availabilities from OPEC so as to cope with world demand. Among other factors, especially those related to the acquisition of technology from the developed consuming countries, pricing policies could help enormously in bringing about a better energy balance through expanded OPEC capacities. Thus, prices should be set at those levels which would encourage oil producers to embark on huge and exorbitantly costly investments for increasing their oil resource base, especially in generating the additional financial requirements for those investments. This would require a stable and moderately growing demand for OPEC oil. Prices should, therefore, be set at levels that encourage consumers not to reduce their dependence on oil in favour of other sources of energy nor to reduce their dependence on OPEC oil in favour of oil supplies from outside OPEC.

(*c*) *Price Administration on the Basis of Market Criteria.* A third option for a long-term pricing strategy is to make decisions on prices on an *ad hoc* basis and in the light of market conditions. If world demand grew at a faster pace than could be met by available OPEC capacities, the oil market itself would take care of the upward price adjustments. In other words, market forces would in this case be the means to achieve equilibrium between supply and demand. If, on the other hand, demand fell short of supply, with the resulting glut in the market, OPEC production adjustments should again be left to the market for readjustment on the basis of a certain price level decided by OPEC.

This is how it was thought that OPEC could set a certain price as a minimum that it could protect against downward pressures, while leaving the price movement over and above this minimum to be determined by the market. The history of OPEC price administration during the 1970s indicates that producers' control of pricing was successful only in keeping the minimum price, below which, in times of over-supply, producers are not permitted to sell. This is how during the 'glut' of 1975 and 1976, OPEC was in fact able to maintain its floor price by leaving its production to follow the downward 'swing'.[25] However, in times of shortage, price administration from any 'floor' has no practical significance, whereas any 'ceiling' set by OPEC for its prices cannot resist the upward market pressures. OPEC successfully endeavoured, for example, to put a ceiling on its price ($23.50 per barrel) during the third quarter of 1979, but no sooner had further market flare-ups taken place early in the fourth quarter of the same year than this price ceiling started to wither in the face of new strains.

Consequently, it is often argued that market forces can, in fact, determine the price, so that market upward pressures resulting from a possible oil shortage in the future would be reflected in much higher OPEC prices whereas market downward pressures, caused by a surplus or over-supply, would be reflected in lower OPEC prices but only to a level which hits the price cushion set by OPEC as a 'floor'. According to this approach, the self-correcting process of supply and demand would be through a market 'cycle' resulting from the reaction of buyers *vis-à-vis* the price movements. Thus, when oil prices in real terms shot up violently and successively as a result of market forces, consumers would naturally tend to reduce demand through various government measures as well as through the natural response of price elasticities of demand. It is also possible that economic reactions, such as, for example, lower rates of growth and lesser economic activity in the consuming countries *vis-à-vis* the very high price, would add a further impetus to the decline in

---

[25] It should be noted, however, that the distribution of the downward 'swing' in OPEC was not equal. Total OPEC production in 1975 fell by about 4 mb/d from that of 1973. Two-thirds of this drop was taken by three member countries, Venezuela, Kuwait and Saudi Arabia.

demand. The market cycle could also be reversed following the fall in demand to levels that might hit the OPEC price. In such a case, lower market prices might generate a revival in demand which would in turn be reflected in higher market prices, and so on. It could be argued that such an approach, based purely on market mechanisms and the reaction of demand *vis-à-vis* price variations, would eventually lead to restoring the equilibrium in the market. Thus the market itself would restore to OPEC its ability to administer its price from a certain price level decided by it.

It is obvious that price administration, according to this 'market approach', is feasible only when OPEC's share of the market corresponds both to member countries' requirements and to the need to retain an adequate proportion of world oil exports. If the fall in OPEC's production continues to lower levels so that OPEC's share may be too small to meet member countries' requirements, the defence of the price would then be difficult to achieve. In this eventuality, prices could well fall below the 'floor' price mentioned above.

This approach does not give enough weight to the far-reaching structural changes which occurred in the world oil industry following the price changes. Generally speaking, demand for oil in the short run is price inelastic in the sense that sharp fluctuations of prices cannot be reflected in commensurate changes in supply or demand. There are already built-in structural mechanisms which would reduce the impact of price changes on demand as it is inconceivable, for example, that consumers would reverse their plans for investment and conservation and/or other sources of energy just as a result of a cycle in the market. Many of the structural changes that took place are irreversible so that the impact of price changes on demand would be reduced. This approach also ignores the political consequences of the market price fluctuations. For both producers and consumers, oil prices are too important a factor in economic growth, the balance of payments and social change to be left to the hazards of the market. Consumers cannot change their plans for such a strategic commodity as energy just because of short-term price changes. Nor can producers allow their development programmes to fluctuate in the light of these short-term market cycles.